# KINSHIP AND POLITY IN THE *POEMA DE MIO CID*

# Purdue Studies in Romance Literatures

# KINSHIP AND POLITY IN THE *POEMA DE MIO CID*

Michael Harney

Purdue University Press
West Lafayette, Indiana

**Library of Congress Cataloging-in-Publication Data**
Harney, Michael, Paul.
Kinship and polity in the Poema de mío Cid / Michael Harney.
p. cm. —(Purdue studies in Romance literature ; v. 2)
Includes bibliographical references and index.
ISBN 1–55753–039–4 (cloth : alk. paper)
1. Cantar de mío Cid. 2. Kinship in literature. 3. Social classes in
literature. I. Title. II. Series.
PQ6374.H37 1993                                        92–46867
861'.1—dc20                                                CIP

Design by Anita Noble

Printed in the United States of America

**For Lucy**

# Contents

# List of Abbreviations

**AA**
American Anthropologist
**AEM**
Anuario de Estudios Medievales
**AESC**
Annales: Economie, Société, Culture
**AHDE**
Anuario de Historia del Derecho Español
**AnnRevS**
Annual Review of Sociology
**ARA**
Annual Review of Anthropology
**BHS**
Bulletin of Hispanic Studies
**CHE**
Cuadernos de Historia de España
**CSIC**
Consejo Superior de Investigaciones Científicas
**CSSH**
Comparative Studies in Society and History
**EDHM**
Estudos de direito hispânico medieval
**His**
Hispania (Madrid)
**HR**
Hispanic Review
**IESS**
International Encyclopedia of the Social Sciences
**JFH**
Journal of Family History
**JHP**
Journal of Hispanic Philology
**JIES**
Journal of Indo-European Studies
**MÆ**
Medium Ævum
**MLN**
Modern Language Notes

**MLR**
Modern Language Review
**NRFH**
Nueva Revista de Filología Hispánica
**O**
Olifant
**P&P**
Past and Present
**PMC**
El Poema de Mio Cid
**PMLA**
Publications of the Modern Language Association of America
**REH**
Revista de Estudios Hispánicos
**RFE**
Revista de Filología Española
**RFH**
Revista de Filología Hispánica
**RH**
Revue Hispanique
**RPh**
Romance Philology
**SJA**
Southwestern Journal of Anthropology

# Introduction

Our reading of the most famous narrative poem devoted to the exploits and adventures of the historical personage Rodrigo Díaz de Vivar has been forever altered by Ramón Menéndez Pidal's scholarly crusade for the implementation of a twofold program in Cidian studies. The first element of this program involved propagating the image of the Cid as a Spanish national hero. This nationalist-historicist premise held not only that the Cid's importance resided in the heroic symbolism of his embodiment of Spanish national character but also that the epic masterpiece dedicated to the tale of his exploits and his triumph was itself essentially valid as historical documentation. As is well known, Menéndez Pidal's position invoked a certain degree of controversy, leading to a debate with Leo Spitzer along the lines of the historical/literary dichotomy. Spitzer expressed an opinion few would now dispute: that a literary work, even where historical accuracy is verifiable, is literary precisely because accuracy for its own sake is irrelevant to the narrative aesthetic. Reversing the terms of Menéndez Pidal's characteristic formulation, Spitzer declared that given the fabulous nature of the plot, it would indeed be risky to postulate the historical accuracy of this epic ("Sobre" 107, 114–17). Much the same conclusion was reached by Colin Smith, who observed that the poet "composed an epic poem, not a historical work." Having created "a drama with a plot, a series of climaxes artistically disposed," he therefore "felt no special duty to record or respect or even to use the facts of history." Such facts, if he was aware of them, were only utilized "when it suited his entirely literary purpose to do so." Bound only by the constraints of "existing traditions and memories," this poet "invented freely" (*Making* 137).[1]

The second element of Menéndez Pidal's program committed the formidable resources of the great philologist to the promulgation of the so-called traditionalist theory of the poem's composition. The work—variously referred to as the "Cantar" or the "Poema" of the Cid—is held by this school of thought to have been produced collectively, anonymously, by generations of folk poets. It was one among an untold number of folkloric compositions of varying length produced by the same communal tradition. Behind each literary masterpiece lie generations of anonymous, collective elaboration—a latent state of popular artistry, endlessly refining, adapting, enhancing. No single author, in this poetic tradition, may claim credit; no single generation can monopolize consumption of the work of narrative art so produced. This, in essence, is the traditionalist premise.[2]

While the nationalist and historicist aspects of his scholarship have lost their power to generate controversy, the second aspect of Menéndez Pidal's approach has been vigorously disputed—or, at any rate, extensively modified—by a number of scholars. Eventually the theory was fortified by fusion with the oralist theory propounded so compellingly by Milman Parry, Albert Lord, and their host of enthusiastic disciples. The field work of Parry, documenting living poetic traditions in Yugoslavia and elsewhere, supported a theory of oral composition in the purest sense, providing the model for a poetic tradition that could compose literary masterpieces without literacy. Master singers transmitted not memorized fixed texts but extensive repertoires of typical motifs (e.g., those of leave-taking, of landings of ships, of sword fights, of homecoming, of banishment, of warriors in council, etc.) and vast inventories of metrical formulae. The song-story, in effect, was an array of such motifs devoted to a specific topic, such as the story of the hero's triumphant homecoming, the victory of one clan over another, the siege of a stronghold. Variable in its specific sequence but consistent in its content, the song, during performance before an audience, was enacted by means of a line-for-line splicing-in of metrical formulae from the singer's vast accumulated store of stock elements, many of which could be fitted, allowing for the constraints of meter and narrative context, to a large number of different motifs. Texts were not memorized in this tradition.[3]

Although the singers may have the impression of singing the same song repeatedly, each performance differs, to a greater or lesser degree, from all others on the same theme. Lord, in a recent summary and updating of his theory, points out that the fundamental medium of communication in the oral world is talk, and that song, a form of talk, is a "specially conventionalized medium that serves to filter out some sounds, [and] to amplify others" ("Merging" 19). Through song, images and ideas ". . . are refracted in the mind's eye, an eye that sees *images* directly rather than through letters and written words." The dimension of talk is necessarily one of "fluidity" and "variability," of "artful speech before codification" (20). In this precodified environment, the storytelling endeavor is characterized by mutability and "multiformity": "One may use the same words as the last time, but the last time was no more formative than any other time" (23). The oral world of manifold variability and the literate world of codified consistency may coexist. Only when the literate elite draws its materials from the oral world is a "bridge" erected between the two realities.[4]

The work that we will designate in this essay as the *Poema de Mio Cid* is the Spanish epic par excellence perhaps chiefly because it is the only more or less complete epic manuscript from a medieval Peninsular language to have come down to us. Its uniqueness has prompted one prominent expert on this poem, Colin Smith, to postulate that the work is the unique effort of a solitary poet working in imitation of French epic style. Smith thus manages to account for formulaic style—he does not deny the possibility of oral formulaic tradition in the French context—while preserving the essential point of authorial creativity for this Spanish masterpiece. The impact of French poetic models on the composition of the *PMC* is so extensive, he argues, that "it is best to postulate [the poet's] residence and study in France, and his learning of the epic art there by both reading and listening" (*Making* 157).[5]

The two foci of debate just discussed—historicist/narratological, traditionalist/individualist—are by no means the only dualities to have plagued Cidian criticism. Another such controversy might be called the philology/aestheticism debate. John S. Geary points out the dangers of such a thematic division in his discussion of Thomas Montgomery's analysis of the *PMC*'s style. While characterizing as "perceptive" the latter scholar's appraisal of the work's primitivism, Geary suggests that Montgomery's contrast of visions—subjective in the *PMC*, objective in chronicle treatments of Cidian themes—supports an unnecessary dichotomy. The evident contrast in styles may indicate not an epochal transition or a cultural transformation, but rather merely a "distinction between poetic and prosaic expression" (Geary 180–81).[6]

Miguel Garci-Gómez chides Menéndez Pidal for his "ex-teriority," suggesting that "en torno" was a most appropriate title for one of the earlier scholar's best-known collections of essays. Menéndez Pidal's approach, according to Garci-Gómez, avoids the "entrañas," focusing as it does on the environment of poet and public. The neotraditionalist school exemplified by Menéndez Pidal is in fact inherently "exter-nalista." It is an "exocrítica" that functions not to study "la médula, el sistema nervioso o endoesqueleto" of the literary work, but rather its "exoesqueleto." This, he affirms, consists of such "disciplinas de soporte periférico" as philology, history (civil, social, economic, ecclesiastical), geography, folklore, jurisprudence, numismatics, and comparative literature. This exocriticism inevitably tends to succumb to "la tentación de salirse de la obra al autor, de la estructura al marco cultural, de los personajes a las personas, de las formas a la materia." In short, he concludes, the critic's attention wanders "de la poesía a la historia" (Garci-Gómez, *"Mio Cid": estudios* 13–14).

As it happens, Garci-Gómez's enumeration of exocritical categories is a fairly complete list of the principal bibliographic rubrics covered by Cidian criticism over the past several de-cades. According to Garci-Gómez's criteria, the vast majority of studies are exocritical. In a bibliographic essay, Miguel Magnotta discusses the history of *PMC* criticism and scholar-ship by dividing his survey into the following topics: date of composition and of the manuscript (Magnotta, *Historia y bibliografía* 17–37); authorship (38–77, with subtopics such as anonymity vs. known author, cleric or layman, originality vs. adaption); origins (78–89); influences (90–117, including French, Germanic, and Muslim); the relation of the *PMC* to both the chronicles (118–35) and the *romancero* tradition (136–45); problems of versification (150–76); aesthetic and critical evaluations (177–207). Appendices address such addi-tional topics as the identity and possible contribution of Per Abbat (208–18), the question of learned vs. popular authorship (219–23), the mythic aspect of the Cid (224–28), and the sense of space and time conveyed in the work (229–39).

The topics outlined by Alan Deyermond exhibit much the same kind of categorization. In his bibliographic survey of work devoted to the *PMC,* he points out the very frequent emphasis on such topics as versification and the relationship between the *PMC* and chronicles ("Tendencies" 14–15). At the same time, he indicates—unlike Magnotta—important gaps, such as the "patchy state of scholarship" in the area of social mobility and related topics. Questions of ideology, he notes, have been "much less intensively studied" than questions of historicity, philology, geography, and other fields solidly represented in his survey ("Tendencies" 28).

Julio Rodríguez-Puértolas, addressing what might be called the "social-science" gap in Hispano-medievalist scholarship, critiques Menéndez Pidal as a "curiosa mescolanza de positivismo, historicismo e idealismo." Emphasizing the *PMC*'s "falseamiento de la historia" ("El *Poema*" 149–57), Rodríguez-Puértolas suggests that the work is conceived as political and social propaganda in service to an emerging social class. Geary, perhaps slightly overstating his assessment, considers this a "somewhat dogmatic position," the result of Rodríguez-Puértolas's determination to regard "epic poetry as little more than the propaganda of an emerging social class against the 'system' and the ruling feudal ranks" (184).

It is tempting to view the conflict dramatized in the *PMC* as one deriving chiefly from the rivalries and confrontations endemic to class struggle. A number of scholars have emphasized the importance of class structure in the work. Eduardo de Hinojosa, for example, contrasted vassalage in the poem with that of the classic feudalism of northern France and Germany. As against the latter's "relación de fidelidad y auxilio recíprocos engendrados por la ceremonia del homenaje," the poem's vassalage, he suggests, represents "el vínculo de los súbditos con el Rey" (vv. 1847, 2905, 2948, 2982), as well as "la subordinación del soldado al caudillo" (249, 376, 568, 806, 1853, 2278). This factor, implies Hinojosa, makes for a more political, more authoritarian polity than that envisioned by conventional feudalism ("El derecho" 549–50). Menéndez Pidal, in essential agreement with this interpretation, considers that "el verdadero tema básico del poema" is that of class confrontation between the lesser nobility of the *infanzones* and the higher nobility of the *ricos hombres* (*En torno* 211). María Eugenia Lacarra and Diego Catalán, while allowing for some degree of class conflict and social hierarchy, emphasize the poet's response to the specific political background of his time: the antipathies of the audience are directed not toward nobles as a class, but only to certain noble factions.[7] Joan Ramon Resina summarizes the persistent school of thought that highlights the Cid's role as rebellious vassal, pointing to the Spanish epic poet's peculiar emphasis on this theme as an indication of intentional appeal to the popular masses and even to the incipient bourgeoisie of that age (419–20).

My own exploration of social mentalities in the poem suggests the emergence in this work not of a particular social class but rather of a sensibility of class and the contradictions that derive from it. The poet's understanding of class struggle is inarticulate, corresponding to what some social historians, notably Anthony Giddens, have defined as a phase of imperfect or partial class consciousness. Focusing on "*the modes in which* 'economic' relationships become translated into 'noneconomic' social structures," Giddens notes the difference between class as "economic category" and class as "specifiable cluster of social groupings." There are innumerable classes of the first sort, resulting from "an indefinite multiplicity of cross-cutting interests created by differential market capacities." Classes of the second type are limited in number. For Giddens, a class is not a "bounded social form," nor does it have a "publicly sanctioned identity" or real "membership" (although he admits that complete avoidance of these concepts is difficult). Least of all does a class "act" or "perceive" in the same way as "an individual actor." Classes as a social reality only emerge with "the formation of common patterns of behaviour and attitude." Classes in this more complete sense "will also tend to manifest common styles of life." The chief symptoms of this intermediate development, argues Giddens, are a denial of the reality of class divisions, and a concomitant accentuation of individual worth and achievement. A willful ignorance of class reality, as expressed through resolute individualism, thus characterizes the "class awareness of the middle class, in so far as it involves beliefs which place a premium upon individual responsibility and achievement." True class consciousness begins with "*a conception of class identity and therefore of class differentiation.*" With time there may materialize as well a "*perception of class unity . . . linked to a recognition of opposition of interest with another class or classes.*" As a catalyst of the emergence of identifiable classes, Giddens identifies " 'closure' of mobility chances—both intergenerationally and within the career of the individual." This closure tends to promote "the *reproduction* of common life experience over the generations." Class structuration, therefore, "is facilitated *to the degree to which mobility closure exists in relation to any specific form of market capacity.*" To each of the three types of "market capacity" ("ownership of property in the means of production," "educational or technical qualifications," "manual labor power") correspond, respectively, the three basic classes of capitalist society: upper, middle, and lower (Giddens, "Class Structuration" 158–64; all italics in original).[8]

Presenting "refinements and enlargements" to Max Weber's concept of "the process by which social collectivities seek to maximize rewards by restricting access to resources and opportunities to a limited circle of eligibles," Frank Parkin accentuates the significance of closure strategies "adopted by the excluded themselves as a direct response to their status as outsiders." The study of emerging class consciousness thus requires investigation of "the countervailing actions of socially defined ineligibles." Organized resistance to "a pattern of dominance governed by exclusion principles" constitutes, he affirms, "the other half of the social closure equation." The implications of this balanced equation have a direct bearing on the conflict dramatized in the *PMC*. Exclusionary closure, notes Parkin, exerts power in a "downward" direction. It entails "the creation of a group, class, or stratum of legally defined inferiors." At the same time, countervailing actions by the outsiders, because they are expressed through "collective attempts . . . to win a greater share of resources," threaten the privileges of "legally defined superiors." Exclusion and usurpation, he concludes, are "the two main generic types of social closure," with the latter always a result of and a "collective response to, the former" (175, 176).

In the midst of a disavowal of class that paradoxically characterizes nascent class structure, we encounter, therefore, an obsession—presumably unconscious—with rivalry as a function of status emulation. If usurpation is the goal of the outsider's resistance to domination and exclusion, the objectives of attempts to turn the tables on the oppressors are defined by things possessed by the oppressors themselves. There can be no question of "resources," however monopolized, as the thing whose possession by the elite defines the unbalanced relationship—not, at any rate, in the sense of subsistence goods. It is not minimal survival we are talking about but rather commodities, luxury items. The outsider covets the things that the insider commodifies by the mere fact of ownership. People, social anthropologists assure us, are never happy in their place. The collective stoicism of the oppressed or the disadvantaged is a self-serving myth promulgated by privileged classes. All notions of positive social mobility are based, in other words, on the imitation of hated role models. The idiom of ambition is learned from the elite, insuring that the outsider in search of acceptance is determined, willy-nilly, to become what he most hates.[9]

If the essence of narrative is plot, as Peter Brooks contends, then the essence of plot—"the organizing dynamic of a specific mode of human understanding"—is desire (7). "Plots," he maintains, are "intentional structures, goal-oriented and forward-moving" (12). This notion of plot as dependent on motivation amounts to more than a mere acting class cliché; we cannot read narratives without some sense of why people do what they do, which requires knowing why they want what they want. What literary characters covet usually has something to do with social things in the most encompassing sense. Thus, such elements as money, sex, status, and a host of other primordial issues, are vitally important motivational—and therefore plot-advancing—factors in all narratives. However, while all narratives are social, some are more social than others. Viewed as narrative, the *Libro de buen amor*, we might hazard, is exceedingly social, and its author (or authorial persona) downright gregarious. But there are many things about the work which attenuate, or deflect, the social focus. Thus, it is not merely in the structural discontinuities of its narrative but also in the content of its digressions that the *Libro de buen amor* deviates from the sociable dimension. Such things as the parody of the canonical hours and the roll call of animated foods in the Doña Cuaresma episode make for narrative aberration. The degree of deviation marks the amplitude of the work's non-narrativity. The very opposite of "storylike," such interludes indicate the *Libro*'s commitment to improvisation, to parodic performance, to delectable inventory. If we seek heuristic analogues in present-day genres, we must turn, therefore, to the digressive improvisation of stand-up cabaret, the manic, genre-blurring potpourri of Monty Python.

In medieval Spanish literature, the *PMC* offers a clear contrast to such ramblings in its use of desire as an engine of narrativity. The hero is nothing if not purposeful, focused, desirous. This conqueror of cities, this vanquisher of armies, this humiliator of *malos mestureros* and dastardly sons-in-law, is above all an ambitious man who gets what he wants. The plot of the poem is the realization of his ambitions. "'Antes fu minguado,'" the Cid exults at one point, "'agora rrico só, / que he aver e tierra  e oro e onor / e son mios yernos  ifantes de Carrión'" (2494–96). The vexations of the Afrenta de Corpes are but a transient frustration serving to enhance the eventual vindication provided by the judicial duels, which disgrace the hero's rivals—"'¡Grado al Rey del çielo,  mis fijas vengadas son!'" (3714)—even as second, greater marriages are arranged: "Los primeros fueron grandes,  mas aquéstos son miiores, ... / ¡Ved quál ondra creçe  al que en buen ora naçió!" (3720, 3722).

We are accustomed to thinking of the Cid as a "medieval man," and therefore as ruled by different motives and drives from those ruling literary personages of later or earlier eras. Without committing the anachronism—or the cultural incongruity—of viewing him as "bourgeois," we may yet point out the degree to which he resembles the "plotted" heroes of a literary tradition such as the nineteenth-century novel, characterized by Brooks as one that takes seriously (rather than parodically or satirically) the notions of "aspiration," of "getting ahead." For nineteenth-century narrative, argues Brooks, ambition becomes "the vehicle and emblem of Eros, that which totalizes the world as possession and progress." Ambition impels to action, "drives the protagonist forward," until the action is resolved through achievement or renunciation. Aspiration as the "armature of plot" is based on the "self's tendency to appropriation and aggrandizement." The ambitious heroes of such writers as Balzac, striving "to have, to do, and to be more," are " 'desiring machines' whose presence in the text creates and sustains narrative movement through the forward march of desire, projecting the self onto the world through scenarios of desire imagined and then acted upon" (39–40).

I have argued elsewhere that the economic mentalities of the poetic Cid, involving economic predation and redistribution, and traditional kinship, amity, solidarity, and reciprocity, are precapitalist and charismatic, and therefore quite the contrary of "bourgeois" in the Marxist sense. In this the poetic Cid typifies social practices observed in a broad variety of contexts.[10] Although the Cid, a defrauder of moneylenders and sacker of towns, can hardly be called "bourgeois," he strongly resembles the typical nineteenth-century novelistic protagonist characterized by Brooks as "a bundle of appetencies" (Brooks 43). The Cid, like the later protagonists, is obsessed with getting ahead, with "appropriation and aggrandizement." His endeavors are grounded in kinship, the foundation of a lineage of his own, rather than an egocentric desire to "be somebody." The Cid is a family man who knows precisely who he is. He does not discover his identity so much as use it to bludgeon his enemies into submission. Focused on kin-minded posterity rather than the egotistical here-and-now, he seeks and attains the foundation of a dynasty of his own, as reflected in the climactic lines: "Oy los rreyes d'España   sos parientes son, / a todos alcança ondra   por el que en buen ora naçió" (3724–25).

A social-science gap exists in Cidian bibliography in that there is a lack of studies devoted to topics of obvious importance to understanding this story of a consummate family man whose principal conflict is with sons-in-law who abuse his daughters and disgrace his lineage. The difficulties begin when we seek to investigate the problem from a socio-historical perspective. Until recently, the history of kinship and family, especially in the Peninsula, has been a limited field. This deficiency is suggested by a glance at the relatively small number of entries in a recent bibliographic survey of historical kinship studies. The shortage of studies on historical kinship in the Iberian peninsula is particularly acute. The bibliographic survey referred to enumerates, under Spanish headings, only 16 items under the heading "Medieval and Islamic" periods, and only 17 for the "Early Modern" period. By contrast Great

Britain and Ireland show 105 items for their "Ancient and Medieval" periods, and 254 for the "Early Modern." France, for the same headings, shows 145 and 328 respectively.[11]

The field has expanded considerably over the past twenty years, as can be seen in collections devoted to extensive comparative analyses of kin-related institutions and practices. Jack Goody, the author of many of the most influential studies of kinship history, has, for example, delineated the outlines of a European marriage system. Numerous practices constitute, in their aggregate, this characteristic pattern: the simultaneous emphasis on dowry and the use of heiresses to recruit "marrying-in" sons-in-law; the exchange of property at marriage and death, leading to the frequent control of land and property by women; the connection between the variable endowment of women and their variable attractiveness as marital partners (a factor often linked with in-marriage of partners within similar categories of wealth and status—hence with emerging class divisions); the tendency to limit participation of junior generations in complete property rights; a connection between matchmaking and monogamous institutions; and the synergetic relationship between traditional European bilateral kindred systems, patterns of property devolution, and the inheritance or transmission of political office (Goody, "Inheritance" 10–13).

David Kertzer and Caroline Brettell point out in a recent survey that considerable progress has been made over the past ten years to remedy the earlier deficiency in historical studies of Peninsular kinship and family structure. The studies they survey pay particular attention to such subjects as inheritance, dowry and marriage, household formation and postmarital residence, and childrearing practices. Sources for this recent scholarship have included genealogies, family histories, settlement charters, customary codes, "censuslike" documents, church and notarial records, and so on. Medieval records, these authors observe, tend to be "occasional and of variable quality and utility" (Kertzer and Brettell 89). William A. Douglass, likewise alluding to considerable recent progress in Iberian family history, stresses the increasingly accurate picture of regional patterns of household organization and extended family structure. While we note, he cautions, such regional emphases as the northern Iberian propensity for "multiple-family households," or central and southern trends toward partible inheritance and neolocal residence (i.e., "nuclear family households"), there is a "general lack of a pan-Iberian . . . perspective." There has been, what is more, a tendency to ignore "transnational commonalities," such as those that might exist in regions straddling the Spanish-Portuguese and Spanish-French frontiers. Douglass observes, in addition, that "both the anthropological and juristic traditions" tend to focus on rural households "to the almost total exclusion of urban ones." Medieval topics, he remarks, continue to suffer from a relative neglect (Douglass 2–3, 7n1).

In view of such gaps, it is often necessary, for the analysis of kinship and related topics in medieval Peninsular literature, to read the works as documents in their own right. To do this requires two necessarily speculative approaches. One involves what I call, for lack of a better term, "retro-extrapolation" based on ethnographic studies of recent or contemporary European and Peninsular communities and populations. Kertzer and Brettell argue: "Even the questions posed by those anthropologists who focus primarily on present-day community relations can provide a context within which to frame appropriate historical questions" (95). Consultation of studies on recent or present-day Peninsular communities helps us, therefore, to formulate a conceptual apparatus for describing and analyzing the behaviors and motives of the personages in medieval tales, at least with regard to kinship practices. An example of this is the occurrence of so-called neolocal residence after marriage, a notion expressed in the Spanish proverb "Los casados, casa quieren." Postmarital residence, as we will see, is a principal issue in the *PMC*. Knowing about present-day norms illuminates past attitudes toward this and related themes.

A comparative viewpoint allows the investigator to select examples and analogues from a broad geographical and temporal range. The anthropological perspective par excellence, this approach assumes, however implicitly, that human behavior is explicable in terms of a finite repertoire of needs and impulses. That is why there are innumerable cross-cultural anthologies devoted to such topics as "the meaning of marriage payments," or "kinship terminology." Expressive of this method are the many studies of dowry and related economic and social issues. Dowry seems to appear, to a greater or lesser degree, everywhere in Eurasia, from Japan to Iceland. Studies of the motives and uses of dowry in widely separated societies elucidate, according to the comparative approach, specific instances of dowry in particular communities. The approach, as applied to the *PMC* or any other medieval text, does not postulate a direct connection between the society depicted in texts and those societies discussed in the ethnographic literature. One single aspect of an account of practices such as primogeniture or the fosterage of children, taken from a context far removed in time and space from the milieu of the literary text under scrutiny, may generate a telling description of the practices and perspectives of literary characters and thus facilitate a socially oriented reading strategy.

For critics dedicated, like Garci-Gómez, to the possibility of a truly text-oriented approach that goes beyond philology and historiography, the present essay merely opens yet another bibliographic subdivision devoted to an exocritical topic, in this case social history. The discussion that follows is designed to demonstrate the imperative need to consider social topics in the reading of epic. One cannot perform aestheticist criticism without knowing what the story is about. I do not therefore dismiss Garci-Gómez as a belated convert to New Criticism, despite the fact that endocriticism as he advocates it cannot be achieved with any purity. His very vocabulary reveals the same traps that numerous critics have encountered in the attempt to read literature of the past as if it were written only yesterday. One cannot, after all, talk of literature without recourse to terminology. All terms, at the same time, are fraught with history—with data or with the assumption of data. Garci-Gómez tells (italics mine, indicating "loaded" terms): that the poem "es una *fábula heroica versificada*" (*"Mio Cid": estudios* 43); that the "escritor *español de juglaría*" is "deseoso del *anonimato*" (47); that "por las *Siete Partidas* nos podemos enterar de la importancia de los *homes bonos*" (68). He constantly assumes—relies on—the presence of society in history, the exterior, extratextual reality he seeks to elude in order to achieve a pure reading. In his harangue, what is more, he ignores such recent critical trends as the New Historicism (which rediscovers the embeddedness of literary and aesthetic enterprise in the ambience of history, and the profound and complex implications this has on poetic composition) and deconstruction (which demolishes preconceived definitions of text and authorship).[12]

As it happens, the present author sympathizes with Garci-Gómez's urgent desire to read the poem as literature, without recourse to cumbersome documentation. It is precisely with the eventual goal in mind of performing more straightforwardly aesthetic criticism that one must verify things about the text that are irrefutable. Before this can be done, the motives of the characters must be clarified. The goal, in essence, is modest: to outline a social reading of the poem. This procedure will consist partly of pointing out the overlooked implications of undeniable facets of the story. Critical perceptions are, it is hoped, enhanced through highlighting the uncertainties presented by an enigmatic text. At the same time, interpretation is expedited by the inclusion of new themes for study. Reading the poem from the only perspective available to us—that of late twentieth-century criticism and scholarship—requires admitting the impossibility of definitive readings. What is needed is an array of simultaneously applicable reading strategies, based on the work's apparent parallels with other social contexts. While the inclusion of cultural common denominators may seem ahistorical, the elucidation of such factors permits us to understand precisely why we call this work an epic. The social orientation explicated in the chapters that follow will, I hope, reveal Alfonso's affinity with Homer's Agamemnon, who likewise must resort to the tool kit of manipulable kinship relationships in order to manage internecine conflict. The Cid will be better understood for his similarity to Odysseus, who, like the Castilian hero, must defend a household and a lineage against the depredations of worthless sons of privilege. Once we define the Cid's social dilemma, generic, temporal, ethnic, and geographic boundaries no longer impede our understanding of his experience of fatherhood, marriage, and leadership—the things, in short, that make him what he is.

This undertaking does not aim to fill a bibliographic gap merely because it is there. The topics of kinship and political sensibility need to be explored for their bearing on the motives and attitudes of the hero and his antagonists, and therefore on the plot and outcome of the work. At the same time, there is no particular need to repudiate any existing school of thought merely for the sake of innovation. Surely the literary work of art, capturing as it does a complex experience in complex ways, can accommodate—indeed, requires—several simultaneous critical approaches. This is particularly true of works from a distant past and a foreign society, as presented in this epic composed eight centuries ago.

**Chapter One**

# Kinship

Kinship is, in general terms, the network of relationships determined by consanguineal links and by associations through marriage. A great deal of literature deals with kinship in this wide sense. Thus, Jorge Manrique's *Coplas* on the death of his father, *The Brothers Karamazov*, *Pride and Prejudice*, and *Père Goriot* are all examples, each in its own way, of kinship-oriented literature. We must narrow our focus if we are to define kinship as it is of peculiar interest in the *PMC*.

We begin by recognizing that kinship is frequently sub-classified into the narrower categories of kinship proper and of descent. According to this distinction, first clearly articulated by Lewis Henry Morgan, kinship is ego-centered in that it focuses, as Harold Scheffler points out, on "each person individually" and divides "the totality of persons . . . genealogically connected to him (his kindred) into a number of lesser categories—categories of kin." Each person is, in effect, "the center or hub of a system of social relations." Descent, by contrast, involves the attribution of common ancestry and thus of membership in a genealogically defined category of persons "recognized as descendants or as some specified type of descendant of . . . selected individuals [who are] deemed to constitute a distinct set" ("Kinship" 756, 760–61).[1]

European kinship, it is generally agreed, was once organized—to a greater or lesser degree, and with wide regional variations—around descent. Primordial European kinship terminology thus divided paternal and maternal lines, with separate terms for each of six roles in the parental generation (father, father's brother, father's sister; mother, mother's brother, mother's sister). Classical Latin continues this usage, while extending its lateral distinctions beyond the parent's generation. Hence such terms as *patruelis* ("of or descended from father's brother," i.e., "cousin on father's side"), *amita* ("father's sister"), *avus* ("maternal grandfather," "forefather"), *avunculus* ("maternal uncle"). This system, notes Jack Goody, emphasized "the unity of parents' siblings of the same sex." A "pan-European" drift toward ego-centered kinship, beginning long before Vulgar Latin's differentiation into the Romance languages, transformed European kinship by unifying the roles of a given generation. There emerged a simplified array of terms for same-sex siblings of parents (uncle, aunt), regardless of lateral affiliation. Kinship relations came to be expressed through a limited set of descriptive affixes (e.g., first cousin, great-uncle) defined with respect to an ego, rather than the more complex scheme of discrete, descent-based terms (Goody, *Development* 262–67). The various medieval pictorial models of genealogical representation—the crucifix, the tree, the idealized human body—are characterized by their bilateral character and, as Goody points out, by their emphasis on "the central notion of *ipse*, that is, an *ego*" (*Development* 142). Such systems, typified by Isidore of Seville and other authoritative ecclesiastical models, are concerned with "genealogical distance between kinship positions" rather than with individual genealogies or "terms of address." Modern European kinship shows the same ego-centered emphasis and "a corresponding focus on the elementary family." This, in Goody's phrase, is the family "of birth and of marriage, of orientation and procreation" (*Development* 267, 268).[2]

The *Partidas*, to take a historically significant Peninsular example, present an ego-centered, bilateral catalogue of kinship terms in the Isidorean style. Terms are positioned above, below, or to the side of an ego, in an imaginary tree. The "quatro grados en el parentesco," states the law in question, are counted "en la liña derecha que sube arriba," and consist, in the first degree ("primero grado"), of "padre et madre"; in the second degree, of "abuelo et abuela"; in the third, of "visabuelo et visabuela"; in the fourth, of "trasabuelo et trasabuela." In the direct descending line ("la liña que decende derecha á yuso") the degrees are those of "fijo et fija," "nieto o nieta," "visnieto et visnieta," "trasvisnieto et trasvisnieta." Collateral degrees ("liña de travieso") are "hermano e hermana," "fijos de hermano et de hermana," "nietos et nietas de hermano et de hermana," "visnietos et visnietas de hermano et de hermana" (Alfonso X, *Partidas* IV.vi.4).

The *PMC* is constructed around the contrast between these two modes: descent and kinship. Although we will frequently have occasion to remark upon what must be described as the work's primitivism or conservatism, kinship is expressed by means of modern ego-centered terminology. We find only the few terms used by modern Spanish, with little trace of more primitive, so-called classificatory terminology. Thus, for example, *padre* (1176, 2594, 2604, etc.; 23 times); *madre* (379, 1599, 1608, etc.; 13 times); *fijo* and *fija* (2106, 2123, 2267/68, 255, 262, 269b, etc.; a total of 124 times for both filial terms); *hermano* and *hermana* (928, 2230, 2319, etc.; a total of 6 times for the two fraternal designations); *sobrino* (741, 963, 2351, etc.; 9 times). A partial and interesting exception to the apparent modernity of this vocabulary, as we will see, is the vocabulary and accompanying social practice associated with cousinship. The term *primo cormano* (as in 3303, applied to the Cid's daughters from the viewpoint of their cousin Pero Vermúez) suggests retention of a primitive terminology of categories encompassing all members of a given generation (thus, siblings of various related nuclear families classed as "co-brothers").

Kinship terminology tends to express itself dyadically. It incites its users to experience relationships in person-to-person terms. Kinship words establish a system of relationships defined by their relative position in regard to corresponding terms. A person's status as a type of kinsman, states Scheffler, is "necessarily a status with respect to another individual who is one's kinsman of the reciprocal category" ("Kinship" 760). Kinship terms thus stipulate emotional response and behavioral performance: they define roles. "The basic logic of kinship terminology," affirms Fred Eggan, "is that particular terms do not imply a status position so much as a relationship: the use of a particular term implies its reciprocal" (392). Father, therefore, is a prompt for son, niece for aunt, brother for sister, and so on.

The *PMC* is particularly attentive to the reciprocal logic of kinship terms. More often than not, when such a term is used, its reciprocal—either by the appropriate counterterm or by reference to the person comprehended by the implied relationship—is contained in the same line. Thus, "Afévos doña Ximena   con sus fijas dó va llegando" (262); "cómmo sirva a doña

Ximena e a la[s] fijas que ha" (384); "A la madre e a las fijas bien las abraçava" (1599); "Amos hermanos apart salidos son" (2319); "amas hermanas don Elvira e doña Sol" (2592); "Félez Muñoz, so sobrino del Campeador" (741); " 'firióm' el sobrino e non' lo enmendó más' " (963); " '¡Ala, Pero Vermúez, el mio sobrino caro!' " (2351). The tendency to express kinship nomenclature in reciprocal pairs occurs as well with affinal terms (i.e., those derived from marital alliance between lineages), as in "Mio Çid e su mugier a la eglesia van" (326); " 'Evad aquí vuestros fijos, quando vuestros yernos son' " (2123). While it is natural to use kinship terms in pairs, or in contexts in which the corresponding terms would be implied, the poem's emphasis on the symmetry of the relationships invoked by familial nomenclature reveals more than mere terminological consistency. Often there is as well a complementary or shared action, tacit or explicit, that emanates from the relationship, as in "nin da cosseio padre a fijo, nin fijo a padre" (1176); "el padre con las fijas lloran de coraçón" (2632). The poem emphasizes, in other words, the emotional solidarity and cooperative fellowship evoked by kinship terms.

Kinship in the *PMC* is ego-centered in the sense that the hero is the focus of an active group of kinsmen and followers. As we will see presently, this pattern, typical of traditional societies, involves the formation of so-called kindreds by incorporation of both relatives and fictive kinsmen. At the same time, the poet is very concerned to present the loving solidarity of the nuclear family. The group formed by the conjugal pair and their children, while nearly universal as an observed arrangement, is not always accorded a privileged function, or even recognized as a distinct unit, in many descent-oriented societies (Eggan 390–91).

The *PMC*, despite a preoccupation with descent that will be examined shortly, assumes the importance of the conjugal pair and their offspring. The Cid loves his wife and daughters: "llególas al coraçón, ca mucho las quería; / llora de los oios, tan fuertemientre sospira" (276–77). In the same scene the Cid declares to his wife: " 'commo a la mi alma yo tanto vos quería' " (279). The charming scene in the second *cantar* (1577) in which the Cid displays his horsemanship before his wife and daughters reveals, in his eagerness to impress them, both passionate devotion to Jimena and filial tenderness toward the girls. The famous lines in which the family members' separation from one another is described as a severing of "la uña de la carne" (375, 2642) confirm the authenticity of feeling among family members and the harmony and stability of the nuclear family. The plot of the poem centers on the desire of the Cid to make a good marriage for his daughters, on the dishonor brought to the Cid's family by a flagrant case of wife-beating, on the vengeance he takes against his abusive sons-in-law, and on the triumph represented by the daughters' second marriages.

We may not, therefore, underestimate the significance of the nuclear family in this epic. At the same time, we must determine how that configuration articulates with the broader dimensions of kindred and clan. The nuclear family is a source of emotional companionship and support, as it is today. At the same time, the poem clearly understands this grouping as an entity that comes into being as the union of two lineages.

Kinship proper, we have seen, centers on an ego (as in medieval charts of the consanguineal degrees), while descent attributes genealogical affiliation to groups of persons. Each person in the ego-centered system becomes the nucleus of a "system of social relations." There are, in theory, as many such systems as there are persons in a society. The principle of descent, on the other hand, divides society into a few groups consisting of the descendants of specified ancestors. Descent classifies persons, observes Scheffler, as "selected persons . . . deemed to constitute a distinct set." Scheffler thus distinguishes between "ego-centric systems of social identities and statuses" and "ancestor-oriented" systems based on genealogical relationships to a "putative founder or apical ancestor." Relations of kinship "relate or oppose individuals to one another." Those of descent, by contrast, "relate or oppose sets of individuals to one another or to other sets of the same structural order" ("Kinship" 756, 760).[3]

Kinship relations of the ego-centered type cannot define groups in the same way as can a principle of descent. The latter concept "signifies group membership of a special kind, handed down, like property and office, from generation to generation" (Goody, "Descent Groups" 401). Robin Fox notes that so-called corporate descent groups use membership to control "relationships between owners and heirs, incumbents and successors." Such groups emerge "when there is some form of group property or obligation, like the ownership in common of impartible land, or the duty to avenge death, or the obligation to avenge ancestors" (51–52). Principles of descent are, in general, most prominently used to recruit group members and to govern the relationship between groups.

Descent groups are based, therefore, on a concept of membership as opposed to relationship. As we have seen, membership so defined is based on descent from a putative founder of the lineage, the so-called apical ancestor. Membership in a descent group is, notes Scheffler, a "status shared with or by others who are also descended from the putative founder of the unit in the same way as oneself." The statuses deriving from such membership involve relations among "co-members of the same unit" and between members of "different descent-ordered units." Descent and kinship can, of course, be present in the same society, and can lead to conflicts of status and of obligation in the same person ("Kinship" 761).

## Kindreds and Cousinship

Although the poem accords considerable attention to the nuclear family, that group is but one element—albeit an important one—within a larger grouping. The action of the poem is organized around ego-centered, cognatic kindreds. To understand the narrative we must therefore explicate the poem's understanding of cognation and its consequences.

The term *cognatic* may take several meanings. It refers, for example, to kin of ego defined through all links on the paternal and maternal sides (thus, *cognati* as opposed to strictly patrilineal *agnati*). This is the primary Latin sense of cognation. In contemporary ethnographic usage, the word thus tends to be used as an effective synonym of *bilateral*, as in the term *cognatic* (i.e., *bilateral*) *kinship*. Much of what defines the "open" nature ascribed by Georges Duby and others to so-called pre-agnatic kinship practices derives from the bilateral character of European kinship patterns. The *PMC* appears to participate to a very great degree in this earlier, more flexible tradition.[4]

*Cognati* can also mean strictly maternal kin. Karl Leyser, in a study devoted to maternal kin in early medieval Germanic society, asserts that *cognati* meant more than simply "kin from both sides," its strict Latin meaning. For medieval writers it very probably signified "matrilateral kin." In support of this contention, he cites Isidore's statement (*Etymologiae* IX. vi.1.2) that *cognati* are the relations that arise through females: "Qui inde post agnatos habentur, quia per feminini sexus personas veniunt, nec sunt agnati, sed alias naturali iure cognati." "Kinsmen," states Leyser, "gathered round and sought to stand as near as possible to their most successful relatives . . . on whichever side, so that the centre of gravity and even the sense of identity of these large families could shift, sometimes within very few generations." Thus, the standing of maternal relatives was often "as high as or even higher than [that of] paternal kin, if they were thought to be nobler and had better things to offer" ("Maternal Kin" 126).[5] Because of the importance of female ancestors, *cognatus*, in other words, came to have the frequent connotation of "maternal kinsman"; *cognatio*, in short, "was heavily weighted on the maternal side" (Leyser, "Maternal Kin" 131).

Even when the *cognatio* is a bilateral kindred, women, observes David Herlihy, "serve as the nodules through which pass the surest kinship ties" (*Medieval Households* 82). Fernand Verkauteren, in his account of kindreds as portrayed in genealogical treatises, notes the bilateral nature of the implied kinship system, and the frequent emphasis placed on the prestige of the maternal line (96–97). The *PMC*, despite its obvious glorification of the masculine adventures of the Cid and his followers, presents just such a matrilateral bias within a bilateral kinship system. Reflecting the emphasis on the maternal side documented by Leyser and eloquently explicated by Herlihy, the poem clearly portrays the Cid as the matrilateral ancestor of the kings referred to in 3724: "Oy los rreyes d'España  sos parientes son." These rulers are the descendants of the daughters whose second marriages make them "señoras . . . de Navarra e de Aragón" (3723). The prestige of the Cid emphatically accrues to these descendants through his daughters: "a todos alcança ondra  por el que en buen ora naçió" (3725).

Yet another sense of "cognatic kin," finally, is that of the assemblage of bilateral kinfolk of an individual. Embodying the distinction introduced earlier, a cognatic kinship network is composed of common relatives rather than common ancestors. The term *kindred* has been applied to groups so defined. A kindred, states J. D. Freeman, "consists of all the recognized stocks of a given individual, these stocks being linked, by marriages, in the generations between this individual and his truncal ancestors" (255). The range of relationships in such bilateral groups is determined by "cousinship." A kindred of first-cousin range is defined as "two stocks linked by a marriage in the first ascending generation," with a second-cousin range of kindred showing three ascending generations, and so on (Freeman 255–56). Because the kindred is always ego-oriented, i.e., "composed of persons related to a particular individual (or group of siblings) bilaterally," the members of a kindred, aside from "the core individual and his siblings," are not necessarily related to one another. Kindreds, by their very nature, thus "necessarily overlap one another endlessly," and cannot, therefore, be regarded as independent units. A society can never be divided into separate kindreds in the same way that it may be "segmented into discrete families, lineages, clans, or communities" (Murdock 239).

Bertha Phillpotts, in her study of kindreds and clans in early Germanic society, used *clan* to refer to "large groups of kindred organized on an agnatic basis." A true clan system, however, as she points out, is impossible in the bilateral context which typifies early Germanic kinship. She uses the word *kindred* in the sense of the "fluctuating group" defined by the consanguineal relations of an individual. This sort of group, she affirms, "can have no name, no permanent organization, and no chief." Because the kindred centers on an individual, it is not a corporation; it is "not permanently organized, and each time that it organizes itself its centre, and therefore its circumference, varies" (2–3). It is generally recognized—as Phillpotts observed in her pioneer study—that such bilateral formations are inherently less stable than strictly defined descent groups. Marc Bloch notes the organizational debility of kindreds in the feudal age: "Since each generation . . . had its circle of relatives which was not the same as that of the previous generation, the area of the kindred's responsibilities continually changed its contours." At the same time, the system was subject to "great internal weakness," with its "zones of active and passive solidarity which . . . were surprisingly large" (1: 138). Stephen Barlau, confirming the limitations of the kindred, observes that its membership "is effectively defined and limited laterally rather than lineally," while its "significant members are contemporaries, linked to their common relative along explicitly traceable paths of kinship." There is, at the same time, usually no consanguineal connection between members of the group so defined: "If two members are related as first cousins to the focal individual through the latter's mother and father respectively," they are not related to each other by blood (101).

Similarly, Marc Bloch argued that "vast gentes or clans, firmly defined and held together by a belief . . . in a common ancestry, were unknown to western Europe in the feudal period." Where the Roman *gens* had persisted over centuries due to the "absolute primacy of descent in the male line," the feudal epoch knew no such durable genealogical entities. The ancient German pattern was for each person to reckon his relatives on both the "spear side" and the "distaff side." Bloch attributes this to the relative weakness of the "agnatic principle," in the face of vestigial "uterine filiation" (1: 140). In assuming vestigial uterine affiliation, Bloch was expressing the notion— once prevalent among ethnographers and social historians—that matriliny was the primordial condition from which later agnatic systems diverged. A consensus of more recent scholarship holds that the bilateral orientation of early Germanic societies was more probably the primordial system, and that this bilaterality accounts for the relatively weak implementation of patriliny. Because the kindred is "ego-focused," points out Herlihy, its composition "is redefined for each new generation." Thus, it does not "continuously accumulate members over time." Because it is bilateral, it "assumes that women, as authentic kin, also enjoy rights of inheritance." Moreover, he notes, in an aside that will take on meaning in the course of the present discussion, such a system "does not impose patrilocal residence upon newlyweds, but allows them neolocal or even matrilocal residence" (Herlihy, "Making" 123).

The transient and occasional nature of the kindred rendered it vulnerable to a number of erosive influences (e.g., the rise of seigneurial domains, the emergence of the state). "A kindred," concludes Phillpotts, "can only be said to exist at the moment when it groups itself round a given kinsman, and a large proportion of this group must merge into other groups if some other

individual is in need" (256). Concerning the deteriorating cohesion of kindreds, Bloch cites Beaumanoir, who, speaking in
the thirteenth century, noted that the circle of people bound up
by vendetta obligations was steadily shrinking in contrast with
earlier generations, whose broadly based recruitment of collaborators extended to distant kinsmen. In Beaumanoir's time
the range had been reduced to second, perhaps only first, cousins (1: 139).

When examining the causal relationship between demographic, economic, or political developments and transformations in kinship structures, it would be well to recall the sensible
caveats formulated by Phillpotts. With regard to the persistence
or weakness of traditional Germanic kindreds, she argues, for
example, that the revival of Roman law, apparently favoring the
emergence of agnatic lineages, bears only a circumstantial
relationship to emerging patriliny. In some areas, such as southern Germany, the adoption of Roman law did indeed coincide
with the disappearance of kindreds. However, in northern
France and northwestern Germany, the kindred persisted despite
the implementation of Roman law, while in still other areas,
such as Norway and Iceland, it disappeared before Romanization.
Christianity, emphasizing individual responsibility, contributed
somewhat to the decay of kindreds, but also valued the kindred
as a means of mediating violence. In any event, kindreds sur-
vived centuries of Christianity in some areas (France, Germany), while becoming extinct in pre-Christian Iceland before
1000. The emergence of the state cannot be the direct cause of
the kindred's demise: under the highly organized French kings,
kindred-related feuds persisted well into the fourteenth century.
While the confluence of these three factors—Roman law, ecclesiastical influence, and emergence of the state—was bound to
weigh ever more heavily on the kindred, Phillpotts affirms that
the cognatic aspect of the kindred system cannot be blamed for
its disintegration: "those regions where the most absolute
equality between agnates and cognates prevails are the very
strongholds of the system," while those areas favoring agnates
(Norway, England) saw the system disappear much earlier. A
pattern of widely dispersed, solitary homesteads—as opposed
to one of villages—would seem to weaken a kindred system.
However, areas characterized by homesteads (Friesland and the

Netherlands) show strong kindreds, while in the village communities of England "kindreds languished" (256–60).

Despite the instability of kindreds, they can, nonetheless, show considerable tenacity as a system, and can wield considerable political power in specific instances. Indeed, their very lack of structure can be a virtue. The kindred, observes Freeman, may avail itself of "a wide range of optative relationships" whose establishment is facilitated by the absence of a "binding descent principle." The very lack of mutually exclusive descent groups permits the individual "to accentuate [the relationships] he pleases." Bilateral societies thus show a predisposition toward "the formation of temporary, kindred-based action groups" whose membership is voluntary. Varying in size from five or six up to forty or fifty and engaging in diverse activities (e.g., trading expeditions), such groups may last several years. Although tending to disband after the collective task is accomplished, the group travels as a unit and reveals, while it lasts, coherent organization, intensive interaction among members, and "a marked collective sense of unity." Its members show a strong sense of "common estate and common purpose." A leader usually gives the group its name and is a "ritual expert" who may take auguries or lead the group in ceremonial rituals. Expressing the "interests and predilections of individuals," such "multifarious" associations constitute an effectual program for cooperative undertakings of all sorts (Freeman 266, 269).[6]

Allowing for obvious cultural differences, Freeman's action groups based on cousinship are analogous to the roving company formed by the Cid and his followers. The Cid's followers constitute a group formed about an individual leader; they are, in their inner circle, recruited from the network of kindreds to which the recruiting individual belongs. The essential feature of improvised yet coherent organization centered on a collective task consists, for example, of the skirmish or warfare of the moment, as in various campaigns of the first *cantar*, and the siege, conquest, and defense of Valencia (Cantar II, *tiradas* 64–75). In the longer term, the collective chore of the group, under the direction of its leader, is—in the *PMC* as in Freeman's examples—to assure the furtherance of the group members' material ambitions. "Del castiello que prisieron," affirms the poet, describing the departure from Castejón, "todos rricos se parten" (540). The substantial success of the Cid's campaigns confirms this aspect of the impromptu action group founded by him. The success is defined as much by the distribution of benefits among all members of the band as by the hero's personal success: "A cavalleros e a peones   fechos los ha rricos" (848); "Tan rricos son los sos   que non saben qué se han" (1086); " 'rricos son venidos   todos los sos vassallos' " (1853).

The collective sense of unity among the Cid's men—the "common estate and purpose," in Freeman's expression—derives from the vassalic bond that links the Cid's men to their lord: "vassallos tan buenos   por coraçón lo an, / mandado de so señor   todo lo han a far" (430–31). As a later chapter on the principle of amity ("kin-mindedness") will demonstrate, non-kinsmen are adopted into the group according to principles of fictive kinship or pseudo-kinship, principles chiefly expressed through the terminology of feudalism. Intensive interaction among group members united by this kin-ordered ideology is conspicuous, as the poem reveals by its emphasis on the unanimous and whole-hearted teamwork exhibited by the Cid's vassals in such matters as—in addition to the obvious collective achievement represented by the poem's many battles—the distribution of booty and the giving of wedding gifts: "Todos los de Mio Çid   tan bien son acordados" (2217); "Los vassallos de Mio Çid   assí son acordados, / cada uno por sí   sos dones avién dados" (2258–59); "Assí lo fazen todos,   ca eran acordados" (2488). The ritual functions of the group leader—to conclude our account of the parallelism between the action group depicted in the poem and the transient associations described by Freeman—find their Cidian analogue in the hero's interpretation of omens (*PMC* 11, 859, 2615).

The reader will have remarked that the majority of the Cid's men are not his kinsmen. However, while recruiting from a broad range of volunteers who respond to the "sabor de la ganançia" (1198), the Cid nonetheless builds his fighting force from a nucleus of kinsmen. While assigning great importance to the vassalic bond, the *PMC* emphasizes kinship as the basic associative principle, with vassalage understood as a kind of fictive kinship. It is natural, therefore, that the nucleus of the Cid's band should be composed of kinsmen, namely, nephews.

Marc Bloch demonstrates that this sort of compound status—i.e., kinsman and vassal—was entirely frequent. The ideal vassal was held to be a kinsman: "Devotion reached its highest fervour when the two solidarities were mingled." Although the *PMC*'s feudalism reveals the deviations from French and German patterns which are to be expected in the Peninsular context, the underlying assumption of an "equality of function between the kinship group and the tie of vassalage" remains operative (Marc Bloch 1: 224, 225).[7] The Cid, therefore, is the link—the "traceable path"—that defines a cooperative kindred made up of cousins. The masculine composition of the group in no way contradicts the bilateral character of the kinship system. Cognatic systems, notes Robin Fox, often have "a patrilineal tinge" and a tendency toward "masculine co-residence for purposes of defense and solidarity in work" (153).

In many traditional societies, persons of the same generation may be called by the same term regardless of whether or not they are, in the modern Western European system, cousins or brothers, or, in the ascending generation, fathers or uncles. Such systems tend, as it were, to "maximize the social roles" of a kinship relation, while "minimizing the biological role." Cousinship is therefore experienced in many societies with the same emotional intensity as fraternity in the strict sense. In Indo-European cultures it was the general pattern that "cousins were considered as brothers" (Schusky 16–17). *Hermano* comes from Latin *germanus*, meaning "true, genuine, authentic." Corominas notes (under the entry for *hermano*) that the expression, from earliest times in Spanish, was reserved for "las relaciones de parentesco, sea para distinguir el parentesco en primer grado o el parentesco carnal." In the Latin Golden Age *frater germanus* had come to mean "full brother" (i.e., sharing the same mother and father) as opposed to "stepbrother" or "half brother"; *germanus* alone thus became a synonym of *frater.*

The Castilian *cohermano* (*cormano* in the *PMC* [3303]) derives, according to Corominas, from *co(n)-germanus*, literally "co-brother," as a synonym for *primo hermano*. The latter expression parallels English "cousin german," Catalan *cosí germà*, French *cousin germain*. Cousin derives from Latin *consobrinus, consobrina*, "son or daughter of mother's sister," "cousin on the mother's side," with variant forms of *cossofrenus*, *cosinus*. The term *consobrinus*, together with the complementary form *patruelis*, "of father's brother," "father's brother's son," thus referred to a terminology of cross-cousins (i.e., sons and daughters of ego's opposite-sex parent). Medieval Latin usage, revealing a long-term shift away from the earlier kinship terminology, frequently employed *consobrinus* and its variants as simple synonyms of *consangineus* (*OED*). Goody notes that *cousin* referred to a very broad category of kinfolk—in fact, "could also include 'nephew' and 'niece,' indeed virtually any 'relative' outside the nuclear kin" (*Development* 271). Robert Beekes attests for *consobrinus* the more specific meaning of "Mother's-Sister's-Son," with the "sobrini . . . [the] sons of consobrini." The term *consobrinus*, argues Beekes, "must have ousted sobrinus, so that sobrinus originally was MoSiSo and came to be used for the next generations only when consobrinus had come into being." The etymology of *sobrinus*, he affirms, derives from the Indo-European *\*suesr-inos*, "he of the sister." *Sobrinus*, therefore, very probably had an original meaning of "Sister's-Son," with *nepos* for "nephew," an ensuing development in Latin (from around 200 A.D.). The earlier meaning of "grandson" is preserved in Spanish *nieto*, Portuguese *neto*, with *sobrino* reserved (assuming a generalization from the sororilateral context) for "sibling's son" (48–52).

A term such as *cohermano* "fraternalizes" cousins, treating them as if they were siblings, thereby reinforcing cousinship as a principle of kin-based collective action. The very ambiguity of the term establishes a usefully broad range of "recruitable" kinfolk. While the *PMC* is not necessarily primitive in its articulation of an ideology of cousinship focused on the emotional equivalence of siblings and cousins, its depiction of a kindred group largely defined by cousinship nonetheless suggests a conservative retention of ancient kinship mentalities, at least insofar as these expedite the engagement of mobilizable kinsmen in cooperative endeavors.

The proximity of cousinship to brotherhood is expressed in the rejoicing in the Cid's camp when Minaya returns from Alfonso's court: "assí era llegado, / diziéndoles saludes de primos e de hermanos" (928). The intimate solidarity of cousins is invoked by the Cid as he charges Félez Muñoz with the guardianship of the newly married daughters as the young couples set out toward the Infantes' ancestral estates. The Cid declares to his nephew: " 'Primo eres de mis fijas amas d'alma e de coraçón' " (2619). The pragmatic equivalence of fraternity and cousinship is dramatized with particular intensity in the scene in which Félez comes to the rescue of his cousins, the Cid's daughters, left for dead by the Infantes (*tirada* 131). Of the twenty-one instances in which the word *primo(a)* is used in the poem, twelve occur in the hundred or so lines (2767–812) devoted to the daughters' rescue. " '¡Primas, primas!' " cries Félez (2778) as he comes upon them, then " '¡Ya primas, las mis primas...!' " (2780) and yet again " '¡Primas, primas...!' " (2786). He addresses them as "cousins" (rather than by their given names) even in this moment of danger: " '¡Despertades, primas, por amor del Criador!' " (2787); " '¡Esforçadvos, primas, por amor del Criador!' " (2792). The fraternal aspect of cousinship is further exhibited by the matrimonial functions of Minaya, who, as his uncle's go-between, gives the Cid's daughters away in marriage to the Infantes (2135–40). After the Afrenta de Corpes and the girls' rescue by Félez Muñoz, Minaya arrives at San Esteban to take the girls home. They welcome him with gratitude bordering on delirium: " 'Atanto vos lo gradimos commo si viéssemos al Criador' " (2860). Pero Vermúez, meanwhile, assures the girls of his commitment to avenge them: " 'Buen casamiento perdiestes, meior podredes ganar. / ¡Aún veamos el día que vos podamos vengar!' " (2867–68).

Solidarity of the kin group, as expressed through the principle of cousinship, is perhaps most intensely revealed in the scene in which the Cid invites his nephew Pero Vermúez to participate in the judicial combat with the Infantes de Carrión:

> "¡Fabla, Pero Mudo, varón que tanto callas!
> Yo las he fijas e tú primas cormanas;
> a mí lo dizen, a ti dan las oreiadas.
> Si yo rrespondier, tú non entrarás en armas."
>
> (3302–05)

The Cid thus declares that although he has been insulted (3270–300) by García Ordóñez and Fernando González, the real target of these slurs, by virtue of the closeness of relationship between cousins, is Pero. The latter responds with a challenge consisting of three pronouncements issued in order of escalating vituperative effect. First, he calls Fernando a liar, revealing to the assembled court the episode in which he had saved the cowardly Infante from a Moor, only to have Fernando claim credit (3313–28). Then he recalls the ignominious episode of the lion (3330–34). Finally, he issues the formal challenge, declaring that he fights on behalf of his cousins: " 'por fijas del Çid, don Elvira e doña Sol, / por quanto las dexastes menos valedes vós' " (3345–46). Similarly, after the challenges of Martín Antolínez and Muño Gustioz, Minaya issues his own challenge to the González clan at large, recalling his role in the arrangement of the marriage: " 'Yo les di mis primas por mandado del rrey Alfonso' " (3438). The poet clearly considers that the mistreatment of cousins is a heinous affront to a man's personal honor. The dramatic tension of Pero's defiant speech thus builds through its steadily heightening emphasis on cousinship.

## Avunculate and Fosterage

The Cid is the uncle of several members of his entourage. The poem, to be sure, exhibits certain historical inaccuracies in regard to the specifics of these avuncular relationships. Pero Vermúez, described in the poem as a nephew (2351), was not historically related to the hero. Other characters, by contrast, are known from historical evidence to have been the real Cid's nephews (e.g., Alvar Fáñez [378, 438, etc.]), although their relationship to the hero is not always expressly recognized by the poet (e.g., Alvar Alvarez [442b, 739, 1719, etc.]). Nonetheless, the presence in the poetic Cid's *mesnada* of characters described as his nephews (such as, in addition to Pero, the apparently fictional Félez Muñoz [741]) confirms the importance attributed by the narrative to practices of avunculate and fosterage that are the correlatives of kindred and cousinship.[8]

The avunculate in Germanic and Indo-European tradition tended to involve fosterage of a young man by either his mother's brother or her father. Jan Bremmer has adduced numerous examples of this type of fosterage from history, folklore, and literature (67–69; e.g., Theseus, reared in the household of Pittheus, his maternal grandfather; Beowulf, raised by his mother's father, Hrethel; and Wodan, raised by his mother's brother).[9] An instance overlooked by Bremmer is that of Odysseus, raised in the household of his mother's father,

Autolykos. In Book 19 of the *Odyssey*, Autolykos names the infant hero, declaring that when the lad grows up and "comes to the great house of his mother's line, he, Autolykos, will freely give of his possessions, to make him happy." Homer portrays a relationship between mother's father and daughter's son in which the former claims the right of naming the new-born male grandchild, plays an important role in the lad's up-bringing, and considers the boy his primary heir (Homer 19.399–412).

Marc Bloch remarks that the "sentimental importance with which the epic invested the relations of the maternal uncle and his nephew" reflects a system for which matrilateral ties "were nearly as important as those of paternal consanguinity" (1: 137). Indo-European societies in fact tend to consider transmission of lineal identity through a man's daughter or sister to be as valid—particularly in the absence of male heirs—as that through his sons. At the same time, the roles of maternal uncle and maternal grandfather tend to be perceived as equivalent. This equivalence of mother's brother with mother's father is reflected by the Latin derivation of the word for "uncle" as the diminutive form of the word for "maternal grandfather": thus, *avunculus* ("maternal uncle") derives from *avus* ("maternal grandfather"). Indo-European avuncular fosterage favors the maternal side: the fostering household is usually that of mother's brother or father (from the viewpoint of the youth in question).[10]

Avuncular relationships in the *PMC*—which, in their cognatic orientation, correspond to the matrilateral emphasis mentioned earlier in connection with the poem's depiction of the Cid as the ancestor of kings—are shown to be important not only in the special, marginalized circumstances of the Cid's nomadic community in exile but also in the society at large. Mistreatment of a nephew is intimately offensive to a man's honor. Thus the anger of the count of Barcelona at the Cid's treatment of the former's nephew: "'Dentro en mi cort tuerto me tovo grand, / firióm' el sobrino e non' lo enmendó más'" (962–63). The relationship between uncle and nephew is typically one of intense affection. "'¡Ala, Pero Vermúez,'" cries the Cid, "'el mio sobrino caro!'" (2351). Trust and mutual reliance are likewise essential components of the avuncular bond, as we see from the Cid's assignment of the most sensitive and important missions to his nephews, such as looking after his daughters (to Félez Muñoz, in 2618 ff.) or guarding the precious sword Tizón (Pero Vermúez, in 3188–90) or defending the family cause in judicial combat (also Pero, challenging Fernando González in 3329–52, before Martín Antolínez and Muño Gustioz issue their own challenges to Diego and Assur, then fighting his opponent, in 3623–45).

The poem does not tell us if the Cid is the maternal or paternal uncle of the personages identified as his nephews. Variations on the avuncular theme permit us to hazard a guess, however, as to what might have seemed obvious to the work's audience. The role of maternal uncle as "friendly counselor" has been pointed out as a frequent theme in European folklore and literature. William O. Farnsworth, taking the old view of the significance of the avunculate, subtitled his study of uncles and nephews in the *chanson de geste* "A Study in the Survival of Matriarchy." A sign of this supposed vestigial matriarchy is the fact that one notes in the texts covered by his survey a "tendency to minimize the intimacy between father and son, while exalting that between uncle and nephew." The uncle-nephew relationship, he notes, reveals "the closest solidarity." The father, on the other hand, tends to show an attitude of "severity and injustice" (21).[11]

Goody demonstrates the deficiency of this matrilineal interpretation of the pattern of inheritance and succession from mother's brother (or father) to sister's (or daughter's) son. "The part played by the maternal lineage (or maternal family, or maternal uncle)," he explains, indicates neither a debility in agnatic relationships nor an earlier phase of matriliny. The mother's brother, and her patrilineage, have "an intrinsic role to play for the members of a patrilineal descent group, a role that is in no way incompatible with the system itself" (*Development* 226).

A. R. Radcliffe-Brown explains the relationship of mother's brother and sister's son in terms of "joking relationships" in patrilineal context. A pattern of "privileged disrespect" toward the mother's brother arises, he asserts, where there is "emphasis on patrilineal lineage and a marked distinction between relatives through the father and relatives through the mother." A member only of his patrilineage, a man is not considered a member of his mother's lineage, although she and her relatives may express affection toward him. Authority and discipline are chiefly vested in the father and other males of the patrilineage. The gentler aspects of child rearing are expressed by the mother, her siblings, and her extended kin. The maternal uncle in this configuration naturally tends to assume the role of nurturing mentor and permissive companion. In some patrilineal societies the maternal uncle is even referred to as "a male mother." "The joking relationship with the uncle," Radcliffe-Brown maintains, "does not merely annul the usual relation between the two generations, it reverses it" (97–98).

Claude Lévi-Strauss summarizes Radcliffe-Brown's analysis in terms of "systems of attitudes" which are "inversely correlated." Where the relationship between father and son is marked by "familiarity" (as in typical matrilineal societies), the relationship between maternal uncle and nephew tends to be respectful, while in systems in which a father is perceived as "the austere representative of family authority" (as in the patrilineal context), the relationship between maternal uncle and nephew is characterized by familiarity. While recognizing the importance of Radcliffe-Brown's contribution, Lévi-Strauss observes that the avunculate "does not occur in all matrilineal or all patrilineal systems," while, at the same time, "different forms of avunculate can coexist with the same type of descent, whether patrilineal or matrilineal." Thus, we may find indulgent fathers and forbidding maternal uncles in patrilineal societies, lenient maternal uncles and authoritarian fathers in matrilineal societies ("Structural Analysis" 43–44).

Despite the incongruities pointed out by Lévi-Strauss, Radcliffe-Brown's theory of the correlation between avuncular relationships and lineage orientation has been supported to a certain extent by subsequent work on matrilineal societies. In such contexts, the authoritarian functions of the mother's brother tend indeed to surpass the "severity and injustice" of medieval French epic fathers. The Ashanti system, for instance, invests the (classificatory) oldest living mother's brother with "sole legal authority" over his sister's children. This avuncular authority encompasses the all-important factor of marriage. The control exercised by the maternal uncle over his sister's children yields a highly ambivalent "asymmetrical" relationship, "particularly," notes Harry Basehart, "with respect to inheritance and succession." He cites a significant proverb: "Nephews are your enemy" (291–92).[12]

The Cid enjoys the jocular, nurturing-figure relationship with his nephews generally associated, according to Radcliffe-Brown's hypothesis, with strict patriliny. We see this, for example, in the scenes in which he jokes with Alvar Fáñez about the *albricias* due to him upon their departure into exile (14), or teases his stammering nephew Pero Vermúez by punning on his name: " '¡Fabla, Pero Mudo,   varón que tanto callas!' " (3302). The Cid's indulgent side is seen in his tolerance of what we must construe to be Pero's extreme disobedience, as in the scene in which Vermúez flagrantly ignores, with impunity, his uncle's order to stay in ranks during the battle with Fáriz and Galve:

> "Vo meter la vuestra seña   en aquella mayor az;
> los que el debdo avedes   veremos cómmo la acorredes."
> Dixo el Campeador:   "¡Non sea, por caridad!"
> Repuso Pero Vermúez:   "¡Non rrastará por ál!"
>
> (707–10)

Pero Vermúez likewise shows himself insubordinate in the episode in which the Cid charges him with looking out for the Infantes during another battle:

> "Yo vos digo, Çid,   por toda caridad,
> que oy los ifantes   a mí por amo non abrán;
> cúrielos qui quier,   ca d'ellos poco m'incal."
>
> (2355–57)

There is no mention in the poem of the fathers of the Cid's nephews, so we cannot say for certain that he is their mother's brother. However, the benevolence of the avuncular relations depicted suggests, bearing in mind the hypothesis of Radcliffe-Brown, a patrilineal context. This may be taken into account with other features to which we now turn our attention.

## Agnation

The consensus among social historians is that traditional kinship in much of Europe was bilateral. From the end of the eleventh century this traditionally cognatic Western European system was challenged by the emergence of a unilineal descent system, that of the agnatic lineage. Before the "agnatization" of noble kinship in the eleventh century, Duby affirms, we note an absence of a "conscience proprement généalogique." An aristocrat in this earlier time conceived of his family as "un groupement . . . horizontal, étalé dans le présent, sans limites précises ni fixes." Made up of both *propinquii* and *consanguinei*, the kin group included male and female relatives linked by blood and by "le jeu des alliances matrimoniales." What mattered most for a person's worldly success and prosperity, "c'était moins ses «ancêtres» que ses «proches», par lesquels il pouvait s'approcher des sources de la puissance." Kinship alliances therefore served to establish and strengthen the individual's relationship to political and economic patrons. This stressed an individual's "relations et non son ascendance." One was, summarizes Duby, "bénéficiaire" rather than "héritier" ("Structures" 283). R. Howard Bloch, explaining kinship and genealogy as elements in an aristocratic "bio-politics," remarks that as agnation became the official genealogical discourse of the nobility, "the kin group as a [synchronic] spatial extension . . . was displaced from within by the notion of the blood group as a diachronic progression." Nobility thus became a matter of lineage, with "linearity . . . the defining principle of the noble house." Nobility became defined by genealogy (*Etymologies* 69–70).

Taking a more nuanced view, Herlihy argues that the agnatic lineage "does not so much replace, as is superimposed upon, the earlier, cognatic gens." This patrilineage, "ancestor-focused, rather than ego-focused," must be considered a unilineal descent group since it traced descent to a common ancestor and "like all ancestor-focused descent groups . . . [tended] to grow with each generation." The emerging patrilineage of the twelfth and thirteenth centuries proclaimed "solidarity with the past . . . through the adoption of an agnatic family name, a coat of arms, mottoes, and sometimes even a mythology." Like agnatic lineages elsewhere, it tended to exclude daughters and their children from inheritance and revealed solidarity among males claiming common descent from the same apical ancestor. The patrilineage constituted, according to Herlihy, "a kind of fellowship of males, stretching backwards and forwards over time." The chief material goal of the patrilineage was "to preserve the wealth and status of its male members over time, by limiting the number of claimants upon its resources or by reducing the size of some shares." The chief mechanism for limiting the number of claimants and the size of claims was the practice of primogeniture ("Making" 124–25).[13]

Duby's highly influential theory of the agnatization of European kinship, and the various modifications and responses to it, must be understood in relation to the older debate involving the nature and influence of Germanic kinship. This was long held to be primordially unilineal and agnatic, then to have given way to cognatic tendencies. Barlau, to cite a recent example, hazards that at some point prior to their earliest appearance in the historical record, the Germanic peoples of history (populations speaking Old Norse, Gothic, Old High German, Old English, etc.) had a unilineal system of the so-called Omaha type, with societies segmented into groups whose membership rules were determined by "statable" descent rules. Hints of such an earlier unilineal Germanic system are revealed, suggests Barlau, in the apparent distinctions between maternal and paternal uncles and aunts (implying a lineality atypical of bilateral systems) as well as in individual terms for parallel as opposed to cross-cousins. On the basis of institutional evidence, particularly that relating to *wergild*, he suggests that early Germanic kinship was essentially patrilineal, although with cognatic aspects.[14]

Barlau's findings agree with the view long held by Germanist philologists and historians, and summarized by H. H. Meinhard, according to which the primordial Teutonic kinship was agnatic, with "discrete corporate descent groups." *Sippe*, according to this consensus, had an earlier meaning of "agnatic descent group"; this changed in historical times to signify "an impermanent Ego-centred cognatic body of kinsfolk" (i.e., a kindred). The meaning assigned to *Sippe* for the supposed primordial context is, according to Meinhard, "a heuristic construct of the nineteenth-century professors." Old sources, he affirms, including the Roman accounts of Caesar and Tacitus, do not indicate the unambiguous presence of true agnatic descent groups. The majority of earlier Germanists nonetheless continued to subscribe to the concept of "an originally agnatic system being gradually replaced by a cognatic one." Tacitus's famous account of the mother's brother / sister's son relationship among the Germans was regarded as "the oldest literary record of an agnatic society gradually admitting the principle of cognation."[15] Early medieval Germanic society, while revealing its characteristic cognation, may well have continued to distinguish patrilineal groupings. Meinhard suggests that vestigial agnation can be seen in such things as the distinction between spear- or sword-kinsmen (patrilineal) and distaff-kinsmen (matrilineal). Patterns in inheritance laws (e.g., a seventh-century reference to an old, "heathenish" custom of daughter disinheritance), contends Meinhard, reveal that the distinction sword/distaff refers not merely to the patrilateral and matrilateral dimensions (a division consonant with kindreds) but to descent groups (15–19).

The presumed cognatic system of early medieval Germanic Europe, referred to by Herlihy, Duby, and numerous others, is thought to have been intruded upon by and to have coexisted with the agnatic innovations of the eleventh century and after. If we embrace the consensus of Germanist historians summarized and partially adopted (albeit with qualifications) by Meinhard, as well as the views of Duby, Herlihy, and others, we are faced with the concept of an evolutionary sequence consisting of a primordial agnative phase in barbarian and early-medieval Europe, followed by an intermediate stage of cognation, and finally by a subsequent reemergence of agnation. The apparent contradiction can be reconciled if we refrain from viewing evidence for either kinship mode as proof of a society-wide transformation or phase. Alexander Murray points out that unilineal structures, "sometimes with a distinct corporate aspect," can arise within some sectors of society, such as the nobility, while "the prevalent forms of society as a whole are personal kindreds and cognatic descent" (5).[16]

We may not interpret references to patrilineage and its solidarities as outright confirmation of the agnatic tendencies postulated by Duby and others. Goody notes considerable confusion in terminology, with historians variously employing such terms as clan, lineage, descent group, agnation, and cognation. Clan, for example, refers in strict anthropological terms to a "non-overlapping descent group" (which is therefore, by definition, unilineal). The problem, affirms Goody (and in this he points out the same distinction that Phillpotts did several decades before him), is that the kinds of membership patterns displayed by the groups called clans or lineages in the historians' analyses do not always indicate unilineal descent groups. Some historians use the word *lineage* to indicate a specific line of ascendants, as in the expression "of noble lineage." For others lineage refers to "an aristocratic 'house' (*maison*) whose identity over time is assured by a landed estate, claims to office, titles or other relatively exclusive rights" (Goody, *Development* 228). It is in this second sense that Duby, for example, employs the term *house,* in his discussion of agnatic lineages, "practicing primogeniture," which emerged in the late eleventh century. These noble houses, he notes, bore names "handed down from generation to generation and from male to male, and [were] endowed with a sense of genealogy" (Duby, "Lineage" 37, 39).

Goody provides a concise definition of unilineal descent groups, such as agnatic (i.e., patrilineal) clans or lineages: "[they are] large ramifying descent groups organized on a unilineal basis by means of recruitment through the father." Such systems, however, are never "entirely agnatic," since ties also exist with and through the other parent, ties that are often "of political and social importance." One may further distinguish between patrilineal and patrilateral kin; the latter are simply all relatives on the father's side, of which true patrilineal kinsmen are a subset. Strict unilineal descent, as in the case of agnation (patrilineal descent), means that relatives may include persons of the opposite sex, but not their offspring. For example, a man's sister in a patrilineal system is his agnate, but her children are not his kin; they pertain to the patrilineage of her husband (*Development* 224–27). The agnatic lineage described by Duby was, Goody points out, "a narrow agnatic line of filiation rather than a branching lineage (descent group) of the African or Chinese kind." The shift to such a hereditary system was prompted, he suggests, by a political stabilization that removed war and pillage as sources of income: "the aristocratic patrimony had to be preserved not by force but by adopting a system of devolution based on primogeniture."

This tenurial practice, making impartible family holdings traditionally shared out among heirs, was one of a number of factors, including the introduction of patronymic surnames, that produced the so-called clanic or agnatic patterns described by Duby and others (Goody, *Development* 228).

The consolidation of the agnatic clan, as typified by the practice of primogeniture, was a reaction to conditions that threatened a deterioration in extended kinship. José Angel García de Cortázar describes the changes in Peninsular society between 1050 and 1300 chiefly in terms of a gradual replacement of extended kinship by "simples asociaciones de intereses comunes pero voluntarios." Focusing on the individual rather than the family or clan, these associations become the "único sujeto de responsabilidades." The extended family, traditionally supported by its cooperative exploitation of the "patrimonio inmobiliario," was eroded by such factors as population growth and the presence of the frontier, which encouraged a dispersal of kin groups through migration to newly settled lands. Family holdings that were traditionally impartible were increasingly distributed among heirs. The isolation of family offshoots and the consequent "división del usufructo de la herencia" insured a fragmentation of lineages into "unidades autónomas y más pequeñas." At the same time, changing agricultural markets and the emerging monetary system contributed to erosion of the manorial estate as the economic foundation of the feudal nobility. Threatened by these conditions, and fortified by the revival of Roman law, the landed aristocracy, emulating royal models, instituted the *mayorazgo* (a Peninsular variant of institutionalized primogeniture) and, again imitating its counterparts elsewhere in Europe, such symbolic practices as the vicinal cognomen and heraldic emblems (García de Cortázar 264).

Subscribing to the more recent consensus view (of agnation supplanting cognation, at least in the upper classes) represented by Duby, Thomas Glick portrays the contrast between Muslim and Christian Spanish society in medieval Spain as one between the "agnatic, patrilineal groups forming a segmentary social system" of the Muslim world and a Christian reality in which we observe "a general drift away from the typical bilateral, cognate structures of primitive Germanic society, towards an agnatic, patrilineal structure." He emphasizes significant differences in kinship structure among classes (with "class differentiation of kinship relations . . . possibly the single point which most distinguishes Christian from Muslim kinship systems"), while noting a "more clear, more deliberate evolution [of] the extended family (whether of cognatic or agnatic orientation) yielding in the face of a socio-economic context that favored the stem or nuclear family" (141–43). Glick argues that the extended family tended to persist among the nobility, while among commoners the nuclear family, due to various social and economic factors, and to the Church's ideological support, came to predominate. Citing both the historical and the poetic Cid (a member of the lesser nobility, but a noble nonetheless) as an example of this upper-class conservatism in matters of kinship, Glick notes the presence in the Cid's *mesnada* of four nephews and his wife's sister's husband—clearly indicating, he asserts, a retention of bilateral kinship. Pierre Guichard, Glick's principal source for this perception of Christian and Muslim social structures, argues that the segmentary, agnatic lineage was pervasive in all sectors of Islamic society of the Peninsula, while in Christian society, the "parentèle bilatérale" (bilateral kindred) was maintained "dans l'aristocratie seulement."[17] Jacques Heers, like Glick and Guichard, suggests that nobles show a tendency to maintain family ties longer, to extend support to wider circles of kin, than non-nobles: "nobles rejected family obligations much later than did commoners" (31).

In line with this class-differentiated view, Alessandro Barbero analyzes lineage and family in the *PMC* in terms of the conflict between the Cid's improvised alliance, based on personal achievement and spontaneous collaboration among group members, and the "compatta solidarietà di lignaggio" of the Infantes de Carrión and their faction. This solidarity on the part of the Infantes and their allies derives from a conscious maintenance of the "parentela organizata" of the Carrión faction; indeed, the very term *parientes* "viene impiegato soltanto in riferimento al bando dei Carrión." This pattern is in striking contrast, he asserts, to the case of the poetic Cid, in reference to whom such terms as *natura* and *parientes* "non sono mai utilizzati" (98–100).

The word *parientes* does indeed apply almost exclusively to the Infantes and their allies. It is often used in collaborative—

or even downright conspiratorial—contexts, as when the Infantes' ally García Ordóñez steps aside for a conference ("con *diez* de sus parientes aparte davan salto" [1860]); or when the Infantes consult with their relatives on the forthcoming *cortes* ("Prenden so conseio assí parientes commo son" [2988; also 2996]); or on the matter of restoring the Cid's swords ("Essora salién aparte . . . / con todos sus parientes e el vando que í son" [3161–62]). On the occasion of the judicial combats, we are reminded of Phillpotts's observation that kin-based solidarity is most frequently evinced in legal proceedings: "Mucho vienen bien adobados de cavallos e de guarnizones / e todos sus parientes con ellos son" (3538–39); "muy bien aconpañados, ca muchos parientes son" (3592). The term *parientes* is used to impart the sense of clanic solidarity among the Cid's enemies. This renders all the more dramatic the single exception to this pattern, the line already mentioned earlier, in which the poet tells us that the kings of Spain are now the *parientes* of the hero (3724).

The Cid of the *PMC*, observes Barbero, is "un uomo solo, senza ascendenti né collaterali che limitino la sua autonomia: tutti gli uomini che lo circondano appartengono alla generazione successiva, e ne riconoscono l'autorità." The evidence of historical documents, suggests Barbero, confirms this contrast. While the genealogy of the Infantes can be reconstructed over six previous generations, that of the Cid—aside from "tratti puramente leggendari"—barely comprises two generations. The "coscienza dinastica" of the "grande nobiltà" of which the Infantes are representative has been collectively maintained, since this nobility "discende largamente dagli antichi detentori di cariche pubbliche." The *infanzones* typified by the Cid, on the other hand, constitute "una classe guerriera che comincia appena a sentirsi anch'essa aristocrazia, en non ha ancora sviluppato forti solidarietà familiari, né ha appreso a conservare la memoria degli antenati" (100–01).

The agnatic lineage in all its solidarity is represented in the poem by the Infantes and their faction, while the Cid and his side reveal an improvised group more flexible and open in its recruitment and organization. The Infantes and their side invoke a principle of lineage; their perception is, in R. Howard Bloch's terms, diachronic. Flaunting the aristocratic stature of their line, they boast of their ancestry in the haughtiest tones:

" 'De natura somos de los condes más li[*m*]pios' " (3354). In this they conform to a salient feature of the agnatic culture. "Almost always in the literature of feudal society," notes Herlihy, "allusions to ancestry have the ring of boasting" (*Medieval Households* 83).

The Cid's group is, by contrast, synchronic in its orientation. This is stressed in Barbero's account, which evaluates the contrast between the Cid's social style and that of his adversaries essentially in terms of a contrast between kindred and descent. Recalling Scheffler, Freeman, and other ethnographers, Barbero emphasizes the lack of ancestral depth on the Cid's side and the dynastic consciousness of genealogical depth on that of the Infantes. We may not, however, construct a neat division between the diachronic, patrilateral mentality of the Infantes' faction and the synchronic, bilateral outlook of the Cid and his people. Agnation dominates the Cid's notions of lineage just as it does that of the Infantes. Agnation as manly solidarity is evident throughout, as we see, for instance, in the frequent use of expressions and descriptions that employ *varón* ("a guisa de varón" [1350, 2576]; "commo tan buen varón" [2006]; "bien semeia varón" [3125]). Female deference confirms the emphasis on masculinity as a principle of social action. " 'Fém' ante vós,' " Jimena tells her husband, " 'yo e vuestras fijas' " (269). The daughters, the text thus tells us, are the hero's, not his wife's. The fundamental importance of paternity is later reaffirmed: " 'Vós nos engendrastes,' " the daughters tell their father, " 'nuestra madre nos parió' " (2595).

These are enunciations of the essential tenet of agnatic ideology, which is, ultimately, that paternity defines group membership. The same ideology is clearly expressed in the fragments of the *Siete Infantes de Salas*. From the union of Gonzalo, father of the Seven Infantes, and the Moorish girl ("mora fija dalgo") assigned by Almanzor to serve the captive, will spring Mudarra González. The use of the patronymic is significant: even an illegitimate child by a Moorish girl is considered a member of his natural father's lineage. On his departure for home, Gonzalo instructs the pregnant girl to send their child— "si fuere uaron"—to him in Salas when the lad reaches "hedat que sepa entender bien et mal." Menéndez Pidal's reconstructed verses of the lost epic, as well as passages from the *Crónica de*

*1344* and the *Tercera crónica general*, the chief sources of the fragments, identify Mudarra's mother as Zenla, the sister of Almanzor. Gonzalo, as he embraces her, declares: " 'conbusco fare el fijo que a los otros vengara' " (Menéndez Pidal, *Reliquias* 214, v. 182).[18]

Ridiculed by the king of Segura as a "fijo de ninguno," an enraged Mudarra hears from his mother the story of his birth: "«Fijo, padre avredes muy onrado . . . / ha nombre Gonçalo Gustioz e es natural de Salas»."[19] The *Crónica de 1344* (*Reliquias* 217–18) accentuates the bilateral implications of this situation, in which Mudarra is raised in the house of Almanzor, his mother's brother (a commonplace, we recall, of Indo-European fosterage). What is more, the boy is his maternal uncle's heir: "non he fijo nin fija que herede despues de mi la mi tierra sinon vos" (218.15). The practices depicted are, of course, folkloric projections of European usage; this is not a medieval Spanish ethnography of Hispano-Arab customs. Despite the nod toward Mudarra's matrilateral affiliation, the focus is clearly on strict patriliny, as we see from his commitment to avenge his brothers: " 'poca sera la mi vida si yo estas cabeças de mios hermanos non vengo' " (*Reliquias*, *Crónica* 220.21). The agnatic principle of descent is further accentuated in the reunion of Gonzalo Gustioz and Mudarra. In the reconstructed verses, Gonzalo, reluctant to acknowledge Mudarra as his son, is chided by Doña Sancha, the mother of the slain Infantes: " 'E por vergüença de min non neguedes vuestra sangre' " (*Reliquias* 221, v. 225).

Despite the agnatic aspects mentioned earlier, which parallel those expressed in the *Infantes de Salas* material, the *PMC* does not convey unequivocal agnation. We have mentioned the importance of the nuclear family. To this we may add that both ancestor-oriented and ego-focused kinship play a role in the social universe of the *PMC*. The dimension of kinship, explicated in our discussion of kindreds, cousinship, and the avunculate, is chiefly that of here-and-now political and military collaboration. It concerns the mobilization of kinsmen and vassals in pursuit of immediate objectives. The Cid's primary goal is not merely the acquisition of wealth and power—these are but the scaffolding of his real project—but rather the establishment of a claim to agnatic legitimacy. The synchronic accomplishment of his conquest of Valencia supports the diachronic ambition to perpetuate his line. From the viewpoint of the contemporary monarchs referred to in the poem's final verses, the Cid is the heroic matrilateral forebear of a patrilineal descent group of which he is the apical ancestor. For the Cid, the poem would have us believe, is no less prestigious an ancestor, with respect to the kings descended from him, than the forefathers of the Infantes, the "natura ... de los de Vanigómez / onde salién condes de prez e de valor" (3443–44).

There remains the problem of how the Cid's descendants can claim him as their ancestor. It is clear that from the perspective of the Cid, descent through his daughters represents a rightful perpetuation of his agnatic line. The fact that membership in the Cidian patrilineage is transmitted through his daughters would seem to be a contradiction, since strict agnation would imply that, while his daughters are members of his patrilineage, their offspring would belong to that of their husbands, the kings of Navarre and Aragon (3723). The contradiction is resolved, as will be demonstrated at length in the third chapter, by regarding the daughters (shown to be brotherless in the poem; the historical existence of the Cid's son Diego is never mentioned) as surrogate male heirs. This practice conforms to a multicultural pattern observed in numerous patrilineal systems, as well as to a specifically Peninsular tradition according to which "a Spanish woman of high birth is able to transmit her patrilineal status to her children" (Pitt-Rivers, "Honour" 69).

The poem is not, therefore, about two rival kinship systems of entirely different type. It is about two lineages competing according to the criteria of a single agnatic ideology that finds expression in both the synchronic and diachronic dimensions. The synchronic kindred of the Cid supports his aspiration to become the putative founder of his own agnatic lineage. The diachronic descent group of the Infantes is used as a principle of kindred mobilization in the confrontation with the Cid and his group.

Descent is best conceived not as a set of rules to be followed but rather as a set of complexly interlocking roles to be performed. The apparatus of agnatic display—heraldry, genealogical chronicles, etc.—provides a set of cues for the consistent enactment of these roles by group members. Pierre Bourdieu speaks of descent, for example, as a kind of accumulated capital of "genealogical markers," of onomastic emblems that provide the members of a lineage with "indices of genealogical position." These markers permit, among other things, the distribution of rights to the group patrimony, and solidarity of action when this is required (Bourdieu 36). Edmund Leach's characterization of a specific genealogical system, that of the Kachin, may be extended to genealogical mentalities in general. Family pedigrees, he argues, "are maintained almost exclusively for structural reasons and have no value at all as evidence of historical fact" (*Political Systems* 127). Genealogy, in other words, even when historically verified and useful, might as well be legendary from the viewpoint of any generation that invokes it for whatever social purposes, since these rarely coincide with those of the ethnographer or historian, whose investigations are descriptive and theoretical.

Genealogy and the principles of descent thus serve more to legitimate the status of an individual than to apportion specific rights and obligations to the members of a lineage apparently so defined. On the other hand, if we adopt Barbero's exceedingly praxis-oriented approach, according to which genealogy is primarily an instrument of political and economic control exerted by the group in conflict with other groups, then we may say that the depth of the Infantes' genealogy serves the same purposes as the shallowness of the Cid's. The Cid's genealogy must be shallow in the sense developed by Barbero: he is the founder of a line, its apical ancestor. The social world of the *PMC* is one of kinship rather than one of descent because it is, genealogically speaking, ego-centered, which is to say, it presents the dynamics of the bilateral kindred. For if genealogy is a deliberate creation of agnatic ideology, then so are the links forged among the members of kindreds. Kinship in the ego-centered sense is both a principle of solidarity and the basis of an "action group" created according to that principle.

The poem's focus (3724–25) on the kings of Spain who are now the descendants of the Cid clearly points to a genealogical perspective. Joseph Duggan documents the poet's possible connection to the Monastery of Santa María de Huerta (favored and frequently visited by Alfonso VIII and Pedro II of Aragon). San Martín de Finojosa, brother-in-law of Alfonso VIII's *alférez* and friend of the monarch, was the nexus of a kinship network of the Cid's descendants and their affines who would have welcomed "the performance and preservation in writing" of a work like the *PMC*. The poet's choice of social and economic themes, his portrayal of historic and pseudohistoric characters, and his "attachment to a well-defined area of Transierran geography" all point to the possibility of performance before an audience composed of the Cid's descendants—or of those eager to proclaim such a connection. These plausible speculations, in connection with a documentary exposition too complex to admit of detailed reference here, lead Duggan to identify the poem's Per Abbat as either Pedro I, abbot of Santa María de Huerta, or Abbot Pedro of Ovila, a nearby monastery. The evidence, although admittedly circumstantial, and leading to "inferential" proposals, permits Duggan to suggest that the poem may have been performed at Huerta in 1199, then copied in May 1207 by one of the two abbots (Duggan 83–85, 99–100, 102–05, 106–07).

Whether or not Duggan's audacious theory of authorship ever finds general acceptance or additional confirmation, his analysis of the poem's audience as a function of its genealogical perspective is substantiated, to a certain degree, by the *PMC*'s notion of descent as a criterion of status verification. The portrayal of the exploits of the legendary founder of a lineage—whether or not members of an original audience regarded themselves as members of said lineage—is to be examined in conjunction with the poem's participation in yet another emblematic practice of the kind referred to by Bourdieu: the naming patterns associated with the European agnatic clans. "Family groups," reports Duby, summarizing his own findings on the aristocratic lineages of the Mâcon region, "were clearly set apart by a cognomen, a family name that brothers and cousins bore in common." While such names could be "nicknames that had become hereditary," most were "associated with the land, that is, with the family's landed patrimony, its inheritance" ("Lineage" 18).

Glick, analyzing the trend away from earlier bilateral kinship toward "a patrilocal, patrilineal, agnatic kinship system," describes the growing use of the cognomen, the family name at first based on that of an illustrious ancestor, then modified to indicate the geographical nucleus of the family fortune (e.g., Haro, Lara, Castro). This, he asserts, reflects the emerging descent-oriented system. The historical Cid's name, he affirms, reflects this vicinal naming pattern: the name Rodrigo Díaz de Vivar contains a patronymic (derived from Diego Laínez, the Cid's father), and the form "de Vivar," representing the geographical locus of the Cid's extended family (Glick 143).

That both sides in the dispute dramatized in the *PMC* subscribe to essentially the same kinship ideology is seen by the poem's obsession with the vicinal cognomina of the two factions. The frequent formulaic epithet applied to the hero, "el de Bivar" (295, 550, 855, 961, etc.) and such variants as "Ruy Díaz de Bivar" (628, 721) and "el bueno de Bivar" (969), must be understood in light of this vicinal fixation. "Vivar" occurs 22 times in the poem. In all but three instances it is a component of the cognominal epithet. "Vivar" as a mere geographical reference appears only once ("a la exida de Bivar" [11]). The other two non-epithetical examples also reflect the cognominal orientation. The Cid, for instance, rejoicing at the numbers of recruits (1263–66), boasts to Minaya: " 'Con más pocos ixiemos   de la casa de Bivar' " (1268).

Glick argues that the historical Cid's surname of "de Vivar" confirms the historical shift "from the community of blood relationships . . . to the common hold of the extended family" (143). Richard Fletcher points out, on the other hand, that the "earliest evidence for the connection (of Vivar to the Cid)" occurs in the poem itself (107). What is of concern here is not the *PMC*'s historical accuracy in the attribution of the specific cognomen to the Cid, but its understanding of the status-affirming significance of this naming practice. The vicinal naming pattern, generalized through the Middle Ages among the European nobility, gave rise to the so-called noble particle, as in French and Spanish *de*, German *von*, Dutch *van*. Karl Ferdinand Werner points out the need for caution in interpreting such shared names as a sign of pervasive clanic solidarity. The use of the cognomen does not necessarily imply an integral endorsement of agnatic ideology. There were, after all, poor members and poor branches of aristocratic lineages. Such naming practices, suggests Werner, should be understood, rather, less in terms of "un dogme du groupe familial et de la parenté," than as a "grammaire de relations de parenté" within the emerging class structure of the later Middle Ages (26).

Vicinal cognomina, therefore, are best understood in terms of status emulation. This does not make the Cid a dysfunctional personage like the modern social climber. It is natural that the Cid take as model in his genealogical project the lineage of his rivals, for the Cid wants what the Infantes have: a lineage perpetuated diachronically. Emulation thus confirms rivalry: the cognomen, indicator par excellence of the stable, geographically localized, diachronically perpetuated lineage, is an emblem of patrilineal prestige. The poem's invidious perception of the cognomen is reflected in the frequent repetition of the toponym associated with the Cid's foes: "Carrión." Used 135 times (versus 22 examples for Vivar), the name occurs in most instances as a component of the cognominal formula "iffantes de Carrión" (1372, 1385, 1835, 1879, etc.), with the cognomen "de Carrión" appearing far more frequently than the patronym González (12, as in 2286, 2527, 2558, etc.), or than the given names of the two young men (Diego, 10 times, as in 2288, 3353, 3658; Fernando, 18 times, as in 2168, 2725, 3634; numerous times they are paired formulaically, as in 1901, 2267, 2352, etc.).

Just as caution is required in interpreting agnatic tendencies in the poem, so also must we refrain from an undue emphasis on apparent class structure. As I have demonstrated in another study, class sensibilities are present in this epic, but are not necessarily self-consciously emphasized by the poet. The presence of named social categories (e.g., *fijos d' algo*, *infanzones*, *ricos omes*, etc.) may be suggestive of differential status among types of persons, indicating what the outside observer might analytically ascertain to be groups defined by shared circumstances (as discussed in the Introduction). However, such differences and potential criteria of association do not necessarily reveal the rigid hierarchy and intergroup confrontation connected with advanced class structure. We find little evidence of a "consciousness of common interests," of the "common class antagonisms" that differentiate Marx's *Klasse an sich* (an incipient grouping without collective awareness of communal identity) from the *Klasse für sich* (the collectively purposeful group capable of communal action in confrontation with other groups). Indeed, the kin-ordered, multifarious nature of political and military collaboration in this poem, as noted earlier in connection with the Cid's recruitment of followers, occurs in disregard of the kinds of economic differences typical of advanced class structure. The Cid's army is composed of a happy few, a band of brothers, and each of the Cid's men, be he ever so mean, will lay down his life for his lord.[20]

Clanic solidarity is inherently eclectic in its deployment of allegiances and resources. Heers, arguing that the notion of class structure is anachronistic when applied to European society before the sixteenth century, suggests an essentially less rigid social structure, contending that "the idea of more or less closed classes" precludes our recognition of "the numerous opportunities for social advancement through the tenure of innumerable royal, princely or municipal posts, through clerkship, the law, or accounting; also through war, or quite simply through marriage." One may speak, he concedes, of social categories such as wealth, way of life, or professional activities. But to speak of classes, class struggle, and "class feeling" leads to "regrettable confusion." He makes the point that the noble clans, always with the presumable purpose of furthering and protecting agnatic interests, engaged in an exceedingly complex game of expansions and contractions, alliances and associations. The game was seldom in mere defensive reaction to the *popolani*, who, through patronage and marital alliance, represented a pool of potential allies and collaborators. They could be recruited, in other words, into what he calls the "suprafamily group," consisting of "associations of individuals who all bore the same name." Such a group could consist of several dozen or several hundred persons. The more powerful families among the commoners, meanwhile, imitated noble ways and sought whenever possible to associate their own lineages with the great noble clans (Heers 5, 10–13, 82).

We will have more to say concerning kindred cooperation, factional recruitment, and the poem's vision of team spirit in the next chapter. For the moment we note that the Infantes, contemplating marriage to the hero's daughters, contrast the Cid's lineage with their own by citing first of all the respective geographical loci of the two houses. " 'Mio Çid es de Bivar,' " observe the Infantes, pessimistic in their matrimonial deliberations, " 'e nós de los condes de Carrión'" (1376). The poem thus confronts the two lineages by juxtaposing the names of the two houses within a single line. Ian Michael, assuming a modern, class orientation on the part of the poet (176n), ascribes the Infantes' misgivings (" 'non la osariemos acometer nós esta rrazón'" [1375]) to the disparity of rank: they are, he reminds us, of the highest lineage, while the Cid is a mere *infanzón*. Nevertheless, their hesitation and the secrecy with which they at first nurture their intentions ("Non lo dizen a nadi e fincó esta rrazón" [1377]) is perhaps more readily explained with reference to clanic confrontation than to class conflict. Again, there are undeniable status differentials at the lineage level in the poem, and the notion of hypergamy (marrying-up by the woman) is of pervasive importance in the work, as we will see in a later chapter. Nonetheless, the Infantes' reluctance to reveal their intentions could very well derive not only from disparities in status but rather from the mere fact of the long-standing rivalry between their lineage and that of the Cid, a rivalry the poem does not explain but clearly takes for granted as a thing known to the audience. The delicacy of the situation stems, therefore, not so much from the snobbery of class sentiment as from the political expediency of the feud.

## Conclusion

Various historians, including García de Cortázar, Glick, and Heers, underscore the persistence of traditional extended kinship among the nobility. There is an implication that the noble classes, prompted by a desire to cultivate mechanisms of group identity and social control, resisted changes through collective retention of traditional kinship. On the other hand, this same nobility is viewed by other historians, notably Duby, as an innovative force in the implementation of agnatic practices that were in fact inimical to traditional European bilateral kinship. The reality was probably more complex. As Goody, Bourdieu, Murray, and others point out, kinship practice is almost always multifaceted, with this or that aspect emphasized in expedient response to prevailing conditions or situations. We may add that characterizing nobility as the collective practitioner of an array of purposeful tactics is perhaps an inversion of terms. Nobility is more an outcome than a precondition: noble families are finalists in a long competition involving numerous elimination rounds. We may just as well say, therefore, that certain families consistently exhibiting solidarity and skill in manipulating advantages—both inherited and acquired—managed to secure a material and political predominance that enabled them to define themselves as noble. Nobility, in other words, is a disguised synonym for clanic solidarity. At the same time, advantages once obtained synergetically facilitate—given the appropriate energy and talent among current clan membership—a renewal of political, economic, and honorific privilege for each subsequent generation.

Referring to a wide body of findings, Herlihy suggests that the agnatic lineage appeared as a result of the "diminishing opportunities and resources available for the support of the elite households." The political and economic stabilization of Europe, reducing "the profits of pillage," left the landed patrimony as the principal economic resource. Thus arose such practices as primogeniture, designed to conserve the clanic holding within the patrilineage. Concomitant to this practice were other tendencies. Elite families, reports Herlihy, "forced their younger sons to delay or eschew marriage, or they sent them forth to make their fortunes." Daughters, if they received anything, "were given [only] the dowries they needed for marriage." Save for unusual circumstances, such as the death of all her brothers, a daughter's dowry "represented the extent of her claims upon the family patrimony." A daughter in the neo-agnatic system is "a marginal member of her father's lineage." Her own children are not members of her father's lineage; instead, "their allegiance passes to her husband's line."[21]

The hero of the *Poema de Mio Cid*, while showing some of the attributes of agnatic culture, such as an obsession with vicinal names and a desire to found a patrilineage of his own, is immune to several of the trends cited by Herlihy. Pillage, for one thing, plays an important role as a source of income and material advancement. On the other hand, primogeniture and related strategies of selective heirship are absent. Dowry plays a role, as we will see, but in no way functions as a disguised disinheritance of the daughters. Not only are the Cid's daughters full-fledged members of their father's lineage, but their descendants as well can lay legitimate claim to membership in the clan of which he is founder. The daughters are perceived to be the primary vectors of agnatic ambition for the Cid and his family. They are the chief means of converting the Cid's descendants into a lineage of *parientes*.

These and related topics are the subject of our chapter on marriage. Before we analyze them, however, we must first clarify an important aspect of the poem's social mentality: namely, its approach to human relationships in general.

## Chapter Two

# Amity

Kinship systems vary in the extent to which genealogical and affinal relationships are recognizable for social purposes. They also vary, as Fred Eggan observes, in "the rights and obligations . . . mediated through kinship." Often, in addition to a primary kinship based on consanguineal and affinal links, "metaphorical and other extensions . . . result in related systems or subsystems." The figurative expansion of kinship terminology derives its metaphorical apparatus from the entire kinship system, not merely from the relationships encompassed within the nuclear family. The latter formation, yielding the so-called primary relationships (i.e., parent, child, sibling), is, while a nearly universal phenomenon, not always the principal focus of the kinship system. Many societies utilize the broader associations of descent for organizing such domestic functions as child rearing, education, and so on. Moreover, birth alone is not the definitive factor in determining a child's status as a member of a lineage or a people, given that it is "the social recognition of parenthood that provides a child with a legitimate position in society" (Eggan 390–91).

Kinship in the broad sense is, then, less a system for determining sets of relationships than an engine for generating and justifying ideologies of relationship. Where, for example, paternal affiliation determines membership in a descent group, the role of *pater* (i.e., social father) tends to prevail over that of *genitor* (biological sire). Whether ego-centered or descent-oriented, kinship does not refer, Harold Scheffler reminds us, to genetic relationships, given that "such relationships are unknown to (i.e., not posited by) the vast majority of the world's peoples . . . [and thus] could not possibly serve . . . as criteria for the ordering of their social relations." The fact that the biology of genetic relationships is unknown to most peoples does not forestall, Scheffler adds, the proclivity of "folk-cultural systems" for devising notions of consanguinity as criteria in the determination of group membership and in the distribution of rights and duties. When "blood ties" are cited, however, they are always the expression of metaphorical bonds—there is no "literal" aspect to traditional kinship (Scheffler, *"Elementary Structures"* 260).

In traditional societies, all relationships tend to be understood as the extension of the consanguineal metaphor. Non-kin relationships are represented not as residential, professional, or confraternal affinities, as they tend to be in modern communities, but rather as ties of fictive or ritualized kinship. Kinship, as it were, colonizes the world by adopting outsiders into the realm of familial relations. Affiliations of all kinds—emotional, political, economic—are thus accommodated to the kinship model. Meyer Fortes has suggested that the basis of this assimilation is a "principle of kinship amity." This amical precept is in turn associated with rules of conduct whose force derives ultimately from "a general principle of kinship morality that is rooted in the familial domain and is assumed everywhere to be axiomatically binding." The concept of amity as kinship morality implicitly divides the world into "two opposed spheres of moral alignment." One is that of "kinship and the familial domain," the other that of "non-kinship." The social universe is thus "polarized into a field in which the rule of amity prevails, and into its contrary, ultimately perceived as the outside world" (Fortes, *Kinship* 232).

While not going so far as Fortes in assuming the ethical uniqueness of kinship relations, Maurice Bloch emphasizes kinship morality as a principle of "political and economic organization" which tends to maintain "the best type of long-term moral relationship." Because morality generally presupposes long-term commitments, "there is no sharp break between kinship and other commitments," argues Bloch, "but rather we should regard kinship as the end of a continuum consisting of commitments of different terms" (Maurice Bloch 77). Viewing the social world as a "continuum of commitments," we may thus regard amity as the organizing principle of the positive extreme, enmity the "anti-ethic" of the negative. Amity in the absolute sense involves unconditional duty, benefaction, and tolerance with regard to those embraced within its circle. All those not within that circle would be the legitimate object of aggressive, selfish behavior or attitudes explicitly forbidden or implicitly controlled by amity. This is why the polarization of the social universe established by kin-based amity—into a dimension of insiders and outsiders, of "us" and "others"—readily gives rise to the ethnocentrism and xenophobia often exhibited by traditional peoples and by isolated or small-scale communities.

The principle of amity assumes two aspects of kinship relationships (and therefore of all meaningful associations). Such relationships are, first of all, mutually binding. Unilateral relations are difficult to imagine in the context of the kin-ordered society. The other characteristic of amical relations in the kin-ordered world is their constancy. Relations of kith and kin are, by their very nature, established in perpetuity. Limitations or conditions transform such relations into something else. Kinship obligations therefore tend to be expressed, notes Maurice Bloch, "as binding, unconditional, and without term." The liabilities and expectations incumbent upon kinship roles are, again, ethical, so that failure to observe kinship obligations brands a person as "the opposite of a moral being," thus as a "murderer, bestialist, lover of death, etc." (78).

Societies may be categorized as more or less kin-oriented according to the degree with which they organize social life in conformity to the principle of kinship amity. The kin-ordered society, however, is not simply one in which the entire social world, even the world beyond the circle of one's kin, is treated as kinfolk. Eric Wolf, while allowing that there are such entities as kin-ordered societies, points out the problematic nature of defining their concept of kinship. "Populations vary," he notes, "in the extent and intensity of their kinship ties." At the same time, "some people have 'a lot of kinship,' others much less." What defines kin-orderedness is, rather, a perception of society and kinship as synonymous. In the kin-ordered society, kinship is the only intelligible principle of social organization. It is not that all men are kinsmen, but that one maintains and establishes relationships with one's kith and kin, while all others are outsiders. All communities must, nonetheless, allow for interaction with outsiders. That is why the "ideology of kinship," and the symbolic function of kinship nomenclature, are employed, as Wolf phrases it, in "the escalation of kinship from a set of interpersonal relations to the political order" (Wolf, *Europe* 92–93).

## Pseudo-Kinship

Fortes speaks of categories of kin "embraced within the orbit of kinship amity." The gravitational field (if I may be forgiven the extension of his metaphor) within which this orbit is described is an "ethic of generosity" that may be broadened to comprise persons and categories of persons far removed from the hub of the system in the "familial domain." The ethical program thus defined is governed by an "axiom of prescriptive altruism" that derives from "the realm of moral values." When a person who is not kin is "metaphorically or figuratively placed in a kinship category, an element, or at least a semblance, of kinship amity goes with this." Moreover, the " 'social recognition' which converts genealogically identified, imputed, or represented connections into kinship relations" imposes the complete kinship role on the recipient of such recognition. Such roles involve "rules and stipulations that regulate rights and duties, privileges and claims." The norms of the assigned role are "thenceforth binding on the persons concerned." Thus, for instance, the adopted child must behave with filial respect toward his fictive parents. He may not, by the same token, marry his adoptive siblings. It is an "incontrovertible principle," summarizes Fortes, "that all classes and categories of genealogically describable connections are ultimately traceable . . . to actual, postulated, or figurative parentage and the reproductive cohabitation which is its prerequisite" (Fortes, *Kinship* 234, 251).

When the primary associative principle of amity embraces persons not related by ties of descent or marriage, it requires a corollary idiom of pseudo-kinship in order to integrate non-kin into the amical sphere. The concept of pseudo-kinship has been explicated in cross-cultural context by Julian Pitt-Rivers. While conceding that, to a certain extent, "any relationship which employs a kin term is kin," he observes that the ascription of kinship status to persons not related by consanguineal or affinal kinship necessarily "depends always upon the individual will of, at least, the initiator." It is the deliberate, often sacramental nature of such relationships that sets them apart from those of kinship proper. Though often ritualistically confirmed, kinship relations are ascribed by birth. Pitt-Rivers distinguishes three types of pseudo-kinship: figurative kinship, fictive kinship, and ritualized friendship. The types may variously coalesce or diverge: "figurative usage becomes an attribution of status when it enjoins behavior appropriate to kin," while ritualized friendship may well exist with no reference or analogy to kinship. Figurative kinship terminology (e.g., the use of "granddad" for all old men) implies "a quality of behavior rather than a status, fraternity rather than the relationship of sibling." Genuine kinship inheres to the person by birth, "whatever the criteria of ascription may be," while pseudo-kinship is an achieved status. The status in question is usually expressed in terms of adoption by or induction into the host group. An adopted person becomes "almost equivalent to one who was born into that status, is linked to all [family] members through ties of kinship, and addresses them by kin terms." The most common function of adoption is to provide heirs, although some societies—such as those that insist on adoption of a captive into a captor's lineage—assign "a kin affiliation . . . where this is essential for the conduct of social relations" (Pitt-Rivers, "Pseudo-Kinship" 408–09).[1]

Adoption, despite its importance in Roman law, virtually disappeared, according to Goody, "from the early legislative codes of the German, Celtic and Romanised peoples in the West." He attributes adoption's thousand-year lapse into desuetude to the Church's dominant influence on family law. A man without heirs who could not adopt was "more likely to leave his possessions for charitable purposes." Thus, the Church "could only benefit by excluding 'fictional' heirs." The details of Goody's theory, which regards the Church as the principal catalyst in the transformation of adoption from a "strategy of heirship" to a kind of spiritual kinship (in the form of godparenthood), are too complex to admit of treatment here (Goody, *Development* 72–75, 99–101, 195–96). Adoption as such plays no evident role in the *PMC*. Whether this reflects Church influence or is simply a matter of narrative irrelevance would be difficult to determine. If the absence of adoption in so kin-minded a poem does indeed reflect the impact of ecclesiastical policy, that impact would have been felt centuries before the composition of the poem—the underlying social transformation might then have been so ancient as to have made the lack of adoption a diffuse and imperceptible element in the social universe of the poet and his audience. On the other hand, as we will see in the next chapter, the poem is ignorant of many policies identifiable with canon law, particularly those associated with marital consent, another element in Goody's cluster of ecclesiastical statutes relating to kinship. At the same time, the fact that adoption plays no role in the *PMC* very probably has nothing to do with legal prohibition. Goody's statement that adoption was "absent from the legal systems of Europe" and was not revived in the West until the nineteenth century is not accurate with regard to medieval Spain, if we may judge from the evidence of the *Partidas*, which allow for adoption in terms predictably reminiscent of Roman law.[2]

## Fosterage

If adoption was infrequent in medieval Europe, for whatever reasons, then another type of artificial kinship was a thriving institution throughout the Middle Ages. This was fosterage. We have already had occasion to mention one kind of fosterage in the *PMC*, namely, that of kinfolk, particularly nephews. Fosterage of non-kin was, apparently, a habitual expansion of this traditional practice. Herlihy notes the tendency of wealthy households to raise a disproportionate number of the surrounding community's children. Orphaned relatives, the illegitimate children of the head of household, adopted children, servants, and apprentices—all these suggest a "massive drift of young persons into and out of the homes of the wealthy." The causes for this influx were various: kinship obligations, simple piety (many households adopted young people, Herlihy notes, " 'for the love of God' "), economic utility. Evidence "from all periods and places of the medieval world," concludes Herlihy, "indicates that rich households were bigger, and presumably more complex, than the poor." Young people tended to circulate among wealthy households before they married (often thereby obtaining the means of establishing their own residence). This "flow of young people among households" was not, however, characteristic only of servants: "the movement was across wealth categories, and up and down the social scale" (Herlihy, *Medieval Households* 153, 155–56).

It is known that the number of persons retained in a lordly household was a symbol of that household's prominence. Orderic Vitalis, in Book VI of his *Ecclesiastical History*, describes the household of Hugh of Avranches, "pre-eminent among the magnates." This notable baron, "a great lover of the world and of worldly pomp," is as famed for his courage ("always in the forefront of battle") as for his munificence ("lavish to the point of prodigality"). The splendor of Hugh's castle is the marvel of all guests, who are well provided for by a host addicted to "games and luxuries, actors, horses, and dogs." His enormous household, finally, is always "full of the noise of swarms of boys of both high and humble birth." Emphasizing both the hospitality of this great lord and the diversity of those attending upon him, Orderic describes Hugh's household as the residence or meeting place of "great lords, simple knights, and noble boys alike" (3: 216).

The size and diversity of a noble household were, then, affirmations of its prestige. The *PMC* partakes of this status-confirming tradition. We know this because of numerous references to both the size of the hero's household and the diversity of its membership. The poet, first of all, uses the same word, *cort*, for the households of both Alfonso and of the Cid in Valencia. Thus, lines such as "Grant fue el día [*por*] la cort del Campeador" (2474) and "Pesó a Mio Çid  e a toda su cort" (2835) are in obvious parallel to the many references to the court of Alfonso (1360, 1384, 1938, etc.). The size and importance of the hero's court are confirmed by the numerous references to the *dueñas* attendant upon Jimena and her daughters. Thus the scenes in which the Cid's wife prays "con çinco dueñas de pro" (239); when the Cid commends Jimena and the girls to the care of Abbot Sancho, declaring, " 'a ella e a sus dueñas  sirvádeslas est año' " (254); and when Minaya sends a message to the Cid assuring him of the imminent arrival of Jimena, their daughters, " 'y todas las dueñas con ellas,  quantas buenas ellas han'" (1412). The ladies in question, we note, are not merely numerous, but high born ("de pro," "buenas"). The prestige of the Cid's household is enhanced by the quality of those who serve in it.

The dimensions and heterogeneity of the hero's court are perhaps most conspicuously indicated in connection with the word *criado*, the term for a person fostered in the household of a lord or prominent kinsman. Thus, in a catalogue of the Cid's entourage, we encounter "Muño Gustioz,   que fue so criado" (737). A close examination shows that many of the Cid's followers are bound to him by ties of fosterage as well as vassalage. Standing with the hero as the Infantes arrive at court are "muchos   que crió el Campeador" (2514). The Cid's court is therefore distinguished by the number of its *criados*. Like all roles in the kin-ordered world, that of *criado* is complementary to other functions. We have already mentioned that kinship and vassalage were not only compatible but desirable as functions fulfilled by the same person. The same holds true for fosterage. Thus, the Cid calls out for Muño Gustioz: " '¿O eres, Muño Gustioz,   mio vassallo de pro? / ¡En buen ora te crié   a ti en la mi cort!' " (2901–02). As with nephews, so also with *criados*: the Cid entrusts to Muño the mission of going to Alfonso to lodge his complaint against the Infantes, as he assigns other, similarly important duties to his nephews. That fosterage establishes a relationship of pseudo-kinship is intimated by the poem's expression of its own version of the nurture/nature division. Its insistence on Alfonso's obligations toward the Cid's daughters reinforces the notion of unbreakable bonds and stringent obligations. " 'Yo las engendré amas,' " the hero reminds his lord, " 'e criásteslas vós' " (2086).

When the Infantes prepare to accomplish their nefarious intentions against their wives, the poet tells us that they send the baggage on ahead, so as to preclude the presence of any witnesses: "adelant eran idos   los de criazón" (2707). The latter expression signifies, according to Michael's gloss, "los de su séquito." These are not, as in capitalist society, servants hired pursuant to recruitment, interviews, and a perusal of references. These are people raised in the household. They are followers because, being members of the household, they are by definition members of the *bando* of the Infantes. The same is obviously true of those assigned by the Cid to accompany Muño Gustioz in his mission to Alfonso: "e con él escuderos que son de criazón" (2919). The poet, by informing us that these squires are "of fosterage," is telling us that they are "of the household."

## Friendship

Pitt-Rivers, speaking on the "kith and kin" as encompassed within a category of "amiable relations," points out that there is a fundamental "antithesis between the notions of jural and moral relations." Morality, he points out, is "seated in the sentiments and conscience of the individual." The "very essence" of morality is free will; coercion can thus play no role in its furtherance. Moral conflicts "cease to be *moral* once sentiments become subjected to jural concepts of right and obligation." Friendship, based on "reciprocity of sentiment" as well as of action, can never be jural (in the sense of being based on rules, incentives, or sanctions). Because friendship involves only "moral commitments," the only sanction in friendship is "withdrawal of sentiment," while "if friendship is placed upon a jural basis it denies its nature: the altruism which is its foundation is revealed to be false." Hence the paradox of friendship: giving must be spontaneous and disinterested, yet at the same time must "be reciprocated if the moral status quo is to be maintained." Friendship is "sentimental in inspiration and instrumental in effects." At the same time, there can never be any question of account-keeping in friendship: "once a tally of favours is kept the amity has gone out of it and we are left with a tacit contract; the relationship is no longer simply moral but implicitly jural." However, the slighted or injured party who protests at unanswered favors "destroys his own reputation by implying that he expected they should be, that he gave them only out of calculation in expectation of a return." Such an admission, revealing as it does that sentiment is not mutual, brings about the irrevocable collapse of the relationship. Pitt-Rivers cites the example of peasant culture in southern France, where neighborly assistance based on a "system of dyadic ties that admits no accounting" ("je ne suis pas regardant" is the common phrase) is "a vital element in the economic system" (Pitt-Rivers, "Kith and the Kin" 96–97).

Friendship is perceived in kin-ordered societies as an association proceeding from kinship feelings. These sentiments are, again, inherently connected with the ethical system of a society and constitute, in Freeman's phrase, "a special morality." The bilateral kindred, a structure defined in the previous chapter, has been described as particularly open to the use of friendship as a supplementary recruiting principle. Members of a kindred, observes Freeman, "admit a special obligation toward one another . . . [to] give help and support in culturally determined ways." By the very openness of its structure, the kindred readily admits friendship as a principle of social cohesion: "the friends of Ego may become the friends of his cousins . . . [and] the development of the institution of friendship is marked in bilateral societies, for the formation of personal friendships is not impeded by loyalties to this or that segmentary descent group" (Freeman 264, 268).

The *Partidas*, reflecting their origin in a society in which kin-minded mentality has not yet been fully eliminated by the diverse forces of modernization, have much to say on the topic of friendship. Revealing little sense of an interpersonal domain that is none of the law's business, they elucidate the nature of relationships considered purely personal by legal codes of later centuries. Like the ethnographers just cited, the *Partidas* show themselves theoretically committed to an understanding of amity. Citing Aristotle, the Fourth *Partida* mentions the Latin term *amicitia* as the proper name for the intrinsically moral virtue of friendship and points out the social utility of friendship. If friendship were the rule, there would be no need of courts or judges (IV.xxvii.1). Friendship is the foundation of mutual interdependence among men. The powerful need friends to sustain them in their position, while ordinary people need friends to support them in poverty and to inspire them in adversity (IV.xxvii.2). Friendship—*amistad*—is, above all, a natural phenomenon. It is the instinctive feeling of parents for their children, of a husband for his wife. The inhabitants of a country, moreover, have a natural friendship for their compatriots that intuitively promotes mutual assistance. At the same time, a higher kind of friendship is one that, while fulfilling all the positive requirements of natural friendship, arises solely from conscious good will rather than from "deudo de natura."

Yet another kind of friendship, however, is inferior to the first two because, being based on mere advantage and the expectation of short-term gain, it tends to dissolve when the material benefit which was the pretext for the relationship is obtained or denied (IV.xxvii.4).

The *PMC*'s conservatism in matters of kinship—as explained in the previous chapter—illuminates its notions of friendship. The latter concept, as is well known, was generally used by medieval folk as a synonym of kinship. Marc Bloch observes that the most prevalent term for relatives, whether by blood or marriage, is *friend* (Fr. *ami*, Germ. *Freund*). D. A. Bullough confirms the use of *amici* and its vernacular derivatives as a synonym for *propinqui, parentes*. The meaning of clanic solidarity, notes Heers, was expressed through the use of the word *friend*. Citing a number of studies and sources, Heers demonstrates that, in the French and Flemish clanic culture that is the focus of his study, the word *amis* meant "relative," which is to say, a member of one's own clan. In cases of conflict or of negotiation, members of a lineage saw to it that they were always accompanied by a maximum number of *amis*. Hinojosa, in his study of fictive brotherhood in Spain, reports the same tendency to equate friendship with consanguinity.[3]

Thus, when Muño Gustioz, the Cid's *criado*, declares to Assur González, "en tu amistad  non quiero aver rraçión" (3380), he very possibly uses friendship as if it were a synonym for kinship. The fact that he is a *criado* and therefore of the hero's household (and historically the Cid's relative by marriage, although the poem does not allude to this relationship) lends credence to this interpretation, as does the poem's expression of the inherently reciprocal nature of friendship, a feature which in many societies leads to a conflation of friendship with blood relationships. The reciprocity of friendship is conveyed by the poem's description of the suffering of the besieged inhabitants of Valencia, in which complementary kin terms are juxtaposed with a friend/friend pairing: "nin da cosseio padre a fijo,  nin fijo a padre, / nin amigo a amigo  nos' pueden consolar" (1176–77).

One's friends are, in essence, one's loved ones. Friendship in the kin-ordered world therefore refers to all persons admitted within the circle of amity. Dispatching Minaya on a mission back to Castile, the Cid exclaims: "'A nuestros amigos bien les podedes dezir: / "Dios nos valió e vençiemos la lid"'" (830–31). If the Cid meant by this friends as opposed to relatives, the omission of the latter would be unusual. The word *amigos* is therefore perhaps more aptly translated as "kith and kin." Friends are defined as those who want to hear of one's triumphs; enemies are, given the appropriate circumstances, those vanquished to provide bread for one's self and friends. The designation of friend is an exclusionary label; those left out are implicitly defined as the contrary, namely, enemies—that is, those omitted from the rolls of amity. We certainly get this notion of an amical elite as the Cid addresses Alfonso and the court at large: "'¡Dios salve a nuestros amigos e a vós más, señor!'" (3038). Later, as the Cid takes his leave, the poet describes his departure in similar terms: "espidiós' de todos los que sos amigos son" (3531).

Friendship in the *PMC*, conflated with both kinship and vassalage, is therefore a kind of fictive kinship, following the three-fold distinction suggested by Pitt-Rivers. The third element in that division, that of ritual kinship, has not yet been addressed. Pseudo-kinship of this sort establishes "ties analogous to kin ties." Such relationships include blood brotherhood and ritual co-parenthood, also known in the Spanish-speaking world as *compadrazgo*. This kind of relationship, argues Pitt-Rivers, should not be considered fictive kinship of the same kind as that expressed in adoption or its analogues. "No fiction is involved," insists Pitt-Rivers, "[since] these institutions are conceptually distinct from and frequently contrasted with natural kinship." Indeed, ritual kinship is itself considered a primordial relationship and is often used as the basis of metaphorical extensions: "just as there are fictive forms and usages of consanguineal kinship, so there are of ritual kinship—and we can hardly speak of fictive 'fictive kinship.'" Ritual kinsmen are comparable not to brothers but rather to brothers-in-law. Ritual relationships, moreover, tend to be limited to the two parties observing the pact. In blood brotherhood, the "intimate identification implied by the exchange of blood represents a bond between two persons . . . [but] does not as a rule entail the acquisition of ties with [each other's] kin." The pact of blood, on the other hand, often settles wars, feuds, and private vendettas. Blood covenants thus "guarantee amicable terms between tribes, kin groups, families, or individuals." Frequently, such compacts expedite "formalizing an instrumental or a purely affective relationship between two men." What Pitt-Rivers calls "covenanted comradeship" is "almost always irrevocable," and "prescribes reciprocal gifts and mutual trust, feelings of amity and the obligation of mutual assistance." It usually involves the ritual "invocation of divine powers who bear witness." The bodily fluids or substances ritualistically exchanged may include, in addition to blood, saliva or semen.[4]

Hinojosa's study of "fictive brotherhood" ("fraternidad artificial"), emphasizing the ritual replacement or imitation of "el vínculo natural de la sangre," points to this institution's origins as a ritual confirmation of the collective exploitation by siblings of the indivisible family holding. Blood brotherhood, Hinojosa notes, is rarely expressed through written law, being a custom observed "principalmente en sociedades políticas poco adelantadas." Basing his study on Leonese documents, he confirms first the persistence of the principle of the indivisibility of inherited property. This collective exploitation was organized according to a notion of corporate utilization and maintenance of the land ("a manera de sociedad"). The corporations of interest to Hinojosa—often consisting of co-proprietors of churches—were those which, based on the model of the fraternal collective, were established by individuals not related by blood (Hinojosa, "Fraternidad" 259–60).

Hinojosa's concept of blood brotherhood does not conform to Pitt-Rivers's distinction of ritual kinship, since the Spanish scholar emphasizes the kinlike aspect of the institution (as opposed to its independent institutional nature). The solidarity expressed by the documents he cites underscores, nonetheless, the character of friendship as a kinlike relationship. Thus, a pact from 1031: "Et sedeamus unus ad allos amicos bonos cum fide et veritate, cum gente, cum amicis et inimicis in totos dies et noctes." *Amici*, as elsewhere in medieval Europe, is a synonym of *hermanos*. Another document quoted by Hinojosa specifically employs the term for friendship when confirming a pact of fictive brotherhood: "Et pro tale actio fecerunt ipsos infanzones inter se *amicitate*." A passage quoted from the *Historia compostelana*, to mention another instance, shows the synonymous use of *germanitas* and *amicitia*. At the same time, affirms Hinojosa, "el estado de hostilidad entre individuos y familias se designaba con el nombre de *inimicitia*." He quotes (recalling the distinction between amity and enmity, alluded to earlier) a text from 1191: "Promissum est nobis pro huiusmodi, ut si *inimicitia* vel infirmitas vel aliud aliquid adversi nobis evenerit, semper auxilium et consilium inveniamus, etc." ("Fraternidad" 269–73, 272nn37 and 38).

Friendship in the amical environment of the kin-ordered community is at once more personal and more official than in modern society. It is not a casual relationship, but a quasi-ritualistic convention. It is, to make use of Pitt-Rivers's terminology, an achieved rather than an ascribed status. The institutional word for the practice that establishes this status appears, in the *PMC*, to be *amistad*. Muño Gustioz, in his challenge to Assur González, exclaims: " 'en tu amistad   non quiero aver rraçión' " (3388). Why would Muño say such a thing, rejecting something never offered him, unless it were presumed to be already in effect? That is, Muño, because he is a *criado* of the hero's entourage, perceives that a relationship has been initiated between himself and his lord's kin, consanguineal or affinal. It is perhaps a relationship by association, but it pertains nonetheless because of his conscious allegiance to the Cid.

The solemn or deliberate nature of friendship explains, perhaps, the significance of *amistad* in ironic or repudiative contexts. The Cid taunts Búcar in the midst of battle: " 'saludar nos hemos amos   e taiaremos amistad.' " To this the Moor replies: " '¡Cofonda Dios tal amistad!' " (2411–12). This seems, as Ian Michael suggests in his gloss of this line, a play on words. However, the pun only works if *taiar*—"to cut, chop, slash, slice"—was part of an idiomatic expression, signifying something like "to hit it off," "to embark upon a friendship." Yet why would "to cut a friendship" mean such a thing, unless there were an underlying imagery of bloodletting—in other words, of blood brotherhood?

The poem's depiction of Abengalbón as the Cid's "amigo de paz" provides an additional hint of ritualized friendship. The Cid tells his men to pass by way of Molina: " 'tiénela Ave[n]galvón,   mio amigo es de paz' " (1464). The expression *de paz*, suggestive of ceremonial confirmation, is reminiscent of the "guest-friendship" relationship of Homeric epic. Later, Abengalbón will employ another expression. The Moor, upon the arrival of the Cid's people, greets them with "grant gozo," exclaiming: "'¡Venides, los vassallos  de mio amigo natural!'" (1479). Alfonso is also several times addressed or referred to as "señor" or "rrey" "natural," as in the lines "'Grado e graçias, rrey,  commo a señor natural'" (895), "'al rrey Alfonso  mio señor natural'" (1272), and others (1885, 2031, 2131). The only other persons called "natural" in this poem—aside from the Cid himself in his Moorish friend's exclamation—are Martín Antolínez ("el burgalés natural" [1500]), and the Cid's daughters, referred to as his "fijas naturales" (1522). The word *natural*, thus meaning "by birth," "by race," as well as "inherent," "genuine," "legitimate," is therefore very possibly tantamount, in the context of friendship, to the expression "by blood." It may well mean, therefore, something like "consanguineal friend"—i.e., "blood brother."

As Minaya escorts Jimena and her daughters to Valencia, Abengalbón meets them on the road and offers them lodging. Responding to the Moor's assurance of his love for the Cid ("'en paz o en guerra  de lo nuestro abrá'"), Alvar Fáñez declares: "'¡Y[a] Ave[n]galvón,  amígol' sodes sin falla!'" (1525, 1528). This affirmation of a separate peace between the Moor and the Cid is evocative of the amical imperatives underlying ritualized friendship, which, in the pre-state world of kin-ordered society, supersede all but the closest ties of blood kinship. The intimacy and trust between the two men is strikingly reiterated. As Elvira and Sol are about to depart with their husbands for Carrión, the Cid entrusts the care of his daughters to Félez Muñoz, charging him with conveying the Cid's best wishes to the Moor: "'saludad a mio amigo  el moro Avengalvón; / rreçiba a mios yernos  commo él pudier meior'" (2636–37). It is clear that friendship entails the obligation to accord unconditional hospitality to the loved ones of a friend.

## Vassalage

The ties of vassalage, as Marc Bloch demonstrates very clearly, were experienced—again to employ the distinction suggested by Pitt-Rivers—as a kind of ritualized kinship. They involved solemn relationships established between individuals; the exchange of "personal substance" (e.g., by means of a kiss, whether on hands or mouth); the calling upon God as witness; the extension of mutual affection and assistance. Jacques Le Goff has likewise extensively documented the minutely detailed attention given to the ritualistic protocol surrounding the ceremonies of entry into and departure from vassalage (Marc Bloch 1: 224–27; Le Goff 237–42).

In its interpersonal (as opposed to its economic) aspect, feudalism is a fictive extended kinship, with the lord acting as a *paterfamilias*, and his vassals, in essence, adopted sons. Feudal vocabulary thus observes the logic of kinship terminology, i.e., that particular terms evoke not a status but a grid of relationships, as embodied by paired reciprocal terms, with each term cueing the use of its match (e.g., father/son, parent/child, brother/sister, etc.). Also as with kinship terms such as *daughter* and *father*, the frequency of occurrence of feudal terms is suggestive of the importance of the indicated relationships. Thus, *señor* occurs 90 times, *vassallo* 39 times.

Vassalic logic and terminology, by virtue of their affinity with kinship, readily conflate with those of friendship. Martín Antolínez, joining the Cid's band, declares his faith in eventual reconciliation with Alfonso: " 'aún çerca o tarde el rrey querer me ha por amigo' " (76). *Friend* here would certainly seem to be a functional synonym of *vassal*. When Muño Gustioz challenges Assur González, his accusation of mendacity is couched in terms of a chronic violation of the principles of amity. The terms he employs are significant: " 'Non dizes verdad [*a*] amigo ni a señor' " (3386). The pairing of *friend* and *lord* suggests, on the one hand, a kinlike reciprocity, if we take the juxtaposition of the two terms as the indicator of a vertical relationship. When one has said such a thing in feudal society, one has said: "everyone, high and low." On the other hand, if *friend* and *lord* are parallel rather than reciprocal expressions, the former term may be taken as *comrade*, perhaps even something like *teammate* in the sense of "co-vassal of the same lord," "co-member of the same *bando*."

The dyadic symbiosis of lord and vassal is expressed in the famous line 20, uttered by the townsfolk of Burgos: " '¡Dios, qué buen vassallo, si oviesse buen señor!' " The notion is repeated, with the Cid himself as the lord (implicitly contrasted, we may guess, with Alfonso), in the scene of the hero's arrival at the final *cortes*: "Bien aguisado viene  el Çid con todos los sos, / buenas conpañas  que assí an tal señor" (3022–23). The reciprocal nature of the relationship is shown to be inescapable: neither factor is complete without the other, as the Cid insistently reminds Alfonso through gifts and through the words of his emissaries. Minaya, for instance, assures the king of the Cid's continued loyalty: " 'rrazonas' por vuestro vassallo  e a vós tiene por señor' " (1339). On the occasion of the third gift, Minaya repeats the vassalic formula with small variation: " 'a vós llama por señor  e tienes' por vuestro vassallo' " (1847). Muño Gustioz, on the occasion of bearing the news of the Afrenta de Corpes, will repeat yet again the symbiotic formula: " 'ele es vuestro vassallo  e vós sodes so señor' " (2938). When the king's pardon has finally been obtained, the Cid himself expresses the symbiotic power of the vassalic relationship: " 'Esto gradesco  al Criador / quando he la graçia  de don Alfonso mio señor; / valer me á Dios  de día e de noch' " (2043b–45).

The fatherly aspect of feudalism is conveyed in the Cid's unflinching acceptance of the role of provider for his followers. He assures Martín Antolínez: " 'yo non trayo aver / e huebos me serié l  pora toda mi compaña' " (82–82b–83). " '[Y]o adobaré conducho,' " he shortly afterwards tells Abbot Sancho, " 'pora mí e pora mis vassallos' " (249). As he releases the count of Barcelona, the Cid explains why he cannot give back any of the booty taken: " 'sabet, non vos daré  a vós un dinero malo, / ca huebos me lo he  e pora estos mios vassallos' " (1042–44). The dependency of vassals on their lord, the correlative of this lordly paternalism, is also clearly revealed:

> ¡qué bien pagó  a sus vassallos mismos!
> A cavalleros e a peones  fechos los ha rricos,
> en todos los sos  non fallariedes un mesquino;
> qui a buen señor sirve  siempre bive en deliçio.
>
> (847–50)

The good lord is he who generously provides for loyal vassals. This allocative function is confirmed by the report of Minaya and Pero Vermúez to Alfonso: " 'Las gananças que fizo  mucho

son sobeianas, / rricos son venidos  todos los sos vassallos'"
(1852–53). Vassalage, however, is more than a unilateral acceptance of largesse. It is an ongoing exchange, a reciprocal generosity. More is involved than goods and services. Vassalage
must be confirmed and continually reaffirmed by symbolic
gesture. One of the poem's most dramatic moments is that
scene in which we witness the final phase in the long process
of reconciliation between lord and vassal, and the ultimate vindication of the symbiotic concept of vassalage. We see this
resolution in the act of absolute trust performed by the Cid as
he leaves for Valencia, not even staying to watch the judicial
combat. " 'Estos mis tres cavalleros,'" he declares to Alfonso,
" 'en vuestra mano son, / d'aquí vos los acomiendo  como a
rrey e a señor' " (3487–88). Alfonso, having presided over the
hearings and having mandated judicial combat, has already
assured Rodrigo that the latter's champions will be in good
hands:

> "Dadme vuestros cavalleros  con todas vuestras guarnizones,
> vayan comigo,  yo seré el curiador,
> yo vos lo sobrelievo  commo a buen vassallo faze señor
> que non prendan fuerça  de conde nin de ifançón."
>
> (3476–79)

The drama of the scene resides in Alfonso's public acknowl-
edgment of the debt owed, a reflection of his understanding that
a good lord must recognize and appreciate the good and true
vassal. The king's transgression has been—aside, we assume,
from his credulity in accepting the testimony of jealous
courtiers—to overstep the bounds of the patriarchal aspect of
lordship. This seignorial immoderation is seen above all in
Alfonso's arrangement of the marriage between the Cid's
daughters and the Infantes of Carrión (1886-93). The king's
political usurpation of the matchmaking function so vital to the
workings of traditional kinship is not of itself incompatible with
the pseudo-kinship role of feudal lord, given that marriage in
traditional society is in many ways a political arrangement. As
*paterfamilias* in the pseudo-kinship network of vassalage, it is
only natural that the feudal lord should practice matchmaking;
historical documents amply confirm that this was the case.

Thus, we may suppose that the filial component of the vassal's role is expressed through the Cid's compliance, however reluctant, with the will of his lord in this matter:

> "A Dios lo gradesco que del rrey he su graçia
> e pídenme mis fijas pora los ifantes de Carrión.
> Ellos son mucho urgullosos e an part en la cort,
> d'este casamiento non avría sabor,
> mas pues lo conseia el que más vale que nós,
> fablemos en ello, en la poridad seamos nós."
>
> (1936-41)

Even as he plays the role of dutiful son to Alfonso's feudal patriarch, the Cid himself assumes the kin-related role of matchmaker. This is revealed in the scene in which he informs Jimena that he intends to arrange marriages between the ladies of her entourage and vassals of his following: " 'Estas dueñas que aduxiestes, que vos sirven tanto, / quiero las casar con de aquestos mios vassallos' " (1764–65). Because the cohesion of the group is what matters most in the kin-ordered universe, it is the system that imposes the matchmaking role on the head of the extended household, which is a community defined by kinship and its surrogates. For the lord to arrange the marriages of vassals and ladies-in-waiting, in the vassalic ideology of the poem, is therefore to fulfill communal expectations. It is, however, one thing to arrange a vassal's marriage, quite another to arrange the marriages of that vassal's own children. Alfonso's error lies in his extortion of his vassal's compliance at the moment of the latter's greatest vulnerability, in the scene of pardon and reconciliation.

## Factionalism

We have already mentioned the importance of fosterage, a kind of pseudo-kinship, in the ideology of the medieval extended household. In addition, we saw in the previous chapter that as Barbero has observed, the term *parientes*, implying an agnatic descent group, tended to be used for the following of the Infantes. The Cid's collaborators, by contrast, are organized around a core of adherents based on the principles of avunculate and cousinship. *Bando*, in somewhat parallel fashion to the pattern shown by *parientes*, is likewise attributed almost exclusively to the faction of the Infantes. Thus, Gonzalo Ansúrez and Assur González, father and brother of the Infantes de Carrión, accompany Diego and Fernando, along with others: "e con ellos grand bando que aduxieron a la cort." The zone of recruitment for the members of this *bando* is a broad one: "De todas partes allí iuntados son" (3010, 3012). A broader, more inclusive concept than that of the vassalic network, the *bando* consists of all who can be mobilized to one's cause. The term *bando* is to the extended feudal clan—encompassing vassals, *criados*, and client lineages—as the word *parientes* is to the consanguineal clan. The *bando* is, in addition, to be understood from the perspective of the noble household, whose multiplex structure we have already mentioned. The faction thus merged easily with "lineage" in the historical sense explicated by Goody, that of the "aristocratic house" or "dynasty" (*Development* 228).

The *bando*, the aggregate faction identified with a noble house, was, as it were, the political extension of the artificial kinship of vassalage. Factions thus defined could be expected to act in unison at public events, particularly legal actions. The Carrión contingent shows this solidarity in refusing as one man, following the example of "el Crespo de Grañón" (García Ordóñez), to rise to its feet in respect for the Cid (unlike Alfonso himself and all others at court): "Nos' quiso levantar el Crespo de Grañón, / nin todos los del bando de ifantes de Carrión" (3111–13). That the *bando* is analogous to but separate from the kinship network is suggested in the scene in which the Infantes confer with their relatives and supporters at the height of the trial: "Essora salién aparte iffantes de Carrión / con todos sus parientes e el vando que í son" (3161–62). It is assumed that factional membership precludes anything like objective judgment, as we see from Alfonso's pointed remarks upon naming judges in the Cid's case. He selects Count Anrrich and Count Remond, " 'e estos otros condes que del vando non sodes' " (3135–36). The formidable power implicit in this factional solidarity is suggested by the request of the Cid's champions before judicial combat begins. Addressing King Alfonso as "king and lord," they ask for fair mediation and protection from injury. They are asking for security in the face of possible aggression by the opposing faction:

"que fiel seades oy   d'ellos e de nós;
a derecho nos valed,   a ningún tuerto no.
Aquí tienen su vando   los ifantes de Carrión,
non sabemos   qués' comidrán ellos o qué non;
en vuestra mano   nos metió nuestro señor:
¡tenendos a derecho,   por amor del Criador!"

(3575–80)

Phillpotts summarizes the practical social importance of the kindred in terms of the possibility of a man's surrounding himself "at any moment . . . with a large group of persons, all of whom are willing to make sacrifices for him." This, she notes, is quite different from the situation of a person "who has to depend on his own efforts and on those of his immediate family for protection against aggression." The "cohesive kindred" she describes—broader in recruiting range but no less coherent than the kindred proper, and rallying above all around a member threatened with a lawsuit—would seem to correspond to the factional grouping called *bando* in the *PMC* (Phillpotts 247–48). Similarly, Heers documents the operations of the extended agnatic clan as a "suprafamily group" of varying size consisting of "associations of individuals who all bore the same name." This extended clan emphasized the flexibility of membership criteria. Heers postulates, in terms of the origin of this formation, a trend away from the bilateral *Sippe* and toward the *Geschlecht*, "a dynasty which brought together all those men who claimed a common ancestor" and in which "wealth and authority were handed down through the male." This group, identifying itself with a geographical locus from which it took its name, corresponds to the agnatic clans described by Duby (Heers 19–20).

The clan as defined by Heers was, however, far more fluid in its structure than Duby's strictly agnatic lineage. The extended clan defined by a common name and ancestor revealed considerable discrepancies of power, wealth, and social prestige among its members. Factional solidarity was in no way diminished by this flexibility of recruiting standards. Indeed, this open, variegated structure is a contributing factor (especially in such areas as Old Castile and Poland), to the rise of a so-called popular nobility, a phenomenon marked by large percentages of a population claiming noble status (and noble names), by a large-scale movement from country to town, and by the "influence of rural structures on municipal ones." In the Basque country and in Castile, suggests Heers, the confrontation and alliances of various factions corresponded to those between and among the clans of other regions. Peninsular lineages, he argues, tended to be "federated into solid, widespread clans, and formed resolutely hostile parties: the *bandos*" (22–25).

While referring to the fourteenth and fifteenth centuries, Heers's model of clanic solidarity may usefully be applied to the social order portrayed in the *PMC*. Indeed, the poem's factional patterns may reflect earlier stages in the social processes that gave rise to the superclans of Heers's study. The power and wealth of the clans, each of whom commanded considerable military power, were not only conducive to armed strife but also inhibited "the very existence of the state." Heers provides a detailed account of patterns of military conflict among lineages (and between lineages and emerging municipalities), involving urban fortresses, the enlistment of dependent or vassal lineages, and paid mercenaries. In the economic realm, the clans "held sway over lands, shores, markets, ports and bridges." In Italy and elsewhere, banking and other financial institutions originated as clan operations. Heers summarizes: "economic cohesion was still, at the end of the Middle Ages, expressed through families."[5]

The *PMC* shows solidarity of the *bando* in the alliance between García Ordóñez and the Infantes: "el conde don Garçía en estas nuevas fue, / enemigo de Mio Çid que mal siémprel' buscó, / aquéste conseió los ifantes de Carrión" (2997–99). Later, Count García will lead the deliberations of the faction: " 'A esto fablemos nós.' / Essora salién aparte iffantes de Carrión / con todos sus parientes e el vando que í son" (3160–62). In the climactic scenes of the poem, García Ordóñez steps forward to be the spokesman of the Infantes and their whole faction. He clearly speaks for the entire group: " 'Quanto él dize non ge lo preçiamos nada' " (3279). As Colin Smith points out, there is no historical evidence "for the poetic alliance of this Castilian with the Leonese Vani-Gómez."[6] The poetic collaboration of the Cid's great enemy and the clan of the Infantes, while perhaps historically inaccurate, is nonetheless clearly suggestive of the supraclanic confederations described by Heers. For the

Peninsular context, María Quintanilla Raso records, in her study of familial and clanic patterns in Cordoban society, the factional rivalries associated with "sólidos linajes, que atrajeron a extensas clientelas de vasallos, escuderos, allegados y criados." The proliferation of "bandos nobiliarios," she observes, was, in Spain just as in other areas of Europe, a principal cause of civic disorder and violence (Quintanilla Raso 347–49).

The term *bando* is never applied to the Cid's group. There is, to be sure, the interesting use of the term in the sense of "help," "assistance," "backing," in that scene in which, in the midst of the battle, the Cid calls Minaya his "diestro braço" and exclaims to his loyal vassal: " 'Oy en este día de vós abré grand bando' " (753–54). *Bando* as a collective term is, however, reserved for the faction of the Infantes. Nevertheless, the Cid is not without his own following. This group is referred to by various terms. A collective word for the vassals of a lord is, for example, *escuelas*. Alfonso uses it to address his court: " '¡Oídme, escuelas e toda la mi cort!' " (1360). Michael glosses this term as a derivation of the *schola regis*, the "séquito de vasallos del rey" (174n). Alfonso himself uses the term in a more general sense, that of "vassalic entourage" (of any lord, and not just of a king), as he excuses the Cid's following of penalties exacted earlier: " 'a todas las escuelas que a él dizen señor, / por que los deseredé, todo ge lo suelto yo' " (1362–63).

Another word used for the Cid's following is *conpaña*, as in the descriptions of the Cid's loyal entourage in terms of "una buena conpaña" (60). The expression is used, on occasion, to convey something almost like "headcount," "recruiting statistics," as in 296 ("quel' creçe conpaña por que más valdrá") or 2165 ("la conpaña del Çid creçe e la del rrey mengó"). Used as a collective term for "company of warriors" (16, 440, 484, 517, 524, 1817, 1829)—as opposed to "companionship" ("dando ivan conpaña" [1385b])—it usually refers to the Cid's men. In 1981, referring to the "grandes conpañas" of the Infantes, it designates simply the total retinue of any important personage.

Likewise used as a collective designation for the Cid's following (and that of Alfonso) is *mesnada*. Referring in ten instances to the troops of the hero and on six occasions to those of Alfonso himself, *mesnada* is a term of broader reference than *entourage* or *retinue*, which imply an inner circle. The word is used by the hero as a term of collective direct address to all his followers: " '¡Oíd, mesnadas,   sí el Criador vos salve!' " (1115). The *mesnadas* of the Cid who plunder the field in 1736 ("Mesnadas de Mio Çid   rrobado an el canpo") clearly represent not an elite corps but the preponderance of his forces. The same inclusive pattern is shown by the poem's use of the term in connection with Alfonso. *Mesnadas* is twice used in contextual proximity to *compañas*, a similarly broad collective term: "el rrey Alfonso   que llegarién sus compañas, / quel' buscarié mal   con todas sus mesnadas" (508–09); "Con el rrey   atantas buenas conpañas; . . . / cuendes e podestades   e muy grandes mesnadas" (1974, 1980). As in the case of the Cid's forces, the *mesnadas* of Alfonso seem to represent a majority of his following, as is suggested by his use of the term in collective direct address (employing a formula reminiscent of the Cid's in 1115): " '¡Oíd, mesnadas,   sí vos vala el Criador!' " (3128). Finally, yet another collective term for the vassalic following of the Cid is *los sos* ("his own," i.e., "his men"), as in "con los sos abuelta *anda*" (589); "Luego llegavan los sos,   ca fecha es el arrancada" (609); "Mio Çid con los sos   tornós' a acordar" (666). This expression is an abbreviated variant of such terms as *mesnada* and *compaña*.[7]

## Reciprocity

The Cid's humility in accepting the marriage arranged by Alfonso (" 'pues lo conseia   el que más vale que nós' " [1940]) is not mere rhetorical posturing. As a man with vassals of his own, the Cid must, first of all, show exemplary behavior toward his own lord. To deny Alfonso incites his own *mesnadas* to deny him; hence the Cid's ostentatious acceptance of the king's seniority. At the same time, the emotional component of the vassalic bond—its amical aspect—is never forgotten. As in the compliance with the arranged marriage, there is an aspect of interested role-playing here. This calculus of public relations is in no way discordant with the authentic emotion aroused by the lord-vassal bond. At the *vistas* on the banks of the Tagus, the Cid speaks to Alfonso (2031–32) with the intensity of a son asking for his father's forgiveness: " 'Merçed vos pido a vós,   mio natural señor, / assí estando, dédesme vuestra amor.'" The Cid humbly begs pardon; the king grants it, thereby reestablishing a disrupted relationship. This is what gives Alfonso the moral leeway to exact a favor of such magnitude, for the renewal of the vassalic dyad reinstates amity in all its complexity. Not the least of the intricacies inherent to the amical condition is an unqualified predisposition to generosity. This mentality, exceedingly common among traditional peoples, has been characterized by Marshall Sahlins as one of "generalized reciprocity."[8]

The formulaic recurrence of supplication and entreaty, often involving the verbs *pedir* and/or *rogar*, expresses this general reciprocity. Examples are found in Minaya's request, on behalf of the Cid, for Alfonso's permission to take Jimena and the girls from the monastery (" 'Merçed vos pide el Çid, si vos cayesse en sabor'" [1351]); or in the Cid's explanation to his daughters ("'pedidas vos ha e rrogadas el mio señor Alfonso'" [2200]); or, yet again, in the daughters' appeal to their father (" '¡Merçed vos pedimos, padre, sí vos vala el Criador!'" [2594]). Supplicatory expressions seldom occur in the context of what we might call unilateral charity. Duggan, in his analysis of reciprocal economic mentalities, demonstrates very clearly that these are experienced in terms of "interested giftgiving." He explains how "generosity in distributing . . . was not simply an option open to the powerful." Liberality was "an obligation, albeit uncodified and often even unarticulated." This concept of the interested gift does not necessarily imply ordinary selfishness. Gift-giving is a bilateral procedure, in which the act of acceptance is no less conscious, no less crucial a gambit in the ongoing game of amity than is the act of offering. The hero's generosity toward Alfonso cannot, therefore, occur without the monarch's receptive collaboration. The hero's generosity, at the same time, compels Alfonso to relent, much as generosity toward his own men transforms Rodrigo's wealth, Duggan observes, "into an instrument of loyalty." The *PMC* likewise expresses, in its depiction of "a devotional and financial obligation between the Cid and the Virgin Mary," a "materialistic view of religion." We see this perspective— perfectly harmonizing, be it noted, with traditional kin-ordered reciprocity—in the Cid's vow to the Virgin Mary, in which he

promises to recompense her for her aid: " 'Si vós assí lo
fiziéredes e la ventura me fuere conplida, / mando al vuestro
altar buenas donas e rricas' " (223–24). In verses 820 and following, the Cid fulfills his vow, consigning to Minaya a quan-
tity of "oro e plata" so that "mill missas" may be said in the
Church of Saint Mary of Burgos. The attitude toward philan-
thropic donations accords with the general system of reciprocal
benefaction that pervades the poem. "Thus," affirms Duggan,
"the gifts, the pardon, and the marriages [of the Cid's daughters to the Infantes] are closely associated in the nexus of events
that leads up to . . . the third *cantar*."[9]

In the world of amity, "balance is not sought in the short term
because the relationship is assumed to endure." Artificial kinship, in this context, provides "a set of social relationships . . .
well adapted to the needs of a particular time but in a sense
too well adapted so that it does not provide a store necessary
for future times." Real kinship ties, by contrast, "go beyond the
economic uses to which they are put at any particular time and
it is this which gives them their economic significance." Kinship relationships, in short, "provide potential cooperation con-
tinuing through the vicissitudes of time." In terms of long-term
planning, "only social relationships which are reliable in the
long term can be used and this reliability comes from morality."
Indeed, it is "the presence of moral cooperation which enables
a man to afford to concentrate on manipulating short term
links" (Maurice Bloch 76, 79–80).

The fact that long-term reciprocity will tend to be the rule
is, argues Maurice Bloch, "an observer's conclusion." Despite
the presumed pragmatic outcome over time of a system of collective altruism, the fact remains, Bloch assures us, that people
in traditional society find themselves "forced into imbalanced
relationships by morality." People in traditional society, in other
words, make ethical decisions in regard to social relationships:
"the crucial effect of morality is long term reciprocity and . . .
the long term effect is achieved because it is not reciprocity
which is the motive but morality" (76). Further defining the
relationship between traditional morality and "delayed reciprocity," Bloch points out that the latter concept means "relationships with great tolerance of imbalance." He characterizes
a vital contrast: "immediate reciprocity is tantamount to the

denial of any moral relationship between the parties while delay between gift and counter gift is an indication of the moral character of the relationship." This illuminates a seemingly unaccountable pattern: that in many contexts, fictive kinsmen are invited to cooperate more often than real kinsmen. Informants explain that " 'real' kinsmen would always come . . . [while] 'artificial' kinsmen would only come if one kept up the typical kinship behaviour of repeated requests for help." Failure to do so leads to a "lapse" of artificial kinship. Bloch notes a tendency to maintain pools of potential cooperators that are much larger than necessary for any given task or project (Maurice Bloch 79).

It is thus not reciprocity alone that makes for kinship, given that reciprocity, as Maurice Bloch points out, "exists with people who do not thereby automatically become kinsmen." Kinship reciprocity derives, rather, from "the categorical moral nature of the dogma." Precisely because this sort of morality "transgresses the reciprocity and exchanges balanced in the short term," it allows adaptation to "the fluid situation of potential labour requirements and varying available personnel." A "central core" of "instrumental short-term relationships maintained by short-term balanced exchange" supports a "periphery" of long-term relationships, the two—core and periphery—making up together a "greater pool of potential cooperators." Bloch refers here to agricultural societies; the logic is equally applicable to the society of the *PMC* (Maurice Bloch 81).

Similarly, Freeman distinguishes, in his discussion of the kindred-based action group, between a field of *de jure* kindred, representing a network of genealogical relationships, and the *de facto* network of relationships activated by appeal to an agreed-upon system of ethical imperatives. Because recruitment and membership in these impromptu action groups focuses on the task or activity "at hand," such groups are ephemeral by nature. It is the pool of kin to whom one turns for help or, to put it another way, the collection of kinfolk categorized or perceived to be reliable, "recruitable," that constitutes the permanent system (Freeman 255). The pool thus formed may be viewed, to borrow Adrian Mayer's expression, as "the kindred of cooperation." This category of active kin, Mayer notes, may be characterized "as a quasi-group formed from a succession of action-sets centred on the individual or his household." In his account of quasi-group formation in India, Mayer discusses the formation of action-sets as a function of the "transactional elements" that underlie their linkages. Such linkages exist, he states, "because they carry transactions furthering in some way the interests of the parties concerned." While, as we noted earlier, it is the interest of a specific ego that forms the nucleus of the action performed with the aid of the kindred, "the interest of the respondent can vary, ranging from specific aims to be fulfilled immediately . . . to a generalized interest of potential help of some sort in the future." Continual recruitment, as Mayer points out, might lead to the formation of what he calls quasi-groups—loosely organized yet durable associations that may in time "crystallize" into still more enduring, "all-purpose" entities. In any case, when kinship provides the pool of candidates, "the outward content of recruitment is always at least partly one of kinship and its entailed moral obligations, whatever other incentives there may be to support ego."[10]

We may hazard, given the reciprocity inherent to the "kin-minded" mentality, that longer- or shorter-term perceptions in the formation of collaborative groups—whether we call them quasi-groups, action-sets, networks, etc.—constitute an important indicator of the degree to which kin-mindedness predominates in a given context. In general, reciprocity is "openly calculated" for non-kin cooperators, while in the case of kinship ties, long-term reciprocity is assumed at the same time that "temporary imbalance in the exchange relationship is tolerated." However, kinship morality as an unconditional, long-term, "imbalance-tolerant" commitment to reciprocity is defined not by abstract categories but by action: "if relatives cooperate regularly they will stress their kinship, if not they will ignore it or forget it, and when individuals cooperate regularly they will search for and reinforce kinship links" (Maurice Bloch 80–81). Pitt-Rivers formulates his perspective on the ethnographic implications of long- and short-term relationships in terms of morality and "legal-mindedness": "the permanence of a relationship," he affirms, "cannot be assured by contract, for jural reciprocity is terminated by the counterprestation."[11]

In the *PMC*, the *mesnadas* of the hero behave like Mayer's "kindreds of cooperation." Theirs is a hearty collaboration, with no need for coercion: "vassallos tan buenos   por coraçón lo an, / mandado de so señor   todo lo han a far" (430–31). Cooperation in the poem is determined by a spontaneous understanding of what needs to be done. This idealized teamwork is expressed through the word *acordado*, as in 2217–18: "Todos los de Mio Çid   tan bien son acordados, / están parando mientes   al que en buen ora nasco." At the marriage of the Cid's daughters, his vassals show the same unconditional unanimity of purpose and instinctive understanding of their roles as they contribute wedding gifts: "Los vassallos de Mio Çid   assí son acordados, / cada uno por sí   sos dones avién dados" (2258). The spontaneous esprit de corps of the Cid's vassals explains why there is never a hint of discord at the division of booty: "todos prisiessen   so derecho contado"; "Assí lo fazen todos,   ca eran acordados" (2486, 2488). To the fellowship is often added a harmony of sentiment, as we see in the response of lord and men to the riches won in battle: "Alegre era Mio Çid   e todos sos vassallos / que Dios les ovo merçed   que vençieron el campo" (1739–40). The men sent to bring back the Cid's daughters show no less zeal and no less solidarity: "Non lo detardan   el mandado de su señor, / apriessa cavalgan,   andan los días e las noches" (2841–42). As the Cid announces preparations for the final trip to Alfonso's court, his vassals show the typical unanimity of word and action: "Respondieron todos:   'Nós esso queremos, señor.' / Assí commo lo á dicho, todos adobados son" (3082–83).

The Cid, in turn, relies absolutely upon the unrehearsed courage and fidelity of his men. This aspect of vassalage is distinctly familial, as when the Cid's vassals instinctively surround their lord in the episode of the escaped lion: "enbraçan los mantos   los del Campeador / e çercan el escaño   e fincan sobre so señor" (2284–85). They are loyal sons solicitous of the welfare of the patriarch. Thus also the alacrity of the Cid's champions in arriving at the site of combat: "cunplir quieren el debdo   que les mandó so señor" (3535). Shortly afterward, the poet underscores the exemplary unanimity of purpose with which they prepare for battle: "todos tres se acuerdan,   ca son de un señor" (3551); then the joyful gratitude shown by the Cid: "conplido han el debdo   que les mandó so señor, / alegre fue d'aquesto   Mio Çid el Campeador" (3703–04). The single-minded teamwork of the Cid's vassals expresses unconditional amity—this is what the poet self-consciously dramatizes. At the same time, prestige accrues to the lord capable of commanding such loyalty—which is to say, capable of mobilizing forces so committed to the ethic of amity. An invidious comparison is invited with the leadership of Alfonso himself: "la conpaña del Çid creçe e la del rrey mengó" (2165).

## Generosity

Amical reciprocity, as we have seen thus far, is expressed through mutual generosity and whole-hearted cooperation. The latter element can in fact also be assimilated to the ethic of generosity: service rendered is, after all, the on-going offering of collaboration. Generosity in the short term may be categorized as limited, conditional, and transactive. This is the realm of the present, the boon, and the favor. Reciprocity of this kind is by definition immediate. Generosity in the long term involves, by contrast, a deferred, unspecified, or optional requital. This is the realm of unconditional altruism and—very frequently in traditional contexts—of a kind of "broadcast" gift-giving which has been characterized as redistributive generosity.[12]

Both aspects of generosity play important roles in the *PMC*. The words *don* and *presentaia* are generally used to express, for example, the modalities of short-term reciprocity. In 192, when the moneylenders contemplate a compensation for Martín Antolínez, it means, essentially, "tip": " 'Démosle buen don, ca él no' lo ha buscado.' " At other times it is straightforwardly a gift, as in 2010–11, where the poet remarks that the "cavallos en diestro" were won by the Cid in battle, "que non ge los dieran en don." At other times *don* may signify "boon" or "favor," as when Bishop Jerome asks for the right to strike the first blow: " 'pídovos un don e séam' presentado, / las feridas primeras que las aya yo otorgadas' " (1708–09). The Bishop's demand is couched in terms of a favor for a favor: his counter-prestation will be a refraining from desertion of the Cid's cause.

Other nuances of the gift present themselves. In the passage describing the disposition of booty taken from Castejón, *presentaia* means, judging from context, something like "offer," "bid," as when the Cid, sending to various local towns, seeks to auction off his fifth of the loot from Castejón. The

Moors of the towns respond: "asmaron . . . *tres* mill marcos de plata"; to which the hero reacts with pleasure: "plogo a Mio Çid d'aquesta presentaia" (521–22). In yet another semantic variant, the term signifies "invitation," as when Abengalbón accepts Alvar Fáñez's offer of hospitality: " 'Plazme d'esta presentaia' " (1532). The verb *presentar*, meanwhile, is used in conjunction with the word *don* to mean "grant," "bestow" (as in Bishop Jerome's demand to strike the first blow). *Presentar* is used in the sense of "furnish" or "provide" with the word *enfurçión* ("tribute in kind," thus, "lodging," "room and board") in the passage describing the hospitality shown by the monks of San Esteban de Gormaz to Minaya and his men (2849). This utilization of the same verb for the presentation of a gift or boon and for the proffering of hospitality accentuates the deliberate and formal nature of the monks' generosity: one does not merely offer hospitality, one makes a present of it. Short-term reciprocity may take on the open-ended, occasional, unpredictable allure of unconditional amity. It is in this light that the hospitality of the priests of San Esteban de Gormaz is to be understood, as they take in Minaya and the others without question: "Varones de Sant Estevan a guisa de muy pros / rreçiben a Minaya e a todos sus varones, / presentan a Minaya essa noch grant enfurçión" (2847–49). We note as a response to this offer (2850) the formal refusal ("non ge lo quiso tomar"), followed by the thanks for hospitality rendered ("mas mucho ge lo gradió"), all of which is followed by the assurance of future reciprocity:

"Graçias, varones de Sant Estevan, que sodes coñoçedores,
por aquesta ondra que vós diestes a esto que nos cuntió;
mucho vos lo gradeçe, allá dó está, Mio Çid el Canpeador,
assí lo fago yo que aquí estó.
Afé Dios de los çielos que vos dé dent buen galardón."
(2851–55)

The poem presents a rich array of detail confirming the political utility of the interested gift. The Cid seeks to remedy the falling-out between his lord and himself by declaring his generous intentions toward his estranged lord: " 'quiérol' e[n]biar en don *treínta* cavallos' " (816). Alfonso replies to Minaya, the Cid's emissary, by reminding him of the short lapse of time since the exile: " 'Mucho es mañana / omne airado   que de señor non ha graçia / por acogello   a cabo de tres semmanas' " (881–83). For each situation in which gifts are sent or accepted between vassal and lord, the poem employs either *don* (1344, 1856, 1922, 2125, 2148) or, as an apparent synonym, *presentaia* (878, 884, 1315, 1813, 1830).

Property in this context lacks its capitalist sense of "accumulated assets." To retain property in the amical universe is to fritter away its true value. The poem clearly depicts this kin-based notion of the volatility of wealth. Verse 516, for example, tells us that the Cid's fifth of the plunder taken from Castejón was so copious that "Aquí non lo puede vender   nin dar en presentaia." Here are the only two alternatives: to sell (i.e., to exchange in direct transaction) or to give away. No other possibilities are mentioned.

Each gift, in this environment of constant circulation of goods, is a move in the chess game of magnanimity between two leaders whose power and standing are largely determined by their ability to dispense and distribute wealth. At the same time, no move may go unanswered: one must always accept or reject an offer made, with acceptance and rejection each significant in its own way. Alfonso, while expressing reluctance to pardon the Cid after only three weeks of exile, nonetheless finds a way to accept the gift of thirty horses conveyed by Minaya (871–74). " 'Mas después que de moros fue,' " allows the king, " 'prendo esta presentaia; / aún me plaze de Mio Çid   que fizo tal ganançia' " (884–85). The escalation of gift-giving marks the stages in an unfolding scheme of emotional blackmail, akin to that engaged in by the lover who sends flowers and candy to the irresolute beloved. Each gift sent by the Cid is a seductive gambit, as is the reiterated formula of vassalic devotion (1339, 1847). When Minaya brings the king one hundred horses, " 'gruessos e corredores' " and all harnessed and saddled (1336–37), Alfonso's response is a countermove designed to communicate his receptivity: " 'rreçibo estos cavallos   quem' enbía de don' " (1344). For the winning of this game is conceived as a mutually satisfactory victory; both sides are losers if the game is overplayed or played ineptly. The Cid, meeting at last with Alfonso, demands "merçed" in the form of "amor." The King does not hesitate, pardoning the hero and granting the most significant boon of all: " 'aquí vos perdono  e dovos mi amor' " (2031–34). The gifts sent and received to this point, through Minaya's offices as go-between, have been feelers, tentative offers to forestall, at each step, the humiliating rebuff. They have prepared and made ever more feasible both Alfonso's offer and the Cid's acceptance: " '¡Merçed! Yo lo rreçibo, Alfonso mi señor' " (2036b).

Hospitality shows another dimension to the game of offer and counteroffer. After the scene of pardon and reconciliation, during which the Cid has reiterated his vassalic pledge by kissing the hands and mouth of his lord, the hero offers: " 'Fuéssedes mi huésped,  si vos ploguiesse, señor' " (2046). To this offer Alfonso replies that the Cid and his men have only just arrived, while he, Alfonso, has been there with his men since the previous night: " 'mio huésped seredes, Çid Campeador, / e cras feremos  lo que ploguiere a vós' " (2049–50). In this game of doing and outdoing, and of avoidance of being outdone, the king now turns the tables, seeking to eclipse his vassal in magnanimity.

The game concludes with the apparently mutual satisfaction of the two parties and the renewal of an invaluable relationship. However, just as the Cid's gifts have served as a prelude to Alfonso's granting of the pardon, so does the monarch's very concession serve as the platform for a boon whose enormity will further threaten the integrity of the vassalic bond. Alfonso's request that the Cid give his daughters in marriage to the Infantes is shown to be a favor exacted for a favor: " 'A Dios lo gradesco  que del rrey he su graçia,' " declares the Cid, " 'e pídenme mis fijas  pora los ifantes de Carrión' " (1936–37). Alfonso, in soliciting and accepting so great a favor, incurs a correspondingly immense moral debt.

Again, the etiquette of the gift involves the most delicate sensibilities on both sides. It is the offer that initiates the sequence—this is the move that communicates generosity of intent, a desire to establish or maintain amity. At the same time, the offerer has to know when to insist, the receiver when to say no, which is to say, when to recognize the moment when the symbolic value of the offer transcends the possible material benefits of an acceptance. Minaya, with typical subtlety, recognizes this as he thanks the Cid for his offer of a fifth of the

booty: " 'Mucho vos lo gradesco, Campeador contado.' "
Minaya's counteroffer in the form of an elegant refusal meanwhile allows him to assert his own generosity, as he suggests
giving the share to Alfonso: " 'd' aquesta quinta que me
avedes mand[*ad*]o / pagar se ía d' ella Alfonso el castellano. /
Yo vos la suelt*o* e avello quitado' " (493–96). The preemptively magnanimous offer, conferring honor on the would-be
donor by its mere utterance, must be as preemptively refused;
the magnitude of the refusal, matching the enormity of the gift,
likewise redounds to the credit of the man powerful enough to
spurn such bounty. Thus, as the Cid prepares to depart for
Valencia, after Alfonso has ruled in his favor, he offers the most
magnificent gift of all, the mighty steed Babieca: " 'y[*o*] vos le
do en don, mandédesle tomar, señor' " (3515). This is both
symbolic and material capital, the perfect gift, the presentation
of which is a prompt generously designed to afford the king an
opportunity of uttering the equally gracious reply:

> . . . "D'esto non he sabor;
> si a vós le tolliés el cavallo non havrié tan bue[*n*] señor.
> Mas atal cavallo cum ést pora tal commo vós
> pora arrancar moros del canpo e ser segudador,
> quien vos lo toller quisiere nol' vala el Criador,
> ca por vós e por el cavallo ondrados somo[*s*] nós."
> (3516–21)

The gambits and countermoves of this gift-giving game—the
gracious offer, the no less gracious refusal, the sensitivity concerning when to accept, when to reject—are familiar elements
in codes of politeness everywhere. However, there is a difference. The tactics of short-term reciprocity in the context of traditional societies constitute an art that only makes sense if
backgrounded by the greater ethical structure of amity. Gifts
conferred without regard for immediate return express more
directly the central principle. The disinterested gift—which is
only that in the sense of its lack of an obvious or immediate
return on investment—is usually given away in conspicuous
distribution of wealth, as when, after the betrothal of the Cid's
daughters to the Infantes, the hero liberally hands out palfreys,
mules, and garments: "conpeçó Mio Çid a dar a quien quiere
prender so don; / cada uno lo que pide nadi nol' dize de no"

(2115, 2117). Gifts such as these are purely amical—they are seeds cast to the wind, to take root wherever they may. They are the material manifestation of the patriarchal generosity that supports a great household, and thus of the fatherly love only the greatest lord may feel. The poet makes a point of the free and indiscriminate nature of this distributive generosity, and of its impact on the recipients: "Mio Çid de los cavallos *sessaenta* dio en don. / Todos son pagados de las vistas quantos que í son" (2118–19). The Cid promises to repeat this performance for the wedding: " 'qui quiere ir a las bodas o rreçebir mi don, / d'aquend vaya comigo, cuedo quel' avrá pro' " (2129–30). The wedding, lasting fifteen days, shows him making good on his promise, distributing horses, mules, palfreys, and rich garments, as well as money, so that "Qui aver quiere prender bien era abastado" (2260). The munificence is confirmed by the fact that all guests depart satisfied: "por pagados se parten de Mio Çid e de sus vassallos" (2265–66). The Cid's distributive generosity is particularly highlighted after the conclusion of the hearing, and before the judicial combat. As the hero prepares to depart, leaving the three champions to Alfonso's assurance of safe-conduct, he offers gifts and money, first to Count Anrrich and Count Remond ("que prendan de sus averes quanto ovieren sabor" [3498]), then to all others who wish to partake, including the king himself:

> A éssos e a los otros que de buena parte son,
> a todos los rrogava assí commo han sabor,
> tales í á que prenden, tales í á que non.
> Los *dozientos* marcos al rrey los soltó,
> de lo ál tanto priso quant ovo sabor.
>
> (3499–503)

As the ethnographers cited heretofore have demonstrated, it is the global morality that supports the episodic transaction of immediate reciprocity as well as the altruism of distributive beneficence. Underlying the microcosm embracing both short-term exchange and long-term generosity, the macrocosm of morality comprises the sine qua non of social relations, to be preserved or restored at all costs. The ruling emotion of this ethical macrocosm is, quite simply, love.

## Love

Functioning as if they were kinship terms, *vassal* and *lord,* as we have seen, imply a kind of dyadic symbiosis: neither term is complete or even meaningful without the other. In his desire to make the king once again his "amigo" and his "señor," the Cid is striving, therefore, not for any merely legalistic reinstatement. He is seeking rather to restore a love relationship as precious, as intense, as that between father and son. Hence the use of the word *amor* in the reconciliation and the scenes leading up to it. The poem's use of the word *love* is one of the principal clues as to its notion of amity.

The *PMC*'s more conventional uses of the word *love* and its affines do not concern us here. The word is used, for example, in formulaic appeal to God and his saints: "por amor de Santa María" (273), "por amor del Criador" (1321, 2787, 2792, etc.). In addition, *love* is used in obviously relevant emotional or familial contexts, such as those of the conjugal family and of amorous relationships. Thus the hero charges Minaya with taking horses and other booty to Jimena and their daughters: " 'por amor de mi mugier   e de mis fijas amas' " (1811), while the poet describes the Infantes, spending the night with their brides in the Oak Grove of Corpes: "con sus mugieres en braços   demuéstranles amor" (2703).

It is love in dimensions now the domain of less emotive terms that is of interest to the present essay. The Cid's is a world where people take things personally. When Bishop Jerome asks for the privilege of leading the Cid's men into battle, the favor he asks is expressed in terms of love: " 'Si este amor non' feches,   yo de vós me quiero quitar' " (2379). The implied negative response to a possible denial by the Cid of this request is, as we have seen, extreme: the abandonment of the Cid's cause. This exchange between the hero and his warrior bishop hints at the emotional blackmail one associates with a family quarrel, rather than the even-tempered deliberations of affairs of state. Revealing a similarly intense perception of what we would consider merely professional relationships, the poet describes the Cid's generosity toward his followers in terms of love: "El amor de Mio Çid   ya lo ivan provando, / los que fueron con él   e los de después todos son pagados" (1247b–48).

The Cid himself does not hesitate to use the word *love*. For instance, as he confides to Minaya the delicate mission of go-between in the matter of his daughters' marriage, he exclaims: " '¡Venit acá, Albar Fáñez, el que yo quiero e amo!' " (2221). When the Cid charges Pero Vermúez with guarding the Infantes in the forthcoming battle, he speaks of the brothers as " 'mios yernos amos a dos, la cosa que mucho amo' " (2353). When the Cid requests an escort for his daughters of the Moor Abengalbón, he tells Félez Muñoz, appointed the girls' guardian: " 'de lo que ovieren huebos sírvalas a so sabor, / desí escúrralas fasta Medina por la mi amor' " (2639–40). The Moor, we are told, responds in precisely the spirit of the request: "Tod esto les fizo el moro por el amor del Çid Campea[dor]" (2658). After the Afrenta de Corpes episode, the exuberant Moor shows what can only be described as impassioned hospitality toward the Cid's daughters: "por amor de Mio Çid rrica cena les da" (2883).

A falling out in this poem is conveyed in terms of unrequited love. Thus the Cid vows not to cut his beard: " 'Por amor del rrey Alfonso que de tierra me á echado' " (1240). The king's wrath, meanwhile, is expressed in terms of love withdrawn. Minaya, as he addresses Alfonso on the exiled Cid's behalf, implores the monarch's forgiveness (" 'quel' ayades mer-çed, ¡sí vos vala el Criador!' "), while recalling the estrange-ment between lord and vassal: " 'Echástesle de tierra, non ha la vuestra amor' " (1324–25). When the Cid eagerly inquires after his lord's health (1921–22), and anxiously wonders how Alfonso has received the gifts conveyed to him by Minaya, the latter reports in characteristically emotional terms: " 'D'alma e de coraçón / es pagado e davos su amor' " (1923–24). Shortly afterwards, when the hero has heard the news of the proposed marriage, Minaya reiterates his appraisal of Alfonso's sentiments, as he informs the Cid of the king's desire to arrange *vistas*: " 'que vos vernié a vistas dó oviéssedes sabor; / querer vos ie ver e darvos su amor' " (1944–45).

When the hero and his king meet, the monarch is embar-rassed by his vassal's show of humility and subservience, as the Cid throws himself at Alfonso's feet and eats grass. Command-ing the Cid to rise, Alfonso declares: " 'besad las manos, ca los pies no[n]; / si esto non feches, non avredes mi amor' "

(2028–29). The hero, remaining on his knees, replies: " 'Merçed vos pido a vós, mio natural señor, / assí estando, dédesme vuestra amor' " (2031–32). To this the king responds: " 'aquí vos perdono  e dovos mi amor' " (2034). Love is what the Cid feels he has lost, and what he wants above all to be restored. When, after the reconciliation, the Cid is the guest of his king, we are told of the monarch's infatuation with his vassal: "non se puede fartar d'él,  tántol' querié de coraçón" (2058).

In the amical universe of traditional kinship, love is more than an emotion. It is the supreme prestation. This illuminates the Cid's declarations in the final court scene. He takes back, first of all, the love he had given to the Infantes: " 'quando dexaron mis fijas  en el rrobredo de Corpes / comigo non quisieron aver nada  e perdieron mi amor' " (3156–57). Having taken them in as sons, having bestowed upon them the gift of his love, with all that this represents in terms of emotional and material support, he thus enacts the harshest reprisal known in the kin-ordered world: the withdrawal of amity. When the Cid seems only to ask for the return of his swords (3158), the Infantes react with disbelief, mistaking the beginning of the hero's judicial complaint for its conclusion: " 'Aún grand amor nos faze  el Çid Campeador / quando desondra de sus fijas  no nos demanda oy' " (3164–65). The passage reveals the Infantes' cynical awareness of the emotional riches they have squandered along with the material capital of their wives' dowry.

When Alfonso, having been empowered to do so by the Cid, marries the hero's daughters to the Infantes, he does so uttering a significant formula of gratitude: " 'Yo las caso a vuestras fijas  con vuestro amor' " (2099). Michael glosses *amor* here as "consentimiento." Of course, the context indicates that this is an adequate translation. But the poem imagines agreement, compliance, in more vividly emotional terms than those implied by the dead metaphor encompassed within "con-sentimiento." We no longer imagine agreement as a "co-sentiment," a literal empathy with the person to whom we give our assent. But this poem does. This is, after all, the tale of a vassal who spends all of his time either recovering the love of his lord—before whose feet he eats grass in sign of homage—or arranging a suitable marriage for daughters whose separation from him causes pain like the rending of "fingernails from the flesh." In this empathetic universe, the emotional urgency of the vassalic relationship insures that injury done to either party in the pact will affect the other. The Cid enjoins Muño Gustioz to convey the message of the Infantes' infamous behavior: " 'cuemo yo só su vassallo e él es mi señor, / d'esta desondra que me an fecha los ifantes de Carrión / quel' pese al buen rrey d'alma e de coraçón' " (2905–07). It is not merely that the king is responsible for having arranged the marriage, but that the Cid— who, as a good vassal has indulged his lord by permitting this usurpation of a sacred familial function—now requires the invocation of the principle of bilateral solidarity: " 'si desondra í cabe alguna contra nós, / la poca e la grant toda es de mio señor' " (2910–11). The solidarity of lord and vassal is therefore above all empathetic. The joys and sorrows of the one are those of the other. Thus the Cid does not ask for anything so abstract as justice. He implores Alfonso, as a preliminary request, literally to feel as he has felt: " 'd'esto que nos abino que vos pese, señor' "; " 'Oídme toda la cort e pésevos de mio mal' " (3041, 3255).

In the world of the Cid, amity is not merely the mild thoughtfulness of modern civilization. It is a full-blown passion—a benevolent infatuation. People do not merely acquiesce in the *PMC*: they give their love. It is in light of this person-to-person fervor that we must understand Alfonso's proclamation concerning the motives of the extraordinary *cortes* called in Toledo: " 'Por amor de Mio Çid esta cort yo fago' " (2971). Later the king will remind all those present of the significance of the occasion. Since he has been king, he recalls, he has only held two *cortes*, one in Burgos, one in Carrión. This third one, in Toledo, he declares, he has called this day " 'por el amor de Mio Çid, el que en buen ora naçió' " (3129–32). The Cid acknowledges the royal favor in the same terms: " 'Mucho vos lo gradesco commo a rrey e a señor / por quanto esta cort fiziestes por mi amor' " (3146–47).

## Small-Scale Society

Generosity in the *PMC* is a virtue, to be sure. But one must understand virtue from the perspective of amity. Morality is the sine qua non of amity; amity without morality is its opposite, namely, enmity. Virtue in the amical universe is not an ethical ideology or even a habit of mind—it is a praxis considered to be indispensable to the social fabric in the same way that hunting, building, or agricultural techniques are regarded as necessary for the physical sustenance of the community.

Summarizing the complex of attitudes of a real people, and correlating it with widespread patterns observed in the anthropological literature on small-scale societies, Colin Turnbull writes (as an introduction to the tragically vanished way of life of the Ik, an East African hunting and gathering people):

> The smaller the society, the less emphasis there is on the formal system, and the more there is on inter-personal and inter-group relations, to which the system is subordinated. Security is seen in terms of these relationships, and so is survival. The result, which appears so deceptively simple, is that hunters frequently display those characteristics that we find so admirable in man: kindness, generosity, consideration, affection, honesty, hospitality, compassion, charity and others. (Turnbull 31)

These attributes, Turnbull hastens to explain, are not virtues in the "tiny, close-knit society" of the hunter. They are necessities, without which "society would collapse." When things happen to a society to eliminate the utility of this complex of moral attributes—as happened in the case of the Ik, a nomadic hunting people obliged, in the political climate of emerging African states, to become agriculturalists in infertile country—these traditional virtues lose their function, becoming personal liabilities that "spell ruin and disaster" for the individual who persists in their observance (Turnbull 31–32).

The society of the *PMC* is not "primitive" in the same way as that of the Ik or any other ethnographically documented people. Nevertheless, the social universe of this poem imitates, by its kin-ordered adherence to the principles of amity, the character of the small-scale, primitive society. That is why teamwork and generosity are not virtues, but rather the very cement of social existence.

Elman R. Service has characterized the so-called primitive society in terms of the dynamics of cohabitation and of the consequent emphasis on dyadic relationships. Powerful mechanisms of social control, he observes, govern "small face-to-face societies . . . where the individual normally spends his whole life among his kinsmen." The force of these mechanisms derives from vicinal as well as consanguineal propinquity. The constancy of personal interactions and the extensive interdependence of community members exerts tremendous moral force: "Since escape is impossible . . . [the individual] cannot recover by moving to some new group the esteem he might have lost by a social mistake in his own group." Things that in large-scale societies involve emotional or ethical options—"cooperation, alliance, love, reciprocities of all kinds"—are not simply a matter of individual decisions in small-scale societies, but rather "totally important to the survival of any individual." This, argues Service, accounts for the evident force of public opinion in primitive societies, and why "people seem so extraordinarily sensitive to the reactions of the group to any social action." The power of public opinion is exercised by the group in the form of definite rewards and punishments:

> Praise and blame, affection and withdrawal, and other such socio-psychological sanctions are extremely powerful reinforcers in small societies of stable membership, and it has been noted over and over by many observers of egalitarian societies how carefully social customs, especially in etiquette, are observed—"custom is king." (Service 83)

The Cid and other personages of the *PMC* reside in a community where, as we have seen, the withdrawal of love is the supreme punishment, and where one lives always in the arena of cruel and inescapable publicity. Public opinion is the mirror that gives the meaning to any action. It is, in other words, shame rather than guilt that drives the Cid and the other characters of the poem. This aspect of the poem is revealed, for example, in the Cid's insistence on a public exoneration, as we have seen in the reconciliation scene, in which the hero demands an announcement of pardon: " 'que lo oyan   quantos aquí son.' " To this Alfonso can only reply: " 'Esto feré d'alma e de coraçón; / aquí vos perdono   e dovos mi amor' " (2032–34).

The dark side of the shame-oriented mentality is revealed by the Infantes' response to the contempt in which they are held at the Cid's court. They must escape the shame incurred by the public ridicule to which they are exposed as a result of their comportment in the episode of the lion: "non viestes tal juego commo iva por la cort; . . . / Muchos' tovieron por enbaídos los ifantes de Carrión, / fiera cosa les pesa d'esto que les cuntió" (2307, 2309–10). The poem's preoccupation with shame is further evidenced by the Infantes' complete lack of remorse concerning their sadistic abuse of the Cid's daughters. So long as they believe they will escape discovery or retribution, they feel no compunction of any kind, nor does the poem show any sense that they should. Their act is, for the poet, unforgivable but perfectly intelligible. Innocent victims of their husbands' wrath, the wives are inevitably scapegoated for the derision undergone by the Infantes: "ellos ívanse alabando: / 'De nuestros casamientos agora somos vengados; . . . / La desondra del león assís' irá vengando'" (2757–58, 2762). The Infantes, in the commission of this outrageous vengeance, are guilty of a monstrous transgression against the vitality and stability of the social order, which is above all a moral order. The ethical standards of the poem, in this sense, are not exotic or primitive. They are common sense exalted. The poet thinks in the same manner as do the social scientists cited in this study— he is himself a theoretician of ethics.

## Forbearance

The principle of amity is the philosophical nucleus of kinship relations. Amity, we have seen, is defined by such things as deferred reciprocity, the tolerance of imbalance in reciprocal relationships, and a willingness to admit principles of inclusion and cooperation in the fabrication of rules of everyday life and of inter-group relations. It is above all the expression of an ethic of altruism that precedes and enables the establishment of systems of kinship relations. An important aspect of "kinmindedness," as Maurice Bloch and others describe it, is a preoccupation with long-term, reciprocal altruism not so much for its own sake as for the sake of the moral system collectively maintained. The kinds of generosity and cooperative behavior typically associated with "primitive" peoples reflect a notion of, as Meyer Fortes puts it, "sharing without reckoning" (*Kinship* 238). So strong are the imperatives of kinship that it is a widely observed fact that kin-based cooperation and help often work, notes Maurice Bloch, "to the disadvantage of the helper." When, for example, a group migrates to an area where it finds no kin, it tends to form "ties of artificial kinship in order to have reliable cooperators." Between artificial kinsmen there tend to emerge patterns of exchange and cooperation that confirm a persistent "tolerance of imbalance" (Maurice Bloch 78–79).

In the *PMC*, the hero and those close to him show the kin-minded forbearance symptomatic of amical mentalities. An admirable deference is expressed in the Cid's compliance with the desire of Alfonso to arrange a match between the hero's daughters and the Infantes. The Cid has his misgivings. The timing of Alfonso's request, as we noted earlier, puts the Cid in the position of having to regard the marriage as the counter-prestation for the favor of the king's forgiveness: "'d'este casamiento non avría sabor, / mas pues lo conseia el que más vale que nós, / fablemos en ello, en la poridad seamos nós'" (1939-41). The Cid's eagerness to accommodate his lord confirms a virtuous humility in his acceptance of vassalic subordination. At the same time, the Cid exercises an exemplary forbearance, a praiseworthy tolerance of imbalance in his relationship with the king.

Forbearance as an eagerness to show one's self conciliatory is seen in Minaya's treatment of the Infantes at the Cid's court. We recall the fraternal aspect of cousinship. The latter phenomenon is better understood not only in light of the bilateral aspect of kinship, a reality referred to conventionally by the term *cognatio*, but with respect to the pervasive influence of amity in this poem. Hence the apparently broader application of *cuñado*. A term derived from *cognatus*, it appears to function like *pariente*, as we see in Minaya's invitation to the Infantes (the husbands of Minaya's cousins): "'Acá venid, cuñados, que más valemos por vós'" (2517).

Forbearance as cooperative generosity is seen in Pero Vermúez's intervention in battle on behalf of the cowardly Infante (2338–43). Pero's generous acceptance of imbalance, as Fernando brays his achievement ("assí lo otorga don Pero cuemo se alaba Ferrando"), confirms a commitment to kin-group solidarity by the Cid's beloved nephew. Fernando's response shows the opposite, in his obsession with the short-term quid pro quo. He speaks the language of reciprocity, but only superficially: " 'aún vea el ora  que vos meresca dos tanto.' "

The Cid's acceptance of the marriage, and his subsequent attempt to "make things work" by showing love for the sons-in-law foisted on him by Alfonso, is a symptom of the forbearing mentality that typifies amity at its most unadulterated. Marital alliance is the Cid's motive: he wants to give the marriages a chance. Prompted, in other words, by a moral and altruistic purpose—generosity without reckoning—he hopes by making the best of a bad situation to fortify the relationship between himself and his lord, between his family and his sons-in-law. Thus his tolerance of short-term disadvantage, his forbearance exercised despite apprehension. The Cid takes the long view of the apical ancestor he is destined to become. For it is the descendant who benefits most of all from both the loyal vassalage and the advantageous marital policy enacted by the ancestor. The complications arising from marital strategies, which link lineages rather than persons, will be the subject of our next chapter.

## Chapter Three

# Marriage

The *PMC*'s understanding of marriage is exceedingly traditional. Hinojosa, in his seminal article on the law in the *PMC*,
points out that marriage as it takes place in this work shows no
concern for the ecclesiastical ceremony of *traditio*, according
to which a priest received the betrothed from the hands of her
father or other relatives and handed her over to her husband. In
contrast to this, the common European usage "en los tres
últimos siglos de la Edad Media," the *PMC* shows the older
practice, prevalent at least until the end of the twelfth century,
according to which the bride is conveyed to her husband by her
father or his proxy (Hinojosa, "El derecho" 572–75). In the case
of the Cid's daughters, it is not the girls' father but rather his
representative, namely, King Alfonso, who makes the marriage.
The king thanks his vassal for assigning the marital decision to
him: " 'Grado e graçias . . . / quem' dades vuestras fijas   pora
los ifantes de Carrión. / D'aquí las prendo por mis manos   don
Elvira e doña Sol / e dolas por veladas   a los ifantes de Carrión.
/ Yo las caso a vuestras fijas   con vuestro amor'" (2095–99).
Shortly thereafter, when the king has placed the Infantes under
the Cid's authority and given the grooms 300 marks as a wedding gift to be disposed of as the Cid sees fit (2101, 2103–04),
the hero reminds his lord: " 'Vós casades mis fijas,   ca non ge
las do yo'" (2110). The Cid is careful to reiterate this attribution of responsibility on several occasions (2200, 2204, 3149).
When the Cid hands over his daughters to Minaya (2222–25),
the latter is therefore acting entirely as the king's agent and
proxy, so that the hero is, in effect, delivering his daughters
into the possession of the king himself. Minaya then gives the
girls away:

"por mano del rrey Alfonso    que a mí lo ovo mandado,
dovos estas dueñas,    amas son fijas d'algo,
que las tomássedes por mugieres    a ondra e a rrecabdo."

(2231–33)

It is only after this ceremony that the two couples proceed to
the Church of Santa María, where Bishop Jerome gives them
"bendictiones" and says mass (2236–40). The poem makes it
very clear that the definitive element in the making of these
marriages between the Infantes and the Cid's daughters is the
transfer of each girl's person from Minaya to her groom. The
priestly blessing, the mass, and the sumptuous wedding feast,
lasting fifteen days (2247–66), celebrate the marriages; they do
not constitute them.

To understand marriage in this poem we must decide between two schools of thought: the legalist and the traditionalist. Colin Smith, speaking from a legalist perspective, contends
that the "poet-lawyer was an expert on the law relating to marriage, as shown by skilled analysts." In a note, he mentions
(without detailed citation) Hinojosa's article on the law in the
*PMC*. There is a certain circularity in quoting Hinojosa to support assertions about the legal content of the poem. Hinojosa,
in his largely descriptive account of the *PMC*, treats the work
as a primary documentary source, quoting from it to justify his
perception of Peninsular legal and social history in the twelfth
century. Smith in turn quotes Hinojosa to support his perception of the poem's legalism. Referring, additionally, to Juan
García González's study of marriage in the *PMC*, Smith points
out that the Cid of the poem fails to consult Jimena about the
marriages. The passive role played by Jimena, and the contradiction that this represents to the law of Castile and León, which
accorded equal rights in marriage arrangements of offspring to
the two spouses, had already been pointed out by Hinojosa.
"One can only suppose an oversight," insists Smith, "by the
otherwise expert poet."[1]

This "oversight" with regard to the wife's role in marriage
arrangements is compounded by an apparent ignorance of or
disregard for the Church's position on divorce. Ruth Webber, a
prominent exponent of the traditionalist approach to marriage
in the *PMC*, points out that the daughters' remarriage at the end
of the poem (3711–23) implies an anomaly involving "both

civil and canon law." The explanation, she maintains, lies not in anachronistic reference to written legal codes but to "matters of custom and precedent"—in other words, to the poet's oral background (Webber, "The *Cantar*" 85).

We need not postulate a legal oversight to account for the *PMC*'s apparently anomalous treatment of divorce and marital consent. The Cid and Alfonso—even, to an extent, the Infantes— act in a manner entirely consistent with traditional marriage practices of the Mediterranean and Indo-European world. These practices are sometimes consonant with written law, sometimes not. Both agreement and discrepancy, as regards the relationship between social practice and legal codes, are a matter not of mere obedience or disobedience of law, but rather of convergent or divergent custom. As is well known, written law sometimes reflects or preserves custom, while at other times it suppresses, circumvents, or supersedes it. What is at issue in this chapter is not the poem's compliance with law, but its depiction of matrimonial practice. As portrayed in the *PMC*, this practice speaks for itself, embodies a logic of its own, and has congeners in other historical and ethnic contexts. There is, moreover, ample ethnographic evidence that the rules of matrimonial gamesmanship are a matter of common knowledge in a given society. Not all players are equally adept, but the community, as an audience, presumably appreciates well-conceived strategies and skillfully executed tactics. An important but largely neglected aspect of the Cid's character as a folk hero is thus his genius as a matchmaker and marital strategist. The lawyerly theory of authorship—concerning which we will have more to say in a later chapter—assumes, on the other hand, a distance between author and audience that is at odds with the populist and traditionalist elements demonstrated in the first two chapters of the present study.

## Divorce, Consent, and Other Marital Issues

Divorce is accomplished in the *PMC* with a minimum of words and without ecclesiastical intervention. The Infantes' abandonment of his daughters, declares the Cid, signifies the dissolution of all ties between them and his family: " 'comigo non quisieron aver nada   e perdieron mi amor; / denme mis espadas quando mios yernos non son' " (3157–58). The marital separation is reaffirmed when the Cid demands the return of the dowry: " 'denme mis averes quando mios yernos non son' " (3206). The marriage is considered dissolved from the moment the Infantes admit their obligation to return the swords, thus recognizing the Cid's assertion that they are no longer his sons-in-law. After the challenges exchanged between the Infantes, their brother Assur, and the Cid's champions (3258–391), the poet immediately depicts the arrival at court of the agents of the princes of Navarre and Aragon, with their proposals of marriage for Elvira and Sol (3392–400). The Cid graciously authorizes Alfonso to arrange the match (3403–08), prompting the king to request, with equal cordiality—and, we may assume, not a little contrition—the Cid's own consent (3410–15). The betrothal is then immediately celebrated: "metieron las fes e los omenaies dados son / que cuemo es dicho assí sea, o meior" (3425–26).

The Church plays no role in this minimalist treatment of divorce and remarriage. The poem shows the dissolution of a marriage on grounds of spousal abuse and public dishonor, followed by a prompt and unproblematic remarriage. This renders somewhat implausible the notion that the author was, as Colin Smith phrases it, "a practicing lawyer." The theory that the *PMC* author was trained in the newly revived Roman law has been advanced by Milija Pavlović and Roger M. Walker, who present a very detailed argument, beginning with the Cid's division of his case into three parts, for the pervasive influence of the Roman *cognitio* procedure as set forth in the revived *Institutiones* of Justinian (Pavlović and Walker, "Roman Forensic Procedure" 97–98, 99). It is equally possible, however, that the tripartite divisions may reflect a well-known propensity of folkloric narrative for things that come in three's: the Cid may present three parts to his case, in the same way that the poet presents three challengers of the Cid (the two Infantes plus their brother Assur). Pavlović and Walker themselves admit, moreover, that "the scarcity of Roman terminology [in the poem] may seem curious." They explain this avoidance of overt legal terminology—odd in an author supposedly steeped in law—by arguing that "the champions of Roman law in the Peninsula had to tread very warily at this period." This timidity was due—in spite of the sponsorship of Roman-trained lawyers by

Alfonso VIII of Castile and Alfonso IX of León—to "the conservatism of various powerful vested interests, especially the nobility and the towns" ("Roman Forensic Procedure" 96, 104).

Yet, we may wonder, if the vested interests feared by the poet are so powerful, why portray potentially offensive legalism at all, in whatever guise? If the nobility and the towns, the constituencies not to be offended, are the readership or audience of the poem, would a poet risk giving affront, by presenting a (supposedly) thinly disguised legal apparatus? And if the audience of the poem is not nobility or townfolk, who then? If either royalty or peasantry (or both), the poet has nothing to fear.

The absence of precise legal vocabulary is indeed significant—precise terminology is one of the characteristics of codified law and lawyerly style. Moreover, a poem about marriage and divorce would presumably make extensive use of the legal terminology on those topics, since marriage law was a core topic of the revived Roman law of the late medieval West. The poet's apparent ignorance of the vital legal issues of divorce and marital consent are conceptual lacunae which, when weighed along with the absence of Latin legal vocabulary, would seem to preclude any notion of the poet as a lawyer trained in Roman law.

The importance of marriage and of the regulation of sexual behavior to the agenda of reformed Church law is extensively discussed by James A. Brundage, who has thoroughly documented the strict guidelines adopted by various generations of reform canonists and decretists from the early eleventh through the crucial later decades of the twelfth century. This was a period that saw the forging of many elements of the canon law on marriage. Among earlier reformists, permissible grounds for dissolution were few: adultery, consanguinity, affinity, impotence. Remarriage was particularly difficult, with, generally, only consanguinity and affinity recognized as legitimate conditions. Only regions "on the fringes of Latin Christendom" failed to implement marriage law based on these narrow criteria for divorce, adhering instead to "Germanic practices that allowed divorce and remarriage for a wide variety of reasons." Meanwhile, traditional lay marriage and divorce, "even at the highest social levels," had yielded to the ecclesiastical paradigm by the mid twelfth century (Brundage 203, 225).

Concentrating on the central themes of indissolubility and exogamy and on the varied uses of Roman law, theoreticians of marriage such as Gratian and the legists of the Bolognese and Parisian schools emphasized, each from his own perspective, a narrow range of criteria for permissible dissolution of marriage. Gratian was strict in his disallowance of divorce, even in cases of fraudulent virginity or financial deception. The Bolognese school, on the other hand, allowed for dissolution in certain cases of *matrimonium initiatum*, but consummated marriage (*m. ratum*) was indissoluble on any grounds. Consensual theorists emphasized such capacity issues as consanguinity or age, as well as "defects of consent," such as fraud, deceit, coercion, or insanity (Brundage 243, 288).

None of these factors, central issues in the family law of social circles touched by the ecclesiastical reforms, is discussed in the *PMC*. Divorce and remarriage in the poem, portrayed as a matter of straightforward routine, do not seem suggestive of an up-to-date legalism. Rather, the poet's treatment of these questions hints at the broadness of criteria of the Germanic practices, mentioned by Brundage, that persisted on the periphery of Latin Christendom. Perhaps even more significantly, marriage in this poem shows itself completely untouched by the consensual revolution of the eleventh and twelfth centuries, whereby the notion of consent by the two individuals became the definitive factor in marriage. Traditional marriage is arranged by the respective families—including the extended families—of the bride and groom. Canon law stresses the freely given consent of the couple, undermining the primacy of kinship in the definition of matrimony, and thereby constraining the use of a principal instrument of political alliance and clanic cohesion in the kin-ordered world.[2]

The *PMC* does not disregard or deny the issue of consent; instead, it reveals a complete unawareness of the problem and of the legal controversy surrounding it. The daughters are not consulted concerning the arrangement of either of their marriages. When the marriage to the Infantes has been finalized, the Cid reports with news of the accomplishment first to his wife (2187–88: " '¡Grado al Criador,   vengo, mugier ondrada! / Yernos vos adugo   de que avremos ondrança' "), then to his daughters (2189: " '¡gradídmelo, mis fijas,   ca bien vos he casadas!'"). The fait accompli of the match with the Infantes foreshadows the scene in which the Cid and his lord refrain from conferring with the daughters on the occasion of the second marriages. It is, as we have seen, the Cid's consent which is sought by the king, rather than that of his daughters: "'que plega a vós, e atorgar lo he yo, / este casamiento oy se otorgue en esta cort'" (3411–12).

This disregard of consent would be remarkable in a poem written by a lawyer during the decades leading up to the Fourth Lateran Council in 1212 (assuming the poem's now generally accepted date of composition in the late twelfth or early thirteenth century). The poet's lack of awareness of the controversy surrounding consent, which was escalating at the time of composition, has far-reaching implications with regard to the work's authorship and audience, and correlates with its approach to other social issues as well.[3]

The consensus-copula debate of the twelfth century, conducted by such influential authors as Gratian, Peter Lombard, and Hugh of St. Victor, was settled by Alexander III (1159–81) in a series of tribunal decisions, and led to the refinement of the Church's concept of marriage and the role of consent in its establishment. Marriage as a sacramental union was defined by the freely exchanged consent of two baptized partners. Sexual consummation, under the preponderant influence of Gratian, was deemed tantamount to absolute indissolubility. "This understanding of when marriage came into being," writes Thomas Doyle in his commentary on this heading of canon law, "has remained the teaching of the Church to the present day" (737).

Charles Donahue, examining the relationship of canon law on marriage to the ethnic tradition which it supplanted, comments that what is conspicuous about the rules enacted by Alexander III is "not what they require but what they do not require." The approval of parents or lords, even sexual consummation, in the case of so-called present consent, are not required. A marriage established through vows of present consent was considered legitimate and indissoluble; the couple's unconstrained mutual consent was the only prerequisite for valid matrimony. Public ceremony and even witnesses were unnecessary (Donahue 145).

For Jack Goody, the consensual rule of marriage was but one of a cluster of precepts making up a program on kin-related issues devised and implemented by the Church over several centuries. These rules, "most of which," notes Goody, "had no scriptural backing," constituted a momentous subversion of traditional patterns of kinship, marriage, and inheritance, and met with continual resistance from the European population. For by inhibiting the possibilities of familial retention of property, such rules "would also facilitate its alienation." The Church, while thwarting the transmission of property to adoptive heirs, illegitimate children of concubines, and stepchildren, simultaneously impeded the formation of marital alliances within a range of kin (a traditional kin-ordered mode of consolidating property within and among lineages). This favored the Church's accumulation of property through "the transfer of rights in land and other goods either *inter vivos* or *mortis causa.*" The Church, protector of widows and orphans, tended to be the beneficiary of those who died without heirs. An innovation particularly erosive of traditional kinship prerogatives was the sacramental concept of marriage, with its emphasis on the mutual consent of the spouses, rather than the approval of their respective families. The concept of consent effectively sabotaged, argues Goody, parental and lineal authority, thus further reducing the influence of kinship.[4]

Goody's hypothesis need not be accepted in its entirety in order to serve as a useful approach to the political unconscious of policies underlying an observed historical pattern with regard to Church doctrine on kin-related matters. However improvised or spontaneous the Church's program of kin-related regulations and policies that materialized over the centuries, and whatever the effect of the program's other components, the doctrine of individual consent in marriage—asserting that marriage was designed for the salvation of the individual soul and was therefore a matter of the individual, freely given consent of the couple—was everywhere resisted by custodians of clanic interests. The Church, concludes Duby, "unintentionally tended to take a stand against the power of the heads of households in matters of marriage . . . and, indeed, against male supremacy, for it asserted the equality of the sexes in concluding the marriage pact and in the accomplishment of the duties thereby implied" (Duby, *Medieval Marriage* 17).

R. Howard Bloch summarizes the effects of the consensual theory of marriage in terms of intergenerational conflict. "It bolstered," he remarks, "the claims of children against parents [while bringing about] a catastrophic short-circuiting of the biopolitics of lineage." The traditional collective arrangement of marriage—focusing on "military, social and economic considerations [such as] obligations to vengeance and to armed service, political alliance, [and] legal and financial responsibilities"—could no longer be carried out with unfettered regard for the complex calculations of clanic advantage (*Etymologies and Genealogies* 162).

While different societies and communities present a wide range of styles of implementing a basic policy of disregarding consent in favor of alliance, the emphasis on relationships between lineages is a common denominator to which the label *traditional* may be conveniently appended. The *PMC*, by its emphasis on the patriarchal aspects of the father's role in the marriage of his offspring, falls squarely in the traditionalist and collectivist side of the threshold demarcated in general terms by the anthropologist Edmund Leach and in specifically medieval European terms by the historian Georges Duby. The first scholar affirms that there are only two essential types of marriage systems: those in which the match is arranged by the lineage, and those in which marriage is contracted by the couple itself. When marriage is arranged by the lineage, it is generally controlled by the senior male members. Women and "remotely situated kinfolk" are not prohibited from participation in marriage arrangements, but co-resident males, usually sharing common descent and representing three generations (i.e., grandfather, father, grandson) constitute the controlling voice in marriage negotiation (Leach, *Rethinking Anthropology* 56). Duby, speaking of the society of twelfth-century France, describes a "lay model" of marriage that coincides in its outlines with the lineal pattern distinguished by Leach. The lay marriage, which Duby contrasts with the ecclesiastic, consensual model, unites two individuals "born of two different houses in order to found a new house of similar form—or rather, to ensure the survival of one of these houses." Marriage of this sort "an ostensible, ceremonial act," was "an agreement, a treaty," the *pactum conjugale* "concluded between two houses." The relationship so established involved an exchange: a woman's "anticipated motherhood" was delivered over to the lineage of her husband. Above all, the marriage, being "essential to the future of both houses," was held to be "too important to be left to the individuals concerned" (*Medieval Marriage* 4–5).

The Cid, as we have seen, does not consult his wife or his daughters. He thereby acts in apparent defiance of both the laws of Castile and León and the ecclesiastical law of marriage. In regard to the wife's prerogatives in marital consent, Heath Dillard documents the "participation of mothers together with fathers" in the arrangement of marriages. Both parents, Dillard affirms, "acted as representatives of both sides of the bride's family, those two sets of relatives to whom a woman was related by blood and inheritance" (42). The Cid, however, refrains from such consultation because he embodies the traditional notion of official, patriarchal, which is to say, unilineal kinship. In this respect he acts in accordance with Visigothic law, as reflected in the *Fuero Juzgo*, which held that paternal authority was the definitive factor in marriage and that a daughter, once betrothed by her father, remained betrothed to the man designated by him, regardless of the intervention of her mother or brothers; indeed, if they contravened the will of the father by arranging or facilitating the daughter's marriage to another, they were subject to fine (III.i.2). If a daughter married without the approval of her father or mother—here a concession to the consultative role of the wife—and her parents did not forgive her, "ella nin sus fiios non deven heredar en la buena de los padres, porque se casó sin voluntad dellos" (III.ii.8).[5]

The Cid does not, however, necessarily "obey" old Germanic laws; rather, he subscribes to the same notion of agnatic control that they express, and by so doing participates in the very broad cross-cultural pattern indicated in Leach's dichotomy. Both the Cid of the poem and the *Fuero Juzgo*, in other words, support the ancient tradition of patriarchal control of marriage. It is for this reason that the poet portrays Jimena and her daughters as showing a dutiful compliance with the will of their lord and master. Informed of the arranged marriage of her daughters to the Infantes, Jimena humbly replies: " 'Todo lo que vós feches es de buena guisa,' " while the daughters respond in unison: " 'Quando vós nos casáredes bien seremos rricas' " (2193, 2195). In this they behave with the same esprit de corps as the zealously amenable vassals described in the previous chapter.

The poem's complete disregard for the wife's consulting role and the daughters' consent reveals the poet's commitment to this aspect of official kinship. The word *official* does not, of course, imply legality in the codified sense, nor may we take the poem's representation of unanimity—on the vassalic or the familial level—as an indication of pervasive consensus in the social reality of the poet and his audience. Traditional clanic notions of group solidarity and stability presuppose marriage as a means of reproducing and perpetuating groups, necessarily taking the view that marriage is an affair between families, lineages, clans. The bride and groom, in other words, represent their respective families in the formation of alliances and the maintenance of collaborative activities between lineages. It is, however, likewise a commonplace of traditional societies that prospective brides and grooms are themselves interested parties. It is, as Bourdieu points out repeatedly, the official system, however locally defined (i.e., as to its bias in favor of this or that specific configuration, this or that emphasis on patrilateral vs. matrilateral, unilateral vs. bilateral, etc.) that presents a public, unitary image of solidarity and cooperation in marital arrangements. In a patrilineal context, the official, lineage-oriented system—represented by the adult males of the lineage—imposes the role of cooperative humility on the betrothed. The unofficial system, the customary province of the clan's women-folk, is fragmented, improvisational, vociferous: it presides over the private family meeting where everyone, including prospective brides and grooms, has his or her say. Viewed from this perspective, a traditional marriage is the outcome not only of negotiations between lineages, but also of intrafamilial negotiations in which marital candidates are more or less successful according to a myriad of chaotic variables. The management of these last is the job—ideally and officially—of the older and wiser heads who represent the traditional, normative concern for the best interests of the group. The variables in matchmaking discussions within the clan include such things as the personality of parents, of the marital candidate, and of siblings; the social standing of the family or the potential spouse's family; the place of the marital candidate in the sequence of siblings (or his or her status as an only child); the age and sex of the candidate; and so on. The final offer or acceptance extended to the spousal candidate from another lineage is a matter (again, ideally and officially) of decorous, harmonious presentation of family policy to the extrafamilial world.[6]

Consent is thus always a factor, however unofficial. In traditional societies it is an issue that tends to be managed or controlled by the two kin groups, and for the maximum benefit of these groups. But youth must have its say. In traditional society consent is the result of intra- and interfamilial negotiations—it is, therefore, an outcome, whereas in modern marriage, it is a precondition, the starting point of a relationship between two persons.

The issues discussed by Duby, Goody, Brundage, and others represent the elements of a public controversy on the subject of marriage that was a constant of the social environment of twelfth-century Europe, particularly among the higher strata of society. The Church established the terms of debate for all questions of marriage, particularly those relating to consent, divorce, and remarriage. Duggan discusses at length the question of legitimacy of royal heirs as an essential component of the historical background of the *PMC*'s composition, describing the case of Alfonso IX of León and Teresa of Portugal, whose marriage was annulled by the Pope on grounds of consanguinity. Similar controversy accompanied the subsequent remarriage of Alfonso to Berenguela of Castile, which provoked Innocent III to impose an interdiction (Duggan 72–73, 76). Innumerable historic episodes confirm that resistance to such influence must have been an obsession with royal and aristocratic families. Yet the Cid of the poem exemplifies the traditional and unquestioned authority of the head of household and lineage, and embodies, with no hint of irony or doubt, the notion of marriage as too important to be left to the children to be married. It is as if Duby's ecclesiastical model never existed. What sort of audience, we wonder, would have accepted such a profile?

## Filiafocality and the Epiclerate

We begin to answer the question of audience by examining in greater detail the role of women in the poem. The *PMC* exhibits what has been called *filiafocality*. The daughters, while they do not play a major role in the action, are the sole motive for the epic's central conflict as well as the pretext for its resolution. The functions of the female characters—daughters and wife—are both central and multifarious. The first marriages, it has been observed, "provide the base upon which the Second and Third Cantares depend," leading as they do to the Afrenta de Corpes, the trial and the ensuing judicial combat, and the triumphant second marriages. The action of the poem is thus "contingent upon the silent impact of the Cid's daughters" (Bluestein 406).

The term *fija* is by far the most frequently used kinship term in the poem. Used 108 times, it occurs more than twice as often as the next most frequently employed kinship term, *mugier* (49 times), more than four times as often as *padre* (23), over five times as often as *primo* (21), and almost ten times as often as *fijo* (12). Other kinship terms, including affinal and fictive terms (we have already mentioned *mugier*), show only a scattered incidence: *sobrino* (9), *hermano* (5), *pareia* (3), with several occurring only once each (*esposa, hermana, padrino, cuñado*).[7] Although mere frequency is at best a crude measure of a word's thematic importance in a literary work, the sheer number of times *fija* is used creates a cumulative effect on the reader or listener. In a poem of just over 3,700 lines, the word *daughter* occurs in roughly 1 line out of every 34. It is interesting to compare the incidence of *daughter* with other words referring to important persons, thus: *yfantes* appears 113 times; the affinal term *yernos* appears with about the same frequency (23 times) as *padre* and *primo*, two other kinship terms of obvious significance in the narrative.

An emphasis on daughters is by no means incompatible with patriliny. Referring to kinship patterns in noble Roman society, Judith Hallett uses the term *filiafocality* to define an "emphasis on ties of blood and marriage through and to men's female children." This daughter-focused "centrality," she argues, insured that Roman daughters, while excluded from official participation in the control of family resources and other "kin-related decision making processes," could, while still in their father's *potestas*, inherit his estate. Traditional Roman society thus emphasized not only "bonds between fathers and sons, but

[also] . . . those between men and their daughters' and sisters' offspring and spouses." A concurrent emphasis on agnate and filiafocal aspects of kinship "is [thus both] possible and logical."[8]

The *PMC*'s analogous emphasis on the distaff side derives not from direct Roman influence (legal or otherwise), but from convergent familial patterns necessitated by patrilineal usage. After their marriage to the Cid's daughters, the Infantes, clearly "marrying in" to their brides' lineage, stay in Valencia to live in the house of their father-in-law and are treated as members of the Cid's family: "el Çid e sos yernos   en Valençia son rrastados. / I moran los ifantes   bien cerca de dos años, / los amores que les fazen   mucho eran sobeianos" (2270–73). This residential pattern reflects, to employ Goody's expression, a "strategy of heirship" designed to perpetuate the agnatic lineage. For families without sons in a patrilineal system, both property and lineal identity may be transmitted through the institution known as the *epiclerate*, in which the inheriting daughter is the transmitter of both property and lineal continuity. The term *epiclerate* as used by Goody and others is, be it noted, modified from its original sense (Gk. *epikleros*, m., f., "heir," "heiress"; lit., "on" or "attached to the estate," thus "unique heiress"). The term *epikleros* originally applied to a woman who, in the absence of male heirs, was temporarily "attached to the estate (*kleros*)" until a man, typically a relative, married her and assumed control of the patrimony, which was eventually to be transmitted to their offspring (Gagarin 67n72).

In a broader sense the term refers to the practice, observed with variations throughout Eurasia, of treating the in-marrying son-in-law as a kind of adopted child, or as an appointed or adopted heir of the bride's family. This is the case of the Japanese *mukoyōshi*, the "groom-foster-son," described by Pitt-Rivers as the "adopted . . . husband for the daughter when there is no son or no suitable son to whom the patrimony can be entrusted" (Pitt-Rivers, "Pseudo-Kinship" 408). Goody employs, in relation to the epiclerate in the broader sense, the expression "filiacentric union," referring to a uxorilocal marriage in a predominantly virilocal system. When children of such marriages are considered primarily heirs of the wife's lineage, the heiress is considered an "appointed father" producing children for her natal group rather than for her husband's lineage. The son-in-law thus recruited is often adopted in a special ceremony that verifies his change of kin group membership. While the epiclerate often implies an upwardly mobile marriage for the man, it may, on the other hand, indicate the bride's hypergamous marriage to a disinherited or otherwise impoverished son of a high-status family, recruited by the materially prosperous but less prestigious family of the bride.[9]

The Infantes are to be considered the Cid's sons because he gives them his daughters in marriage. This reflects the adoptive concept underlying the epiclerate. " 'Los yernos e las fijas todos vuestros fijos son,' " declares Alfonso to the Cid (2106). The king places the Infantes in the Cid's custody, reminding the hero of their new status: " 'Evad aquí vuestros fijos, quando vuestros yernos son' " (2123). Later the Cid will confirm the filial status of his sons-in-law: " '¡Venides, mios yernos, mios fijos sodes amos!' " (2443). Still later the Cid relates to the court how, at the time when his sons-in-law had departed with his daughters for their lands in Carrión, he had loved them " 'd'alma e de coraçón' " and had given them the swords Colada and Tizón so that they could bring honor to themselves and better serve Alfonso. Their treatment of his daughters provokes his withdrawal of paternal affection: " 'comigo non quisieron aver nada e perdieron mi amor; / denme mis espadas quando mios yernos non son' " (3152–58). Their misdeeds have canceled all the ties that had bound them to him when they were married to his daughters, as we see from his demand that they return the girls' dowry: " 'denme mis averes quando mios yernos non son' " (3206). In keeping with the ethical system of amity outlined in the previous chapter, the Cid speaks in terms of love. Again, his is not a metaphorical passion, but reveals instead the genuine emotional intensity of kinship relations.

After the humiliation of the episode of the lion and their ignominious performance on the battlefield (2278–310, 2338–54), the Infantes decide to move back to Carrión, taking their brides with them: " 'Vayamos pora Carrión aquí mucho detardamos' " (2540). The poem clearly portrays their sense of having lived as mere appendages to their wives' natal household, and therefore under the domination of their father-in-law: "Sacar las hemos de Valençia de poder del Campeador" (2546). They think that their petition will be expedited if they provide a good reason; the one they provide would seem to be obvious (that of going back to their family's estates): " 'Pidamos nuestras mugieres al Çid Campeador, / digamos que las levaremos a tierras de Carrión'" (2543–44). But the Infantes insist too much—why would they need to mention their desire to return home with their brides, to ask permission to take them away, unless to do so were somehow out of the ordinary? The fact that in requesting to depart with their wives they are in some way deviating from customary expectations is suggested by the formality with which they request permission to take their leave, as they address their father-in-law directly: " 'Que plega a doña Ximena e primero a vós / e a Minaya Albar Fáñez e a quantos aquí son: / dadnos nuestras mugieres que avemos a bendiçiones'" (2560–62). At the moment of departure, the lamentation of the Cid and his people is significant: "Grandes fueron los duelos a la departiçión, / el padre con las fijas lloran de coraçón, / assí fazían los cavalleros del Campeador" (2631–33).

## Hypergamy

Throughout the *PMC*, the marriage of his daughters is uppermost in the Cid's mind. The urgent need to provide them with good husbands is mentioned immediately upon his achievement of financial and political independence after the capture of Valencia, in the scene in which the Cid guarantees dowries and husbands from his entourage for the ladies of Jimena's household: " 'quiero las casar con de aquestos mios vassallos; / a cada una d'ellas doles *dozientos* marcos de plata'" (1765–66). After he has made this promise, he reassures her: " 'Lo de vuestras fijas venir se á más por espaçio'" (1768).

The Cid has only daughters (the poem ignores or is unaware of the historical existence of the Cid's son).[10] He must, in Bourdieu's terms, arrange a marriage for the integration of the lineage as well as for advantageous alliance. "Any particular marriage," notes Bourdieu, "is meaningful only in relation to the totality of simultaneously possible marriages"—which is to say, he adds, the "range of potential partners." The continuum of marital alternatives runs from the completely secure and integrative parallel-cousin marriage (with European analogues in cousin marriage, increasingly controlled by the Church from the eleventh century on) to the hazardous yet potentially beneficial and maximally prestigious union with a member of a distant tribe. The former possibility is safely intimate and relatively risk-free, requiring little ostentatious expenditure and no risky negotiations. The latter exposes the clan to any number of perils, both social and economic, but offers a potentially greater payoff in terms of both expanded alliances and lineal prestige. The two types of marriage, defined by the extremes of the suggested spectrum, thus

> represent the points of maximum intensity of the two values which all marriages seek to maximize: on the one hand the integration of the minimal unit and its security, on the other hand alliance and prestige, that is, opening up to the outside world, towards strangers. (Bourdieu 57)

The Cid accomplishes the remarkable feat, from the perspective of the traditional kin-ordered community, of engineering marriages for his daughters that satisfy the needs of both integration and alliance. He finds sons-in-law who will marry in, who are at the same time of a prestigious and well-connected lineage. He has the best of both dimensions in a situation characterized by Bourdieu as a choice between "fission and fusion, the inside and the outside, security and adventure." The integrative marriage implied by the epiclerate solves essentially the same problems as the parallel-cousin marriages discussed by Bourdieu, while avoiding the risk posed by the latter type of union, namely, that of "squandering by [its] redundancy the opportunity of creating new alliances which marriage represents." At the same time, the Cid stage-manages the situation so as to avoid the dangers of distant marriage, which "secures prestigious alliances at the cost of lineage integration." Bourdieu emphasizes the public appreciation accorded to the families who manage to bring off marriages with distant non-kin. Such unions, evoking the logic "of the exploit, prowess, prestige," are, as it were, heroic in themselves, requiring "great prestige and wild audacity" (Bourdieu 57–58).

The daughters' first marriages are noble, the poem says, because the king has arranged them. Thus the Cid's emissary,

Muño Gustioz, declares to Alfonso: " 'alto fue el casamien[*t*]o
ca lo quisiestes vós' " (2940). That invidious comparisons may
be made among different possible matches is expressed in Pero
Vermúez's speech of reassurance to the aggrieved daughters
after the Afrenta de Corpes: " 'cuidado non ayades / quando vós
sodes sanas e bivas  e sin otro mal. / Buen casamiento perdiestes,  meior podredes ganar' " (2865–67). Pero's speech
prepares us for Alfonso's declaration to the agents of the princes
of Navarre and Aragon:

> "este casamiento  otórgovosle yo
> de fijas de Mio Çid  don Elvira e doña Sol,
> pora los ifantes  de Navarra e de Aragón,
> que vos las den  a ondra e a bendiçión."
>
> (3418–21)

The propriety and distinction of the second matches are verified: "metieron las fes  e los omenaies dados son / que cuemo
es dicho  assí sea, o meior" (3425–26). After the emissaries of
Navarre and Aragon present their "pleitos" to Alfonso, the girls'
second marriages are confirmed:

> fizieron sus casamientos  con don Elvira e con doña Sol.
> Los primeros fueron grandes,  mas aquéstos son miiores,
> a mayor ondra las casa  que lo que primero fue.
> ¡Ved quál ondra creçe  al que en buen ora naçió
> quando señoras son sus fijas  de Navarra e de Aragón!
> Oy los rreyes d'España  sos parientes son,
> a todos alcança ondra  por el que en buen ora naçió.
>
> (3719–25)

The good marriage, then, is one that yields *ondra*—honor, prestige, enhanced standing—but to the father and, through him, to
kith and kin and all members of his *bando* ("¡Ved quál ondra
creçe  al que en buen ora naçió," "a todos alcança ondra  por
el que en buen ora naçió"). The caliber of the second marriages,
therefore, is the Cid's supreme accomplishment, one for which
he is solely responsible and therefore one which redounds first
and foremost to his personal honor. The good marriage, we
note, has nothing necessarily to do with the personal qualities
of the spouses; it is an accomplishment in its own right, a feat

of diplomatic savoir faire by which a family earns the envy and the admiration of its community.

The Cid's concept of the good match must be viewed in the wider context of upwardly mobile marriage for women. Menéndez Pidal emphasizes, with respect to this question, the conflict between the inferior nobility of the *infanzones*, represented by the Cid, and the "jerarquía superior de los ricoshombres," represented by the Infantes and their allies. Despite this conflict, he argues, there was a fluidity of boundaries between the greater and lesser nobility: "Estas dos clases no estaban radicalmente separadas." The daughters of *infanzones*, he affirms, often married into the families of *ricoshombres*, while the "ricoshombres más linajudos" could marry their children to the sons and daughters of kings. "En esta intercomunicación," contends Pidal, "surge el drama político y familiar de nuestro poema."[11]

The "marriage up" by the Cid's daughters exemplifies *hypergamy*, a general term for upward-bound marriage by women. In the Indian context for which the term was originally coined, hypergamy comprises, according to Louis Dumont, a "slight inferiority of the wife's family in relation to the husband's." Hypergamous marriage is usually prescribed within narrow limits of permissible categories of eligible husbands, defining a relationship between endogamous caste groups invidiously ranked with respect to one another, rather than a mechanism for individual social climbing through marriage. A preferential rather than an obligatory rule, the practice thus implies "a strong recommendation for the girl's parents to find her a superior partner" (Dumont 116–17). The more common pattern, however, may well be that of isogamy within the endogamous caste group. Adrian Mayer remarks for the central Indian context, that "there is hypergamy only to a minor degree between some subcastes of the same caste." These limited marriage relations can be reciprocal as well as hypergamous. Subcastes are, in turn, divided into exogamous sections functioning as clans based on "agnatic ties, putatively assumed from the patrilineal succession to a common clan name" (*Caste and Kinship* 29, 156, 161).

Dumont has detailed the consequences of obligatory hypergamy within the context of a caste divided into a number of clans, "strictly hierarchized in relation to each other." Assuming clan exogamy, one cannot marry an equal "since one must marry outside the clan." Because men may not marry women of superior status, "hypergamy will be obligatory." Theoretically, therefore, men are "supernumerary" in the inferior segments of the endogamous group, since women prefer to marry into a superior group. Women, on the other hand, would be superfluous in the superior categories, "unless recourse were had to large-scale polygyny." The situation is typified by the Rajputs: "infanticide of the daughters at the top of the ladder, breakdown of endogamy at the bottom, polygyny among the powerful" (Dumont 118).

Associated with hypergamy is a patrilineal notion of clanic membership and inheritance: "All children born in wedlock belong to their pater's caste." Thus, children born of a woman marrying down are customarily assigned to the legal father's caste (Mayer, *Caste and Kinship* 25–26). Medieval Europe offers many expressions of a similar mentality. The *Partidas*, to cite a prominent example, reveal a hypergamous and patrilineal concept, declaring: "Pero la mayor parte de la fidalguia ganan los homes por la honra de los padres; ca maguer la madre sea villana et el padre fijodalgo, fijodalgo es el fijo que dellos nasciere." The son born of a noblewoman's union with a *villano,* by contrast, is decidedly not an *hidalgo*: "... mas si nasciere de fijadalgo et de villano, non tovieron por derecho que fuese contado por fijodalgo" (*Partidas* II.xxi.3). When the *Partidas* seem to endorse patriliny over matriliny, they in fact expound a principle of hypergamy:

> nin otrosi la madre nunca le serie ementada que á denuesto
> non se tornase del fijo et della, porque el mayor denuesto que
> la cosa honrada puede haber es quando se mezcla tanto con
> la vil que pierde su nombre et gana el da la otra. (II.xxi.3)

This law imparts a disguised marriage rule: the daughter shall not "marry down" by marrying a non-noble. The stipulation of partners "of good family" remains more or less consonant with the matrimonial prescriptions of kin-ordered societies, including caste-structured ones. When we speak of caste in the extended sense—that is, extrapolating from the supposed Indian model, with wider application to apparently analogous systems—we refer to more or less endogamous groups invidiously stratified in a single system defined both by the tendency toward group endogamy and, it has been suggested, by the apparent consensus of the members of the total group—a consensus often difficult of verification. One of the tests of consensus, however, would be the very existence of hypergamy. Its prevalence as a preferential rule of marriage demonstrates that the members of the total supposed "program" understand and accept the invidious distinctions upon which the system is based. At the same time, a specific configuration of relative positions in the hierarchy would be subject to disagreement, thus leading to the jockeying and disputation concerning rankings which so characterize such systems. Such contentions, as we will see in the next chapter, paradoxically express the intimacy between groups which typifies feud and vendetta.

Hypergamy has also come to refer to "marrying up" by individual, social-climbing women. One study of marriage patterns in the United States found indications that among members of the higher social strata there is indeed a tendency toward hypergamous marriage in this broader sense (Rubin 641–42). However hypergamy in the Indian, interclanic sense and hypergamy as individual social climbing through upward-bound marriage are not the same thing. The "gold-digging" marriage of the modern, Western type represents not a relationship between lineages but a method of female social mobility.

Hypergamy in the *PMC* is clearly not of this ego-centered, dissociative type. It is not a vector of mobility for the daughters, but rather a means of status enhancement for their father and his line. Nor is he himself mobile, as will be demonstrated in detail in a later chapter. Daughters are exchanged for prestigious relatives—the interfamilial alliance *is* the achievement.

In strictly patrilineal societies, release of women to another lineage is considered dishonorable. "Givers" of wives consequently tend to be lower on the social and economic scale than "takers." In part this is because wealthier, more prestigious lineages tend to be relatively immune to the economic circumstances that oblige a lineage to "marry out" its women. Traditionally, a woman's marriage to a man of lower status results in violent intervention by the men of her lineage. Hypergamy may therefore additionally be defined as a relationship between endogamous groups, with one side only taking, never giving wives. Or to be more precise: the principle involved is not that inferior groups give wives, nor that superior groups take them, but that wife-giving makes for deference, the admission of inferiority. When perpetuated as a relationship between lineages (the relationship between *infanzones* and higher nobles described by Menéndez Pidal seems to fit the pattern), unidirectional wife-giving may be considered a kind of vassalic tribute. Differential prestige between patrilineal extended families conduces to a tributary relationship, of which hypergamy is but one aspect. Where the donor lineage enjoys less prestige than the receiver, this is only partly because receiver lineages tend to be of traditionally higher status. The mere act of "giving up" one's women to another family is status-reductive: the very practice of giving away daughters, more even than the status of the donor family, confirms its lower social standing.[12]

The possibility of hypergamy is diagnostic of an "endogamous unit [which] tolerates notable differences of status within itself" (Dumont 117). However, the principle of group identity and continuity generally prevails over the principle of hierarchy. Marriages outside the group, even apparently upwardbound ones within a larger, more encompassing association, are subject to the supervision and approval of elders. Hypergamy, moreover, often takes the form of a customary relationship between two groups, as in the case of the wealthy landed families of Rajputs, who "marry girls from the petty headman level of Rajputs, but give no girls in return." Such configurations reveal the frequently contradictory nature of hypergamy. On the one hand, the bride's lineage is deemed to benefit from an upgrading of its ranking and from an advantageous political connection. On the other, the surrender of daughters to a family of higher rank is often perceived as demeaning.[13]

The foregoing discussion provides a set of terms applicable to some aspects of marriage as portrayed in the *PMC*. With respect to hypergamy, we note that by offering marriage the Infantes elevate the Cid's family into the category of families deemed to be suitable wife-givers—the Cid's family is thereby included in the circle of marriageability. By their subsequent repudiation of the match, on the basis of disavowals of this amelioration of the Cid's status (2759–60, 3275–76), the Infantes renege on the promise inherent in their initial proposal.

The Cid exults that his daughters have found suitable husbands from among a genealogically prestigious lineage. At the same time, he feels misgivings about the Infantes' character and resentment about his king's imposition of the marriage. Duby notes the growing friction, from the early twelfth century on, between lords and their vassals over "the usurpation of the right to control the dynastic strategies of his vassals by the feudal seigneur." Kings and great lords, using kinship functions for political and diplomatic purposes, sought to "tighten the bonds of vassalic friendship by using marriage as a means of making alliances and of providing their most faithful followers with wives."[14]

The life of the famous William the Marshall portrays, in just such terms as those outlined by Duby, the king or lord as marriage broker of his followers. In the verse biography of William, King Henry promises him a wife, "la pucele / D'Estrigoil, qui fu bone et bele" (Meyer 8303–04). Upon the death of Henry II, the woman, Isabelle de Clare, countess of Striguil and Pembroke, is given to William, along with her lands, by Henry's heir, the future Richard I (9364–71). It is significant that the first order of business, in the very presence of the dead king, is the action taken by the chancellor to guarantee the heir's confirmation of the marriages and distributions promised by Henry to the members of his retinue (9373–409).

From the viewpoint of the vassal, lordly matchmaking could be desirable or intrusive, depending on the circumstances. In the Cid's case, the vassal's reaction is one of ambivalence bordering on resentment, as seen in the passage where, while pondering his rise from disgraced exile to wealthy lord in his own right, he reveals his ambivalence concerning his prospective sons-in-law:

> "Echado fu de tierra,   é tollida la onor,
> con grand afán gané   lo que he yo.
> A Dios lo gradesco   que del rrey he su graçia
> e pídenme mis fijas   pora los ifantes de Carrión.
> Ellos son mucho urgullosos   e an part en la cort,
> d'este casamiento   non avría sabor,

mas pues lo conseia   el que más vale que nós,
fablemos en ello,   en la poridad seamos nós."

(1934–41)

The Cid's misgivings are those of the patriarch determined to uphold the honor and dignity of the clan. We may detect, therefore, a notion of "our lineage may be less prestigious, but we have our honor." Thus he apologizes to his daughters at the very moment he announces their betrothal (2197–204). Although the match promises status enhancement ("'d'este vu[e]stro casamiento   creçremos en onor'"), he, the Cid, is not responsible ("'non lo levanté yo'"), but rather the king ("'que yo nulla cosa   nol' sope dezir de no'"), who is solely answerable ("'que él vos casa, ca non yo'"). Later, however, the Cid will rejoice that the Infantes are married to his daughters: "'que he aver e tierra   e oro e onor / e son mios yernos   ifantes de Carrión'" (2495–96). This optimism and the paternal forbearance he shows the Infantes—a function of kin-ordered amity—are not incompatible with his initial apprehension.

The hero's uncertainty in the matter of the daughters' first marriages is the marital correlative of the genealogical rivalry mentioned earlier. The Infantes have what the Cid wants; their marriages to his daughters allow an approximation to that goal. At the same time, the uneasiness of the situation is intensified by the Infantes' own ambivalence about the marriages. In conformity with the demographic implications of a hypergamous system, they need wives of lower social standing than their own. Women of their stratum marry up, leaving their male peers with reduced chances of marrying appropriately. The situation provokes status anxiety. For hypergamy, from the viewpoint of the down-marrying male, is a second choice. A woman of equal or higher standing is, however unlikely of attainment, the ideal. The Infantes, therefore, make the best of a disagreeable situation by securing at the very least an economically advantageous match.

Duby, however, argues that statistics may not have been against the quality marriages desired by the Infantes. He notes that "social superiority in the wife" was in reality the practical rule in aristocratic marriages. The disparity in rank, he suggests, "exacerbated men's fear of women," an apprehension largely caused by the prospect of absorption into the wife's family.

Duby's view of aristocratic marriage is based on the likelihood of a superabundance of wives in the marriage market, giving eligible males a consequent "buying power."[15] Thus, the demographics of aristocratic marriage might indeed have justified the Infantes' pretensions to upward-bound marriages: " 'podremos casar con fijas   de rreyes o de enperadores, / ca de natura somos   de condes de Carrión' " (2553–54). Fernando González reminds all present that he and his brother are of " 'natura . . . de condes de Carrión' " and insists that they are more properly married to the daughters of " 'rreyes o de enperadores, / ca non perteneçién   fijas de ifançones' " (3296–98). It is on these grounds that the Infante Diego justifies the Afrenta de Corpes and denies the charge of *menos valer* (infamy). Because he and his brother are, he insists, of the lineage ("natura") of the " 'condes más li[m]pios,' " their marriages to the Cid's daughters were not " 'apareçidos, / por consagrar   con Mio Çid don Rodrigo' " (3354–56).

The poem seems as unaware of Church policy on concubinage as it is of the primacy of consent and the impropriety of divorce. The Infantes tell themselves, in another element of their self-deceptive scenario, that the Cid's daughters were *varraganas*—i.e., concubines—rather than legitimate wives: " 'non las deviemos tomar por varraganas   | si non fuéssemos rrogados, / pues nuestras pareias   non eran pora en braços' " (2759–61). García Ordóñez, speaking on the Infantes' behalf, alleges the same concept in their defense:

> "Los de Carrión   son de natura tal
> non ge las devién querer   sus fijas por varraganas,
> o ¿quién ge las diera   por pareias o por veladas?
> Derecho fizieron   por que las han dexadas."
>
> (3275–78)

Duby notes the decades-long controversy, in the eleventh and twelfth centuries, over the issue of concubinage. Even as it forbade sexual unions of any kind for priests, the Church aimed "at trapping the whole of the laity in a net in which each mesh was a duly consecrated marriage." Concubinage came officially to be viewed, long before the *PMC*'s composition, as "no different from fornication." When cases of de facto concubinage were verified, they were to be redefined as marriage: "if a man treated a concubine as if she were a wife, then their union was indissoluble," so that "it was no longer permissible for a man to dismiss a concubine in order to remarry" (Duby, *Knight, Lady, Priest* 117–18, 144, 164).

Marriage in the ancient Germanic context, summarizes Brundage, was a union "created by cohabitation, rather than by formal act." Marriage in fifth- and sixth-century Germanic society was, therefore, "a social fact, not a legal status," with polygyny a common practice, particularly among royal families and the higher ranks of nobility. The distinction between marriage and concubinage was unclear, "both in practice and in law." For practical purposes, argues Brundage, Germanic concubinage can be defined as a "quasi-marriage . . . without full legal consequences," and "a long-term and more or less permanent relationship between a man and a woman of unequal social status . . . [which] was common in early Germanic societies." The offspring of concubinage could have no share in their father's estate. Marriage tended to be defined as a sexually consummated union accompanied—in contrast with concubinage—by the intention of having children and forming a permanent union. Germanic law held the first year of marriage to be a trial period that, if it ended without children, could be terminated. Men, even when the union produced children, had considerably more latitude in obtaining divorce than women (Brundage 129–31).

Significantly, neither the Cid nor his champions question the validity of concubinage as a recognized type of sexual liaison with its own customary status. The Infantes' allegation in vv. 3276–77—that the Cid's daughters have been their *varraganas* and not their *pareias* and *veladas* (concubines as opposed to proper wives)—is taken seriously and answered as stated. The Cid and his champions argue that the daughters are not concubines but legitimate spouses. A truly legal-minded poet such as the one postulated by Colin Smith and others would have discredited the very notion of alleged concubinage as a defense.

## Dowry and Other Prestations

Dowry and other marital prestations must be seen as elements in the total system of donative practice, rather than as isolated expressions of legal obligation. The gift-giving system manifests itself, for example, in the scene in which the moneylenders Rachel and Vidas conclude their deal with the Cid. Rachel makes an unabashed request, reminding the Cid of "grandes . . . gananças" he is destined to win: " 'una piel vermeia, morisca e ondrada, / Çid, beso vuestra mano en don que la yo aya' " (178–79). To this the hero replies with a promise to fulfill the request, assuring Rachel that if the gift should fail to arrive, its value may be deducted from the amount contained in the chests (180–81). Martín Antolínez's behavior shortly thereafter suggests that not only gift-giving but the straightforward solicitation of gifts was the norm. As Martín delivers the chests, he declares to the moneylenders: " 'yo que esto vos gané bien mereçía calças' " (190), obliging Rachel and Vidas to agree (" 'Démosle buen don, ca él no' lo ha buscado' " [192]) and to grant him a gratuity of 30 marks (196).

Other reciprocal gifts include the swords exchanged at the moment when Alfonso confirms the betrothal (2093) and the 200 marks mentioned by the king as a gift given to him by the Infantes from the 3,000 marks of the girls' *axuvar*: " 'D'estos *tres* mill marcos los *dozientos* tengo yo, / entr'amos me los dieron los ifantes de Carrión' " (3231–32). The latter gift is explained by Hinojosa as an example of the "regalo que el marido hacía en señal de gratitud al que le transmitía la potestad sobre la mujer, según el antiguo derecho germánico." The Germanic peoples he mentions as practitioners of this so-called *launegild* are the Lombards and the Scandinavians. García González points out, however, the absence of evidence for this custom in medieval Spain. He suggests, furthermore, that it would be illogical for the king to accept a present of 200 marks from the Infantes after having already presented them with a gift of 300 marks, on the occasion of giving the sons-in-law into the Cid's keeping: " 'Trezientos marcos de plata en ayuda les do yo / que metan en sus bodas o dó quisiéredes vós' " (2103–04). Rather than a token of gratitude for the king's offices as go-between and matchmaker, the sum represents, in his view, a fine levied against the Infantes for having repudiated their wives. Pavlović and Walker endorse García González's interpretation, adding that the king gives back the 200 marks to facilitate the Infantes' repayment of the dowry sum to the Cid.[16]

Despite García González's citation of passages from the *Fuero de Cuenca* which would seem to support the notion of the 200 marks as a fine (one must multiply by 2 to obtain this sum for the *PMC*: thus, 100 per Infante), it must be noted that the king would indeed be guilty of illogic to show the sternness needed to impose such a penalty, then to cite pity as the reason for immediately reimbursing the fine: " 'tornárgelos quiero, ca *tan* desfechos son' " (3233). Furthermore, if the trial at the end of the poem involves the refund of the 3,000 marks to the Cid, the 200 marks cited as coming from that amount (" 'D'estos *tres* mill marcos los *dozientos* tengo yo' ") cannot be regarded as a fine, since they are specifically mentioned as coming from the dowry fund; one cannot, presumably, take the amount of a fine from a specific sum claimed by a plaintiff. As for the notion that the refund of the amount significantly reduces the Infantes' liability, while helping them avoid total bankruptcy, it must be remarked that 200 marks seems, from the viewpoint of impoverished, debt-ridden young noblemen, a very insignificant percentage of the total sum.

The 200 marks apparently given by the Infantes to Alfonso, as well as the 300 marks given by the king to the Cid's sons-in-law, clearly express the logic of amicable reciprocity. This is the same kind of give-and-take portrayed in the scene in which the Cid promises a "tip" to the moneylenders and the latter present a gratuity to Martín Antolínez. In the context of Alfonso's matchmaking intervention on behalf of the Infantes, and of his gift to them of 300 marks, the absence of a return gift incurs loss of face. The three principal obligations of reciprocity, Marcel Mauss states in his famous essay, are giving, receiving, and repaying. Amounting, as he expresses it, to a "total system," they may not be viewed as singular, isolated, or idiosyncratic, but rather as the elements of a regime quite different from that of "pure individual contract, the money market, sale proper, fixed price, and weighed and coined money" (37–41, 45).

The *PMC*, attentive to the nuances of reciprocity, pays particular attention to marital assigns. The principal payments depicted are the dowry, devolving upon the bride from her family, and a payment from the groom to the bride, which apparently corresponds to prestations variously termed, in medieval codes, the *dos ex marito, donatio ante nuptias,* and *donatio propter nuptias*. Goody points out the need to distinguish by a special term "a present or gift by a man to or for his bride." The dowry proper ("direct dowry" in Goody's terminology) is the money or assets brought by a wife into her marriage, as well as the portion devolving upon a bride as a share (although not necessarily the totality of her share) in the estate of her natal family. A payment by groom to bride, according to Goody, is indirect or reverse dowry. The term *bridewealth*, he points out, is more appropriately reserved for a prestation conferred by the groom or his kin on the bride's kin (Goody, *Development* 241–42). Bridewealth is destined not for the bride but for her kin: "it is," affirms Goody, "wealth for, not to, the bride." Dowry, by contrast, goes to the bride herself, or to her husband for safekeeping, or to both spouses jointly. It is therefore misleading to use bridewealth as a synonym for so-called reverse dowry, whereby a husband endows his wife at the time of betrothal or marriage.[17]

The *Partidas*, accentuating the reciprocity of marital prestations, define the latter as *dote* and *arras*. The dowry (*dote*), they acknowledge, is, while given by the wife to the husband "con entendimiento de se mantener et ayudar el matrimonio," nonetheless to be regarded "como propio patrimonio de la muger." Donations should be "fechas egualmiente, fueras ende si fuese costumbre usada de luengo tiempo en algunos logares de las facer dotra manera." The *Partidas* affirm that a man's donation to the bride at marriage, the Latin *donatio propter nuptias,* is referred to in Spanish by the term *arras,* although, it is noted, "las leyes de los sabios antiguos" considered this term to refer to the pledge (*peño*) guaranteeing the fulfillment of the marriage contract (IV.xi.1). In Latin usage the *arrhae* constituted earnest money exchanged between the parties at the time of betrothal. In late Imperial times there arose a tendency to conflate the two originally separate prestations of the *sponsalia* or *donatio ante nuptias* (prenuptial gift to the bride, amounting to indirect dowry), and the *arrhae,* the prenuptial earnest money or deposit.[18]

The *Partidas* observe the Latin distinction between *adventitia* (prestations from bride to groom derived from property or wealth accruing to her personally from sources other than the patrimonial estate) and *profectitia*, defined as property which "sale de los bienes del padre, ó del abuelo ó de los otros parientes que suben por liña derecha." The patrimonial nature of the dowry is reaffirmed in another law stipulating that the husband may acquire his wife's dowry outright only through contractual agreement, or by reason of the wife's adultery, or "por costumbre" (23). In the case of the wife's death in a childless marriage, dowry given as *profectitia* reverts to her father (30); if she has children, they inherit the dowry (31). The dowry, then, is a thing over which the husband has control and usufruct, including whatever increased profit it realizes (18, 25). It is, however, transmitted from the woman's paternal kin to her and to her children.

The modern Spanish word for dowry, *dote*, does not appear in the *PMC*. Instead the poem uses the term *axuvar* (mod. Sp. *ajuar*). Corominas observes that the term *axuvar*, in the *PMC*, signifies "heredad que la esposa recibe de sus ascendientes." The term *ajuar* for trousseau was not common usage until the sixteenth century, according to Corominas (1: 98–99). The poem uses this term, in other words, to refer to the asymmetrical prestation called *dowry* in modern ethnographic parlance. When the Cid's men arrive in Valencia with copious plunder, he proudly announces to his wife: " 'Riqueza es que nos acreçe maravillosa e grand, ... / por casar son vuestras fijas,  adúzenvos axuvar'" (1648–50).

It is clear in 2571 that the amount of the dowry is considered to have been given to the daughters, rather than the sons-in-law (" 'yo quiero les dar axuvar  *tres* mill marcos de plata' "), but it is also evident that the Infantes have control and usufruct of the amount. This is the point of the Cid's complaint in the *cortes* scene:

> "quando sacaron de Valençia  mis fijas amas a dos
> en oro e en plata  tres mill marcos les di [y]o,
> yo faziendo esto,  ellos acabaron lo so;
> denme mis averes  quando mios yernos non son."
>
> (3203–06)

The Infantes cannot refund the dowry, because they have already spent it: "los haveres grandes son, / espesos los han  ifantes de Carrión" (3218–19). They can only offer to liquidate some of their hereditary estates: " 'pagar le hemos de heredades   en tierras de Carrión'" (3223). From the amount of the dowry, as we have seen, they have already given Alfonso a portion; he offers to contribute this money (3229–34), in view of the justice of the plaintiff's cause (" 'que derecho demanda el Çid Campeador'"), and the penury of the defendants (" 'ca *tan* desfechos son'"). When Fernando González confesses that the two brothers have no cash (" 'Averes monedados non tenemos nós'" [3236]), they are told by Count Remond, one of the judges, to pay in kind: " 'páguenle en apreçiadura   e préndalo el Campeador'" (3240). The payment, consisting, among other things, of horses, mules, palfreys, and swords, is made, but only by recourse to borrowing: "enpréstanles de lo ageno,   que non les cumple lo suyo" (3248).

In the Mediterranean system of marital prestations, according to Diane Hughes, contributions from the groom's family (payments, material or symbolic, for the bride) and dowry (devolving upon the wife from her kin) frequently coexist within a broad range of matrimonial endowments and exchanges. Roman practice emphasized the betrothal guarantee, or *arra sponsalicia*. Among the Romans, marriage with *manus* originally insured that dowry "fell totally into the husband's control." In contrast, dowry functioned in ancient Athens as an "avenue of benefit [to a daughter] from her father's patrimony." A woman's husband controlled rather than owned his wife's dowry, administering it "in trust for sons borne to him by the wife who brought the dowry with her." The dowry, a "separately accountable" entity, was either "vested in the sons of the marriage, or returned to the woman's former *kyrios*" (i.e., her father or the senior agnate of her lineage).[19] The Mediterranean groom and his family are generally outdone by the bride and her family in the variety and value of gifts and expenditures. Traditional Mediterranean gifts from the groom and his kin tend to be "minimal or trivial," while the bride's dowry, by contrast, is usually a "weighty and substantial settlement on which prospective bridegrooms might cast greedy eyes" (Hughes 263–64, and 264n7).

It is just such a fund, established for the marriages of the Cid's daughters, which makes them attractive partners to the Infantes. The motivation of the latter may be deduced from their attitude on the occasion of the Afrenta de Corpes. Their

self-deception encompasses both the blame for their predicament—they tell themselves that the marriages were foisted
upon them ("'De nuestros casamientos   agora somos vengados'" [2758])—and the realities of the marriage market.
They look to use their wives' dowry as the means to financial
independence: "'los averes que tenemos   grandes son e sobeianos, / mientra que visquiéremos   despender no lo podremos'" (2541–42). They even view the girls' dowry as a platform
for future advantageous marriages:

> "Averes levaremos grandes   que valen grant valor,
> escarniremos   las fijas del Canpeador.
> D'aquestos averes   siempre seremos rricos omnes,
> podremos casar con fijas   de rreyes o de enperadores."
>
> (2550–53)

But for the detail of their brides' inferior social status, the
Infantes de Carrión clearly fit the pattern of heiress-hunting
soldiers of fortune and prodigal upper-class wastrels—one of
the Western world's perennial literary and folkloric themes.
Here we must introduce a distinction. These characters are
very possibly not realistic, true-to-life wastrels, but rather
*señoritos*—"upper-class twits," to employ the satirical idiom
of the Monty Python troop—as a poet of non-noble origins
scathingly lampoons them. Their initial motive is vaguely
status-enhancing: "'demandemos sus fijas   pora con ellas casar, /
creçremos en nuestra ondra   e iremos adelant'" (1882–83). Here
the Infantes themselves, through their use of the word *ondra,*
acknowledge the honor and prestige accruing to the Cid's
heroic achievement. They wish to partake vicariously in this
honor. Only secondarily does the more general concept of
"getting ahead" take its place in the Infantes' calculus of motives. Later, as an afterthought, they will seek to minimize the
Cid's meritorious honor through invocation of their ascribed
status as descendants of a noble ancestor (2549, 2554, 3275,
3296, 3354). In issuing his challenge, Alvar Fáñez recognizes
their honorable ancestry, emphasizing by his very acknowledg-
ment the unworthiness of the young men (3443–44). Even as
their own personal honor decreases, the Infantes concentrate on
the material benefits of the marital alliance with the Cid's
family. Fernando admits to the Cid: "'tanto avemos de averes

que no son contados'" (2529). As we have seen, the enormity of the fortune gained through their marriage encourages them to look forward, as they contemplate their revenge, to a life of ease (2541–42).

Before asking the Cid's leave to depart with the daughters, the Infantes agree: " 'digamos que las levaremos a tierras de Carrión / [e] enseñar las hemos dó las heredades son'" (2544–45). The Infantes promise their wives "villas" (manorial holdings) as a wedding gift in the form of estates ("'por arras e por onores'" [2565]). When they ask the Cid's permission to take Elvira and Sol back to Carrión, the Infantes again refer to these properties: " 'verán vuestras fijas lo que avemos nós, / los fijos que oviéremos en qué avrán partición'" (2566–67). That the Cid and his family understand this offer as a gift of land to the daughters is demonstrated by Jimena's farewell: " 'Id a Carrión dó sodes heredadas, / assí commo yo tengo, bien vos he casadas'" (2605–06). When the Cid charges Félez Muñoz with accompanying the girls, he declares: " 'verás las heredades que a mis fijas dadas son'" (2621). As the Infantes are about to commit the Afrenta de Corpes, they taunt the Cid's daughters: " 'Oy nos partiremos e dexadas seredes de nós, / non abredes part en tierras de Carrión'" (2716–17). After the successful outcome of the judicial combat, the Cid declares: " '¡Grado al Rey del çielo, mis fijas vengadas son! / Agora las ayan quitas heredades de Carrión. / Sin vergüença las casaré o a qui pese o a qui non'" (3714–16).

Pavlović and Walker comment that the Roman practice of *donatio*, a contribution provided by the husband either before (*d. ante nuptias*) or after the wedding (*d. propter nuptias*), insured the wife's financial security in case of widowhood or divorce. The amount was considered the sole property of the woman. They suggest that "*arras* as it appears in the *PMC* shows many interesting similarities with . . . the *donatio*." They point out that the Infantes' contribution consists of land (" 'villas por arras en tierras de Carrión'" [2570]), while the Cid bestows a cash gift (2571). Although the recovery of the *axuvar* is relatively straightforward, the outcome with regard to the *arras* is, they suggest, unclear. Arguing, with García González, that the Cid's daughters have a legal claim on the *arras* (2605: " 'Id a Carrión,'" Jimena urges the girls, " 'dó sodes heredadas'"),

and that it would be "out of keeping with the Cid's character
... to renounce voluntarily money or property to which he is
legally entitled," they assert that the *arras* are not an issue in
the court case "because the innocent party was only required
to bring an *actio* in order to recover his or her own matrimonial contribution, not in order for him or her to retain the
contribution of the guilty party" ("Money, Marriage and the
Law" 201–02).

Pavlović and Walker conclude by an interpretation of the
Cid's exclamation on hearing the outcome of the judicial combat (3715: " 'Agora las ayan quitas  heredades de Carrión' ").
Far from being "an ironic expression of relief by the Cid that
his daughters are now completely rid of all connection with
Carrión and the evil Infantes," the Cid's utterance, they contend, reveals his thankfulness for the fact that the Infantes were
defeated but not killed. Had they died, the daughters would
have no further claim on the estates comprising their *arras*.
According to such codes as the *Fuero de Molina*, a wife lost all
claim on property not handed over to her in the lifetime of a
deceased husband. The Cid's exultation over the higher quality
of the second marriages is thus enhanced by the notion that the
girls bring to their new husbands not only the original *axuvar*
of 3,000 marks, but "the additional *axuvar* consisting of the rich
estates of Carrión" ("Money, Marriage and the Law" 202–03).

*Arras* means, according to Corominas, "lo que se da como
prenda en algún contrato," as well as "donación dotal" (1: 349).
To understand the Cid's attitude in 3715, however, we must
determine the precise nature of the bargain implied by the term
and the marital prestation it comprises. In the Germanic system of the early Middle Ages, the husband's donation was the
significant matrimonial prestation. Diane Hughes argues that
the legal commonplace of the early Middle Ages, *nullum sine
dote fiat conjugium,* referred not to dowry proper but rather to
the Germanic custom of the husband's gift—in other words, to
bridewealth. Citing Tacitus (*Germania* 18), she notes that marriage gifts in this system are not for women or women's tastes;
they are destined not for the bride but rather for her male kin
(Hughes 265).

*Arras* in the *PMC* are paid by the groom, as in the Germanic
pattern. However, departing from the ancient practice, they do

not compensate the bride's family. Instead, the *arras* constitute an endowment of the bride by the groom. In this the *PMC* reflects the pattern shown by the marriage of the historical Cid and Jimena, which provides an example of the prospective groom's *donatio* accompanying betrothal. The document confirming this prestation, witnessed by Pedro Anzúrez and García Ordóñez, speaks of "omnes ipsas hereditates qui sunt in territorio kastelle," promising to "Scemena" Rodrigo's "porciones" in numerous towns and places. "Et sunt quidem istas *arras* tibi uxor mea Szemena," affirms the charter, "in foro de Legione." In addition, the historical Cid endows his wife with other lands not included in the *arras* ("dono tibi illas alias meas villas . . . qui non sunt in tuas *arras*"). Both parties name the surviving partner beneficiary of the deceased partner's estate, with their children inheriting after the death of the survivor.[20]

The *Fuero Juzgo* takes this notion of *arras* as prenuptial pledge very seriously:

> Depues que andar el pleyteamiento de las bodas ante testimonias entre aquellos que se quieren desposar, ó entre sus padres, ó entre sus propinquos, é la sortiia fuere dada é recibida por nombre de arras . . . por nenguna manera el prometimiento non sea crebantado, ni nenguna de las partes non pueda mudar el pleyto, si el otra parte non quisiere; mas las bodas sean fechas, é las arras sean complidas. (III.i.3)

The *Fuero Juzgo* makes it clear that the *arras* are destined for the wife and are considered her property. Should, for instance, a man die after the betrothal ("las esposaias") and the transfer of the *arras*, the surviving woman "deve aver la meetad de todas las cosas quel diera el esposo, y la otra meetad deven aver los herederos del esposo" (III.i.5). Control of the *arras* lies entirely with the woman who receives it: "á las muieres era mandado que fiziesen de sus *arras* lo que quisiesen" (IV.v.2). This implies that *arras* as conceived by the *Fuero Juzgo* refers to what the modern ethnographer calls indirect dowry.

The *Fuero Viejo*'s reference to the third of a man's estate consigned, in pledge, to his wife's usufruct or possible inheritance, also falls under the rubric of *arras*. A *fijodalgo*, it is stipulated, must give "el tercio del eredamiento" to his wife, "en arras." She, having lived "una buena vida," is entitled to keep this on his death. If her husband's heirs wish to deny her this inheritance, they must indemnify her to the amount of "quinientos sueldos." The woman is also entitled to the husband's "mula ensellada o enfrenada," as well as the furniture and clothing she brought into the marriage and "la meitat de todas las ganancias que ganaron en uno" (V.i.294). The *donadio*, a separate prestation given by an *hidalgo* "a la ora del casamiento, ante que sean jurados," could consist of a "piel de abortones" long enough to allow "un cauallero armado entrar por la una manga e salir por la otra," as well as, among other things, a saddled and harnessed mule, a silver plate, a Moorish slave woman, or simply a cash payment to the "quantia de mil maravedis" (V.ii). The *donadio* could be taken from the amount set aside in trust before the marriage, with half of the total destined for the wife, half for the husband (V.xiv) (San Martín, *Códigos españoles* 294–96).

Law codes and the marriage agreement of the historical Cid support the contention of Pavlović and Walker that the Cid's daughters might well have a right to the lands promised them by the Infantes. But the point of the Cid's reaction in 3715 is that he renounces all further claim against the Infantes, thereby sharpening, by his utter contempt for any continued association with them or their line, the bitter sting of their humiliation.

Acceptance of the gift, in the world of amicable reciprocity, makes for a contractual relationship. Reverse dowry, in other words, compromises the woman as much as it compensates her. To disengage himself from the lingering entanglement represented by the lands promised as *arras*, the Cid must see that they are taken back. The Infantes are caught in a contradiction: you cannot allege that your women are mere concubines, then keep their dowry. The Cid avoids the mirror-image contradiction. He cannot allege that he has not accepted the *arras*, since to do so would deny that legitimate marriage took place. He must contend that the marriage is legitimate, so that his daughters will not be disgraced. Only by proving that legitimate marriage did take place can the Cid expunge, by the marriage's annulment, the lingering compromise represented by his acceptance of the *arras*. The outcome of the combat insures that the daughters are thus indeed quit of the *arras*, so that they can now remarry unencumbered. After the duels, no one can say that the Infantes have any further hold on the Cid or his family.

Minaya's gracious refusal of the Cid's offer of a fifth of the spoils provides a clue to the meaning of 3715 ("'Agora las ayan quitas'"). Again, the reciprocal logic of amity is the clue: "'d' aquesta quinta . . . / Yo vos la suelto e avello quitado'" (494, 496). An offer, we see, is a formal act which cannot be ignored by the intended recipient. Indeed, to remain silent is to tacitly accept the proffered benefaction, thereby accepting the ethical obligation and the social encumbrance it represents. Viewing marriage as an element in this exchange system, we better understand the use by the Cid and Minaya of the same verb—*quitar*—to express the action of releasing a prestation from a specific dyadic contract, thereby returning it to the infinite stock of potential offerings. In the amicable game of give-and-take, in which marriage is but another gift, abrogation of a contract requires—publicly, legally, dramatically—that any counterprestation, such as the *arras*, be formally taken back by the donor.

Whereas the *arras* represent a guarantee, dowry is more multifunctional. Often characterized as an ostentatious status display, especially in connection with hypergamous match-making, the dowry was a frequent mechanism of effective daughter disinheritance. In this latter aspect it was in many ways an extralegal patriarchal scheme accomplished in defiance of laws and customs that protected women's rights. The dotal regime, concludes Hughes, "drew attention away from the conjugal bond to focus it instead on the relations between the couple and the wife's kinsmen." The principle of marital consent emerged "at precisely the time when the net of dotal marriage was catching daughters ever more firmly in the marital schemes of their kinsmen." For medieval dowry was "almost from its beginnings . . . part of a status, rather than an inheritance system." Dowry, in other words, was a way of using rights over daughters "as a way of asserting status or competing for it." It thus comes to constitute "a form of disinheritance within a social group whose organization had become significantly *less* bilateral." Dowry thus increasingly came to function as another item in the tool kit of political and economic strategies designed to promote the interests of the agnatic lineage at the expense of all but designated heirs (Hughes 284, 290).

Hypergamous marriage and dowry are naturally complementary aspects of donative practice. Viewed as exchange, dowry often accompanies marriage in which the groom's side may provide various kinds of symbolic capital. "While dowry-giving households lose daughters and wealth," observe Alice Schlegel and Rohn Eloul, "they can gain status." Alliance with a powerful or prestigious clan is frequently obtained by recruitment of "a high-status son-in-law," with the concomitant honorific and political advantages afforded by such a match ("Marriage Transactions" 301). According to Dumont, the practice of hypergamy expresses the "Brahmanic-classical" notion of marriage as a "gift of the maiden." The bride represents a meritorious gift "on the condition that no payment is received for the girl," while giving her away is "accompanied by material gifts and by as lavish receptions as possible." At the same time, the superior status of the bridegroom's family encourages it to be "demanding about the prestations it receives with the girl, as if it would only accept marriage into an inferior family on condition of receiving hard cash." Thus, summarizes Dumont, a bride's family exchanges "a daughter and goods . . . for . . . the prestige or consideration which results from intermarriage with [the superior group]" (Dumont 117–18).

Stanley Tambiah, examining dowry in India and Ceylon, argues that the practice is governed by the "twin principles" of "female rights to property" transferred at the time of marriage "as a sort of pre-mortem inheritance" and of dowry as an establishment of "a relation of affinity between the bride's family and the husband's family." While this affinal relationship occasions "gift-giving which persists long after the marriage rite," the central prestation remains dowry itself, which "lends itself to being dressed up as a 'gift' that accompanies the 'gift of the virgin' (*kanya dana*)," thus facilitating "hypergamy whereby a family of lower social status but not necessarily of inferior wealth attempts to raise its position and its prestige by contracting a superior marriage for its daughters and sisters." Such unions imply, asserts Tambiah, "an exchange of status for wealth." The receiving family is, in a way, beholden to—and outdone by—the giving family. But there is at the same time, argues Tambiah, an implicit notion of a kind of pool or floating fund in the society at large: dowry-givers may "get their return" by exacting higher dowries from the families of their wives or daughters-in-law (Tambiah 64–65).

A less hierarchical and less transactional view may be taken, both of hypergamy and of marital prestations. Gloria Raheja, for example, examines the "almost universal assumption" that hierarchy is the "dominant ideological feature" underlying the relationship between "wife-givers" and "wife-receivers." Affinal endowments have been interpreted, she argues, as a recognition by wife-givers of "the 'superiority' of wife-receivers." This approach, she suggests, is inadequate on several grounds. It restricts analysis of prestations to "an arbitrarily drawn domain of 'kinship,'" thus ignoring, among other things, the ritual and linguistic aspects of such donations. Analyses focusing on the merely hierarchical element fail to appreciate the crucial importance of *dan*, the most important prestation in an Indian customary system dating from Vedic times. The giving and receiving of *dan*, particularly with respect to such groups as the Gujar landholders of the study, transcends mere economic, political, or hierarchical power. Assuming the "proper ritual contexts" and the "appropriate recipients," the giving of *dan* "transfers inauspiciousness and brings about the auspiciousness, well-being, and protection of the person, the family, the house, and the village." The giving and receiving of *dan* is "the ideological core" of the standing and influence exerted by the dominant caste (Raheja xi–xii, 118–19).

Certain areas of India, Raheja allows, do reveal "a ranked relationship between lower wife-givers and higher wife-receivers," which may "sometimes appear as a formalized ranking of clan groupings." At the same time, some regions in North India show a tendency toward "hypergamous directionality in marriage," while in other areas "there is no formalized system of rank within the caste, and it is only the marriage itself that establishes the hierarchic superiority of wife-receivers over wife-givers." In this contest, "givers and receivers are ranked only with respect to each other and only with regard to a specific marriage." In still other areas, formal definition of "hypergamous entities" is minimal, with little or no restrictions on clan intermarriage. Aversion toward "reversals of directionality" in the giving of daughters is not expressed in terms of "an undesirable reversal or neutralization of a ranked relationship that might have previously existed between wife-givers and wife-receivers." Such exchanges, rather, are avoided because they imply the purchase of a bride. Such a transaction "contravenes the fundamental purposes of *dan*, inasmuch as inauspiciousness can never be transferred in a reciprocated exchange." Only the "unreciprocated gifting away of a daughter" assures the "well-being" and "auspiciousness" that are the intended effects of *dan*. When asked about the connection "between rank and affinal prestations," informants assert both the importance of the groom's obligation to receive gifts and the "ritual centrality of the giver of *dan* rather than his hierarchical position vis-à-vis the recipient" (Raheja 119–21).

A recent cross-cultural study, supporting Raheja's contention that there is more to the marriage gift than status asymmetry, questions transactive theories of dowry. Dowry, in contrast to bridewealth (which functions in some societies as an effective payment for a woman), "creates a conjugal fund legally belonging not to the extended family of which the new couple is a part but to the couple itself" (Harrel and Dickey 108). Dowry, therefore, does not necessarily recompense a high-status family for the alliance thereby formed with the bride's kinfolk. Moreover, the supposed political, economic, or honorific benefits of an affinal relationship between lineages of bride and groom has been refuted by others. Even if cost-benefit ratios could be verified, argues John Comaroff, "the co-existence of two phenomena does not itself establish that the one motivates the other." The meaning of marriage payments such as dowry cannot be illuminated by merely "economistic" models, which assimilate prestations into "undifferentiated categories," and overemphasize "the commercial logic of conjugal transactions" (Comaroff, Introduction 6–7). In agreement with this approach, Steven Harrel and Sara Dickey demonstrate that dowry occurs even in isogamous marriages, in which affinal ties do not represent a clearly unbalanced transaction. They cite as an example the marriage patterns described by Carmelo Lisón-Tolosana for Belmonte de los Caballeros, in which both spouses bring important shares of property to the marriage.[21]

Dowry, furthermore, is not necessarily a mechanism of daughter disinheritance. Many patrilineal societies, such as those of sub-Saharan Africa, bequeath the daughter little or nothing. Why do Eurasian families give their daughters anything at all, and "why," ask Harrel and Dickey, "does it take some kind of dowry to disinherit them?" Discrepancy in the timing, amount, and kind of inheritance between daughters and sons does not necessarily mean disinheritance of the former, but simply that a community "has two ways of devolving property; one for sons and one for daughters" (107, 118). Dowry is not, they affirm, a transaction but a "social statement" and an exhibition of status by the family of the bride. The ostentatious expenditure represented by dowry thus characterizes those societies in which wealth confers status (many societies, despite economic inequality, do not recognize status based on wealth). In general, "a family's ability to compensate for its lower status by making a large, publicly displayed gift of dowry to its daughter is clear evidence that wealth matters." Dowry is therefore typical where "there is some competition or possible disagreement about whose wealth is indeed superior." Where social mobility is limited, dowry will be less likely, while in "fluid and competitive status systems," by contrast, dowry functions as a "public statement of a family's wealth and status, meant to be noticed, discussed, and taken into account whenever questions of relative status arise." Dowry, conclude Harrel and Dickey, transfers to a daughter "all or part of her share in inheritance," while displaying "the status of the family that gives it and, to a lesser extent, of the family that receives it" (112–13, 119).

Acknowledging the Infantes' gift to their brides of landed estates in Carrión, the Cid proposes to bestow a handsome counterprestation. We note that his speech expressly defines the girls as a gift—they are the direct object of the verb *dar*. The dowry, furthermore, is transmitted simultaneously along with the daughters:

> "Dar vos he mis fijas    e algo de lo mío;
> vós les diestes villas por arras    en tierras de Carrión,
> yo quiero les dar axuvar    *tres* mill marcos de plata;
> dar vos é mulas e palafrés    muy gruessos de sazón,
> cavallos pora en diestro,    fuertes e corredores,
> e muchas vestiduras    de paños de çiclatones;
> dar vos he dos espadas,    a Colada e a Tizón."
>
> (2568b–75)

Both the Infantes and their father-in-law present gifts to Elvira and Sol. The daughters are the recipients of largesse both as brides and as heiresses. The amount of the Cid's dowry to his daughters, three thousand marks, corresponds to a sum mentioned earlier in connection with the amount of booty taken after the defeat of Yusuf (*tirada* 95): "Mesnadas de Mio Çid rrobado an el canpo, / entre oro e plata  fallaron tres mill marcos, / las otras ganançias  non avía rrecabdo" (1736–38). The dowry, again, goes to the girls; the "algo de lo mío" promised by the Cid to his new sons-in-law consists of mules, palfreys, horses, clothing, and the two swords.

Ostentatious status affirmation is revealed at the wedding (2247–70). "[R]ricas fueron las bodas," the poet tells us. There is jousting, with seven mock castles built and destroyed. During the wedding feast, which lasts fifteen days, the father of the brides shows conspicuous generosity toward all his guests:

> entre palafrés e mulas  e corredores cavallos,
> en bestias sines ál  *ciento á* mandados;
> mantos e pelliçones  e otros vestidos largos;
> non fueron en cuenta  los averes monedados.
>
> (2254–57)

Wealth, in other words, in distributed to all comers, in a public display of generosity: "Qui aver quiere prender  bien era abastado; / rricos' tornan a Castiella  los que a las bodas llegaron" (2260–61).

What, we may ask, does the Cid gain from all this generosity? The wedding, for one thing, serves as the occasion for a public relations coup. For the guests, it is a source of gifts, a spectacle for their edification. The feast described is, then, in every way a multipurpose political event, cementing relationships between the Cid and his guests, between the Cid and his family, and the new sons-in-law. It provides the Cid with the opportunity of presenting his clan in a favorable light, as he completely eclipses the Infantes and their kin by the magnitude of his liberality. He who gives, receives—generosity, a powerful leveling agent, thus allows the Cid to surpass his sons-in-law in personal standing.

## Matrimonial Strategies

In testing their hypothesis concerning dowry, Harrel and Dickey specifically cite Peninsular examples, noting that communities showing relative economic egalitarianism also show "[limited] distribution of productive property at the time of marriage" as well as a strong tendency toward parental retention of ownership and control of land during the parents' lifetime. Even where considerable differences in wealth exist, a given community may show collective reluctance to regard such differences as significant indicators of relative status: "It is not the fact of economic distinctions, but the recognition of such distinctions as at least partially determining social status, that is necessary if a community is to have a significant dowry system." Thus, in the Aragonese community studied by Lisón-Tolosana, families provide daughters with both household furnishings and a plot of land "so as not to be outdone." In all the Spanish communities studied, inheritance is bilateral and egalitarian among siblings. The issue, therefore, is not one of transmission through females but rather "of the timing of the transmission and of the assertion and validation of a family's status in the community through its display of wealth given at its daughter's or son's marriage" (Harrel and Dickey 115–16).

There is a historical tendency—stronger at some times and in some communities than others—to regard dowry as an effective substitute for a daughter's normal share in the paternal estate. The consequence of medieval dotal practice as "the daughter's effective disinheritance" was a "preference for cash dowries throughout the western Mediterranean" (Hughes 278 and 278n47; 279–80, 281). Dowry as a so-called pre-mortem inheritance for daughters tended to function along with other elements in the agnatic system prevalent in Europe after the eleventh century, such as primogeniture (an essentially tenurial practice designed to maintain patrimonial holdings within a lineage) and patronymic surnames (Goody, *Development* 228–29). Herlihy suggests that exclusionist tendencies emerged as the natural concomitant to such agnatic practices. Families thus compelled their younger sons "to delay or eschew marriage, or . . . sent them forth to make their fortunes." Daughters, if they received anything at all, "were given [only] the dowries they needed for marriage." Save for unusual circumstances, such as the death of all her brothers, a daughter's dowry "represented the extent of her claims upon the family patrimony" (Herlihy, "Making" 124).

Dillard reports a resistance to this trend, as well as to that of primogeniture, in Leonese and Castilian territory throughout the Reconquest. There was a strong general tendency in most towns for the persistence of partible inheritance among heirs and heiresses, "with preference for women in a closer relationship to the deceased relative." Inheritance was transferred "irrespective of children's sex, age or order of birth." Moreover, it was generally considered "highly illegal to prefer one child, especially a male child, over another in inheritance" (Dillard 26–27).

The *Fuero Juzgo* does not distinguish between prestations from the families of the husband and the wife. Forbidding families to demand back from their children "lo que les dan á sus bodas," it decrees that

> si alguna cosa recibieren los esposados delos padres en tiempo de sus bodas en siervos, ó en vinas, ó en tierras, ó en casas, ó en vestidos, ó en otros ornamientos, ó en bodas ó depues de sus bodas, ó por escripto, ó por testimonio, que todo esto sea en voluntad de los fiios lo que quisieren ende tomar. (IV.v.3)

The donations described do not correspond to dowry as defined by Hughes, Goody, and others, namely, as a prestation destined for the bride and falling under her control. The *Fuero Juzgo* here discusses items applied to a conjugal fund. Neither man nor wife is privileged by this law; both apparently share in control of the total amount of goods and property given to them by their respective families. The endowments referred to therefore cannot be construed as a stratagem of disinheritance of the bride. Again, such contributions are held to pertain to the patrimonial holdings of the donating families. After the death of the father (presumably of either the bride or the groom), the law stipulates

> que vengan todos los hermanos egualmientre á la buena del padre ... Et aquello quel diera el padre al fiio ó á la fiia en tiempo de sus bodas, puede fazer dello lo que quisiere en la vida del padre é depues de su muerte, todavia en tal manera, que lo quel dió el padre en tiempo de las bodas que sea asmado, é que los hermanos tomen al tanto por ello, é lo

que fuere demas de la buena del padre pártanlo egual
mientre. (IV.v.3)

Dillard reports that the general trend in medieval Leonese and
Castilian codes viewed the "advances on a child's share . . .
commonly bestowed at marriage" as part of the total patrimony,
to be shared out after the death of the parent. At the death of a
parent, married heirs and heiresses accordingly were obliged
to "return or evaluate parental wedding gifts" for partition
among siblings and the surviving parent. "The reintegration of
parental marriage gifts or their value," Dillard notes, "was the
traditional mechanism for assuring an equitable and final
redistribution of a parent's property among all the children."[22]

As noted earlier, the most frequently mentioned kinship term
in the story is *fija*. In the hypergamous system, assuming social and political advantages conferred on wife-givers, daughters are the all-important conduit of lineal honor. This fact
neither denies them individuality, nor minimizes their other
possible roles (for example, as bearers of grandchildren for both
lineages). It simply means that insofar as marriage alliance is
concerned, they are bargaining instruments, poker chips, of the
highest value. The affinal relationship established between the
men of two lineages is, if anything, even more important. Marriage contracts, David Rheubottom has observed, "can be read
as if marriage was a relationship between father-in-law and
son-in-law in which the bride was a third party." The *pacta
matrimonialia*, he concludes, established a complex and "economically and socially consequential" alliance between individual men and their families (367).

The matrimonial pacts in the *PMC* are between the Cid and
Alfonso, with the brides a third party in both the first and second marriages. Amid all these male negotiations and agreements, the daughters are the beneficiaries of nothing uniquely
their own—even dowry and *arras* are to be shared. This, in a
way, confirms the urgency of their usefulness to the Cidian lineage. Despite his initial misgivings (2083: "'. . . non han grant
edad e de días pequeñas son'"), the Cid's willingness to marry
his daughters at a young age is entirely in accordance with time-
honored ethnic patterns. Marriage takes place, argues Bourdieu,
as a function of a lineage's "products on the matrimonial

market." Largely determined by such "secondary characteristics" as matrimonial status, age, and sex, a man's marriage market value variously affects the types of marriage arranged for him, according to his status as a marriageable or over-age bachelor, "an already married man looking for a co-wife, or a widower or divorcee wanting to remarry." Women are analogously classified, except that the "depreciation entailed by previous marriages is infinitely greater." A man, if willing to accept the possibility of marrying a social inferior or a previously married woman, may bide his time, since men are generally more likely than women to find a spouse. A father with daughters, by contrast, "can play with time so as to prolong the conjunctural advantage he derives from his position as the receiver of offers . . . only up to a certain point." The father who waits too long "will see his products devalued because they are thought to be unsaleable, or simply because they are past their prime." The marriage market value of a daughter, therefore, is chiefly determined by her age. The sooner and younger married, the better (Bourdieu 68).

Extrapolating from the North African context that provides Bourdieu with the material for his account, we may characterize the Cid's dilemma and accomplishment as a patriarchal father with daughters. He is, first of all, lucky that his divorced girls are immediately graced with new, better husbands. This happy ending may indeed be characterized as a fairy-tale element in the story. These ideal second marriages into royal families are the matrimonial equivalent of manna from heaven. In another way also the Cid's family escapes cruel necessity. He is allowed to be egalitarian in the marriages arranged for the girls, showing no differentiation between his offspring. Reality tends to be brutally indifferent to fair treatment of siblings. Bourdieu notes that the marriages of siblings are never treated as if "each marriage [were] an isolated unit." The timing of each marriage among a group of siblings is largely determined by "the marrying of all the others, and thus varies as a function of each child's *position* (defined mainly by sibling order, sex, and relationship to the head of the family), within the particular *configuration* of the whole set of children to be married, itself characterized by their number and sex." A son's function in matrimonial strategies, for example, is influenced by the number and sex of his siblings. The eldest male sibling, generally favored "to the detriment of his younger brothers," is likely to be married "first and as well as possible," and "outside rather than inside the lineage." Younger sons, on the other hand, are kept in the lineage, appointed "for work on the land rather than the house's external politics." A family with numerous daughters and few or no sons is, meanwhile, "in an unfavourable position and finds itself forced to incur debts toward the families which receive its women." A family "rich in men," by contrast, can "invest" its sons in a variety of ways, thus responding more flexibly to economic and political change (Bourdieu 68–70).

Rheubottom, addressing a different historical context, makes comparable observations concerning differentiation of siblings and their relative age at marriage. The younger the daughter, the "greater the number of potential husbands." Her family, in such circumstances, has "more choice and a longer period of time in which to exercise it." He confirms the prevalence of a "sisters-first" policy in the society of fifteenth-century Ragusa, and in Italian towns of the same period, which tended to increase the marriage age of brothers, while insuring that siblings of the same sex married in order (Rheubottom 360–70).

The Cid faces the supreme dilemma outlined by Bourdieu and Rheubottom—that of a father with only daughters. He is, at the same time, determined to obtain the best possible marriage, which is to say, one involving maximal alliance with a lineage of superior status. Despite this problem and these aspirations, the Cid, again, knows nothing of age-differentiation among siblings, with regard either to inheritance or to deployment on the marriage market. In this also the *PMC* seems to ignore historical patterns. The hero's daughters are neither selectively circulated within, nor withheld from, the marriage market. The Cid's equal treatment of his girls must be viewed as old-fashioned, defying as it does verifiable trends in the noble society of the time.

The breakdown of the manorial economy, in the Peninsula as elsewhere in Europe, provoked among the nobility an essentially defensive move toward agnatization (and away from bilaterality). In Spain the *mayorazgo,* whereby a lineage established "un orden de sustitución por vía de primogenitura," permitted the foundation of inalienable estates, often including towns as well as lands. Transmitted *mortis causa* from eldest son to eldest son (or, lacking a male heir, to eldest daughter or nearest male relative), *mayorazgo*, while devised to reinforce the stability of "la familia amplia o parentela," actually promoted lineal fragmentation, as younger sons sought "un patrimonio como para no tener que someterse al cobijo del «pariente mayor» del linaje." Ironically, achievement of this objective— "su establecimiento en otro lugar y por la fundación de su propio mayorazgo"—only worsened the economic position of noble houses (Quintanilla Raso 338–41; 346–47).

The *Partidas*, reflecting social trends, endorse primogeniture by declaring that the sons of kings must learn "como amen et teman á su padre, et á su madre, et á su hermano mayor, que son sus señores naturales por razon del linaje" (II.vii.9). Primogeniture is further explicated (II.xv.2) in terms of the "mayoria" of eldest sons as a "muy grant señal de amor que muestra Dios." Younger brothers must therefore reverence and safeguard the first-born heir "como á padre et á señor." Citing the Old Testament ("segunt él dixo á Moysen en la vieja ley, todo másculo que nasciese primeramente serie llamado cosa santa de Dios"), the *Partidas* maintain that the integrity of the lineage requires the devolution of inheritance upon the eldest son, despite the equal partition among heirs provided by ancient custom: "los padres comunalmente habiendo piedat del los otros fijos, non quisieron que el mayor lo hobiese todo, mas que cada uno dellos hobiese su parte." A more exclusive testament provides for the common good: "esta particion non se podrie facer en los regnos que destroidos non fuesen, segunt nuestro señor Jesu Cristo dixo, que todo regno partido astragado serie."

The *Fuero Juzgo*, reflecting the specific influence of ancient Germanic customs of bilateral inheritance, and the general tendency of kin-ordered societies toward equitable distribution of inheritance, shows itself flatly egalitarian with regard to treatment of heirs: "las ermanas deven aver egualmientre la buena del padre con los hermanos" (IV.ii.1). Inheritance rights, moreover, are thoroughly bilateral. A woman, declares the *Fuero Juzgo*, should "venir egualmientre con sus ermanos á la buena del padre, é de la madre, é de los avuelos, é de las avuelas de parte del padre é de parte de la madre." For it is right, states the *Fuero Juzgo*, that "aquellos que natura fizo egualmientre

parientes, egualmientre vengan á la buena" (IV.ii.9). Disinheritance of a son or daughter is an extraordinary sanction,
not to be accomplished without exceptional provocation: "El
padre non puede desheredar los fiios ni los nietos por lieve
culpa" (IV.v.1).

The Cid, apparently participating in the egalitarian tradition
of inheritance, knows nothing of the principle of sibling differentiation, whether as primogeniture, or as sequential marriage
of offspring. From a transactional viewpoint, he "squanders"
his daughters on the marriage market by marrying them both
in a straightforward matrimonial exchange: i.e., two (daughters) for two (sons-in-law). The case of the Infantes also
suggests that their own people know nothing of primogeniture
or of other age-differentiating principles in the deployment
of siblings on the marriage market. Otherwise they would
have been unable to offer lands of their own as *arras* (although
we may also assume that they might simply be lying about
these properties).

The Cid appears, as we have just noted, ingenuously committed to a symmetrical exchange: two sons for two daughters.
He "spends" his daughters on the marriage market with no regard for their differential value. More accurately: he ignores the
very existence of such a market. But there is more to it than that.
With whom is the exchange accomplished, in the Cid's mind?
Not with the lineage of the Infantes, but with the young men
themselves. The Cid declares: " 'Mios fijos sodes amos    quando
mis fijas vos do' " (2577). Again, the epiclerate recruits surrogate male heirs who will perpetuate their brides' patrilineage,
only secondarily securing the lineal alliance and honorific enhancement represented by hypergamy. The essence of the Cid's
matchmaking coup, in both the first and second marriages, is
that he obtains maximal internal coherence by recruiting two
"sons-in-law marrying in," while acquiring at the same time
maximum status through alliance with high-ranking families.

The Cid is shown as having the advantage in negotiations.
The idea for the Infantes' marriage to the Cid's daughters
comes, we recall, from the Infantes themselves rather than from
their family, as we see in their solicitation of the king's media-
tive offices (1882, 1888, 1901–02). Both sides thus avail themselves of the third-party brokering customary in traditional

matchmaking. But the Infantes, as suitors, endure the psychological disadvantage of the supplicant. The Cid, by accepting the negotiatory offices of his king and lord, enjoys the highground position of the decision maker. By appointing Minaya as the girls' *padrino*, he assumes the similarly powerful role of the person for whom third parties perform:

> "pues que casades mis fijas    assí commo a vós plaz,
> dad manero a qui las dé,    quando vós las tomades;
> non ge las daré yo con mi mano,    nin de[n]d non
> [se alabarán."
> Respondió el rrey:    "Afé aquí Albar Fáñez,
> prendellas con vuestras manos    e daldas a los ifantes,
> assí commo yo las prendo d'aquent,    commo si fosse delant,
> sed padrino d'ellas    a tod el velar."
>
> (2132–38)

The Cid, far from showing himself naïve or inept, accomplishes several things by relinquishing his patriarchal prerogatives. Very shrewdly, he allows Alfonso to assume responsibility for the marriage, as we see when the king, seeking to persuade the Cid to assent to the match, declares: "'Seméiam' el casamiento    ondrado e con grant pro, / ellos vos las piden    e mándovoslo yo'" (2077–78). At the same time, the Cid's relinquishment of the matchmaking role severely compromises Alfonso with regard to his vassal. This is accentuated by the touching scene in which the Cid, after his daughters' rescue, begs their pardon:

> "¡Venides, mis fijas,    Dios vos curie de mal!
> Yo tomé el casamiento,    mas non osé dezir ál.
> Plega al Criador,    que en çielo está,
> que vos vea meior casadas    d'aquí en adelant.
> ¡De mios yernos de Carrión    Dios me faga vengar!"
>
> (2890–94)

Alfonso is thus deeply in the Cid's moral debt regarding the events that follow from this match. The Afrenta de Corpes is an affront to the royal honor, as well as an affair between the Infantes and their father-in-law. "' que me pesa de coraçón,'" Alfonso later admits, " 'ca yo casé sus fijas    con ifantes de Carrión; / fizlo por bien    que fuesse a su pro. / ¡Si quier el casamiento    fecho non fuesse oy!'" (2954, 2956–58).

Lévi-Strauss's explication of reciprocity illuminates the game being played between the Cid and his lord, between Alfonso and the Infantes, and between the latter and their father-in-law. The exchange system does not, Lévi-Strauss insists, simply support or facilitate marriage; "the system of prestations *results in* marriage" (italics in original). He goes further: "Exchanges are peacefully resolved wars, and wars are the result of unsuccessful transactions." The gift that is the centerpiece of exchange is, therefore, never merely a transaction, but rather a pretext for the establishment and maintenance of "the artificial kinship relationship of brothers-in-law" (*Elementary Structures* 67).

Alfonso, to be sure, is not the Cid's blood relative. But given the amicable extrapolation of kinship ideology, the king—as the Infantes' "godfather"—makes himself their surrogate father. Thus, through the marriage of the Cid's daughters to the Infantes, he becomes a metaphorical affine of the Cid. The purpose of Alfonso's intervention, from his viewpoint, is to strengthen the vassalic network by making it more complex, that is, by providing it with greater redundancy. The best vassal, we recall, was one who was also a kinsman. By mediating the Infantes' marriage proposal, Alfonso becomes, in effect, the hero's father-in-law, thereby making himself the apex of an affinal triangle, with the Infantes and the Cid at the other angles.

While Alfonso seeks to shore up the system over which he presides, the Cid attains, by his acquiescence to Alfonso's matrimonial brokering, another kind of security. Where the king's matchmaking consolidates, the Cid's cooperation makes for a reaching out, in the sense of the use he makes of his strengthened alliance with the monarch. In the game of matrimonial negotiations, affirms Bourdieu, prestige is conferred upon the lineage by the eminence of those officially designated as guarantors of the match. Such "explicitly authorized spokesmen" constitute a "striking testimony of the symbolic capital possessed by a family capable of mobilizing such prestigious men" (Bourdieu 59). By submitting to the royal will in this imposed marriage, by permitting the king himself to broker the marriage, the Cid, perhaps in spite of himself, scores a public relations coup. Mediation and intercession, always comprehended, in the dimension of amity, as kinship functions, are viewed as particularly kin-oriented in the context of marriage and marriage negotiations. Alfonso, already enmeshed in the fictive kinship network of vassalage and vulnerable to the Cid's adroit management of the compromising logic of tribute and its implied reciprocities, becomes, in essence, a kinsman of his vassal by playing the role of go-between. Again, while this is the king's intention, the primary beneficiary is the Cid. The enhanced kinship role, redounding through its royal prestige to the honor of the Cid and his lineage, is affirmed by the Cid's gracious appeal on the occasion of the second marriages: " 'afé mis fijas, en vuestras manos son; / sin vuestro mandado nada non feré yo' " (3407–08).

We can be sure that the audience richly appreciated the gambits and stratagems of the Cid. His shrewdness is an aspect of the Cid's heroism that has gone unappreciated by modern scholarship. But even marriage, pervasively important though it is, is part of a bigger picture. The Cid is equally shrewd and righteous in this larger dimension, that of political relations. These also, governed by the principle of amity, are an integral component of the Cid's heroism, as we will see in the next chapter.

# Chapter Four

# Polity

Previous chapters have dealt with various aspects of communal solidarity: kinship, amity, marriage. The present chapter is largely concerned with authority. In light of the multitude of possible definitions of the latter term, we will limit discussion to those meanings that reveal some degree of analogy to the poem's concepts of government and social order. We may therefore adopt a notion of authority as legitimated power, as a recognition of the right to control or influence accorded by the governed, through enactment of law, decree, or by collective resolution. Authority, furthermore, is inevitably linked with a notion of power. The latter term is usefully applied to the *PMC* in Max Weber's sense, that of an ability to achieve one's desires in social context, even against the resistance of others. Power may be enforced through domination, as when law is "upheld by a specific staff of men who will use physical or psychical compulsion." Power may also be implemented through more distributed means, as through political influence, legislative statute, or bureaucratic policy.[1]

Authority may therefore be further defined as "the capacity to exact compliance or to induce behavior." But this definition could equally be applied to straightforwardly aggressive means of exacting obedience. Conformity as a response to mere belligerence cannot serve as an associative or cooperative principle of polity. The latter phenomenon can be defined, for the purposes of this essay, as a system of organizing allegiances above the level of amity, which, we recall, involves interpersonal relationships. If kinship thinking is extrapolated far enough beyond the domain of small-scale, kin-based relationships, it loses its metaphorical value, transmuting into something quite different. The purpose of kinship ideology is solidarity.

Amity, the philosophical essence of kinship thinking, is designed to hold the community together. Authority, we may hazard, is designed to mobilize communal activity. Amity leads; authority manages.

Polity, in the formulation of Talcott Parsons, is "concerned with the selection, ordering and attainment of collective goals, rather than the maintenance of solidarity (including order) as such" (25). Polity, then, is a level of organization that collectively mediates, codifies, surrogates, and stratifies. Imposing a vision of the big picture, it makes indirect that which had been direct. Supplanting amity with charity, it shifts the focus of altruism from the individual level to that of the group. It seeks compromise where the kin-ordered world prefers conflict; it keeps the peace, where the rule of amity demands satisfaction. Polity is about both control and corruption: it seduces as often as it compels, by its promise of security and order. In fact, the less coercive force is required, the more authoritarian the polity.

Anthony Giddens presents a synthesis of views on polity and its relationship to power, according to which the latter term refers both to the efficacy of the social actor's will in attaining its goals (the Weberian concept) and to a "property of the collectivity." Neither concept, argues Giddens, "is appropriate in isolation." Social structure, he contends, can be understood in terms of the "mediations and transformations" it makes possible in the "temporal-spatial constitutions of social systems." The efficacy of mediation—its ability to "bind" the arrangement of social space-time—may be determined by reference to what Giddens calls the "presence-availability" of actors. Where interaction is primarily of a face-to-face kind, mediation is facilitated by physical contiguity. When geography or demography prohibit amicable solutions, the group is organized by more diffuse, indirect means (*Central Problems in Social Theory* 69, 103).

It is the purpose of this chapter to refute, to a certain extent, the long-standing notion, prevalent since Hinojosa, that the *PMC* exhibits a highly authoritarian society, with Alfonso and the Cid each as *caudillo* in his respective sphere. Thomas R. Hart and Roger M. Walker, each from a different perspective, support this view, arguing for a hierarchical reading of authority relations in the poem. The latter critic even goes so far as to contend that after the reconciliation between the Cid and Alfonso, "the Cid's active role . . . is more or less over," while "the King's is just beginning." The *vistas* "confirm the Cid's vindication as a true vassal," while their later meeting functions "to confirm Alfonso's vindication as a true lord." The Cid uses the *vistas*, Walker points out, to dramatize his vassalage to the maximum, and to publicly contrast his "extraordinary humility" with his "material power." The poet stresses above all the importance to the Cid of vassalic integrity. The Cid "may be the King's near equal in riches and power, but neither he nor the poet wishes to suggest that he has become his equal in status, since this would upset the natural hierarchical harmony even more than the Cid's exile had done."[2]

The *PMC*'s concept of society seems almost to actualize Giddens's account of circumstances conducive to face-to-face interaction. The poem's world is the small-scale community of the village or camp, rather than the modern, stratified world often pictured as a pyramid of invidiously differentiated groups, each successively smaller as one reaches the apex of the structure. The poem's society is a macrofamily, with each person having the impression of direct, person-to-person access to the patriarch of the clan. Leadership within this familial domain, to cite Morton Fried's description of political authority within small-scale, kin-ordered societies, "lacks connotations of power, and is transient and situational" (*Evolution of Political Society* 83). The society of the poem is guided by just such a principle of command. The Cid is therefore patriarchal, but patriarchy is less domineering than one might at first suppose. The poem reveals a very diffuse authority structure in keeping with the pre-state, pre-stratified, kin-ordered nature of the society portrayed.[3]

## Feud and Arbitration

The poem tells the story of a feud between two clans. The poet chooses sides and assumes that we will sympathize with the hero in his conflict with the Infantes and their *bando*. But there is a greater society outside the context of the Cid's family and outside the arena of interclanic disputes. It is this greater sphere that oversees the arbitration and judicial resolution at the end of the poem. This realm is that of polity.

Feuds are defined as conflicts between groups within a recognized system of reprisal, arbitration, and compensation. Chronic feuds are symptomatic of a weak state, but their very presence—defined as they are by arbitration of some kind, however minimal—indicates the existence of an organized, supraclanic polity, however tenuous. The nature of feud and intergroup conflict in the *PMC* is a clue to its perception of political and legal reality. Parallels with other epic texts, furthermore, may help to decode the social reality of the Spanish poem. Referring to the role of kin groups in Homeric epic, M. I. Finley points out that "When criminal acts were involved, the family, not the class (or the community as a whole), was charged with preserving the standards of conduct and with punishing any breach." There is, he points out, an "inverse relationship between the extension of the notion of crime as an act of public malfeasance and the authority of the kinship group." Public responsibility for punishing an offender, he reminds us, is an unknown concept in primitive societies, where vengeance is the exclusive prerogative and responsibility of the victim's kin. There was no punitive instrumentality save for those kinsmen. The history of the concept of criminality is "the history of the chipping away of that early state of family omnipotence." Where homicide is "a private affair," there can be no distinguishing between malicious, justifiable, or accidental homicide. This is why the suitors' death at the hands of Odysseus almost brings about a feud (prevented only by the intervention of Athena) between his lineage and the lineages of his opponents.[4]

In the case, then, of both Homeric epic and the *PMC*, notions of publicly mediated justice and of criminality reveal some degree of deterioration in the influence of kinship. On the other hand, the greater community implied by such notions imposes judicial combat as a peacekeeping solution, with the community as mediator, as a rough and ready arbitrator—not as an imposer of law and order. The litigants are, as it were, allowed to "fight it out once and for all," to "get it over with." The ancient notions of "may the best man win" and of an expedient arbitrator who, like a sports referee, functions as a facilitator of the contest, rather than as a dispenser of abstract justice (let alone as an interpreter of textual precedents), express this underlying, essentially dyadic, concept of conflict and arbitration.

Feud has been defined as a conflict arising between two groups within an encompassing larger polity. As the legal anthropologist Leopold Pospisil has noted, a consensus definition of feud would include the two somewhat contradictory concepts of violence and intimacy between related groups. The latter criterion is particularly problematic, since it is usually difficult to define the kind of relationship that constitutes "intimacy," while at the same time taking into account the escalated violence that so often characterizes the feud. To put the matter another way: it is often difficult to distinguish between war and feud. The acts that initiate and perpetuate the latter are, to quote Quincy Wright, designed "to secure revenge, reprisal, or glory for a particular individual or family within the group."[5]

The *PMC* presents just such a scenario of revenge, reprisal, and glory for an individual or family. At the same time, there is intimacy between the Cid's family and the *bando* of the Infantes. For all their mutual hatred, the two groups maintain a sense of belonging to an encompassing, endogamous group. As demonstrated in the previous chapter, they constitute a kind of marriage circle. The controversy that provokes enmity—over their status relative to each other—is the very question that unites them in the intimacy of competition for a common goal.

Where war is conflict between unrelated groups, the intragroup confrontations of feud occur within a context of a designated higher authority whose jurisdiction is recognized by the feuding parties. It has even been suggested that feuds, by necessitating arbitration, tend to promote solidarity and cohesion among the members of the larger group. Pospisil observes that

> wherever feuds do occur, there exists a politically influential authority (a formal chief, an informal headman, a council of important men, or an individual of very limited power, such as a go-between), who is usually too weak or disinterested in controlling his constituents, with the result that prolonged fighting is not prevented. The weaker the political control, the longer the feuds last and the harder it is to conclude them. (Pospisil 6)

Although we may not be accustomed to thinking of Alfonso in the *PMC* as a "weak" or "disinterested" ruler, the limited nature of his power is evident. As mentioned earlier, nowhere in the *PMC* is there any hint of an interiorized law of the land that all feel constrained to obey. Alfonso must personally guarantee the safety of the Cid's champions (3476–79) and spirit them away by night after their victory (3698–99) for fear of an attack by the Beni-Gómez faction. The very fact that Alfonso must employ matrimonial strategies to shore up his vassalic network suggests that he is nothing like the absolute monarch of later centuries. The concessions he so readily grants, as, for example, to the choice of site for the *vistas* and *cortes,* are further indications of the negotiated and conditional nature of royal authority in this poem.

## Law and Order

The tendency to characterize law in the poem as "Germanic" has been very convincingly critiqued by Alfonso García Gallo. He asks, assuming the retention of Visigothic law, where and by whom was this law maintained, from the fifth to the eleventh, twelfth, and thirteenth centuries? How was this law of a minority ever imposed on the Hispano-Roman population? Toponymy and archeology, he points out, offer scant proof of any significant impact of Visigothic culture. Because of the depopulation of the Meseta during the Arab occupation, the first centuries of the Reconquest afford little sense of a "continuidad de lo gótico." If such a spirit reflected pride of race, it would presumably appear as spontaneous popular expression, indicating density of population. This is not the case. Castilian epic, for instance, never attributes Gothic origin to its heroes. The Basques and Cantabrians who repopulated the Meseta were never imbued with the "espíritu germánico." The Germanic thesis is based, therefore, on an unfounded notion of Visigothic concentration in Castile. The thesis insists, moreover, on an image of a legal system's being retained, while all other institutions—language, religion, culture—are abandoned. In the face of such discrepancies, he suggests, occasional and variable textual coincidences with this or that Germanic country do not make for a coherent, durable "Germanism" in medieval Hispanic law codes. García Gallo admits the importance of such elements as blood revenge, collective guilt, "co-swearing" of oaths, and judicial combat. But parallels may equally well be established, on the basis of such factors, with the law systems of Ancient Rome, the Iberian peoples, and the Muslims, as well as with many primitive peoples (García Gallo 608–10, 619–21, 627, 629–37).

The "Roman" theory of the poem's legal sensibility, as we saw in the previous chapter, may be assessed in similarly skeptical terms. The fact is that there is no single ethnic or national law to which all legal aspects of the *PMC* may be attributed. On the one hand, as García Gallo points out, many of these aspects are exhibited by a wide range of societies. On the other, the obvious multiculturalism of the poem's social background precludes any assignment of a single ethnic origin to its social practices, legal or otherwise. This cultural multiplicity must constantly be borne in mind in the case of an epic whose Christian hero sports a Semitic nickname and whose personages derive from at least three distinct ethnicities and a dozen regional cultures.

In an appraisal of Colin Smith's legalist theory of the *PMC*'s authorship, Ruth Webber points out that the great Spanish legal codes had not yet been compiled in the first decade of the thirteenth century (the consensus date of composition for the *PMC* as we know it). Customary law, she states, "determined by usage and habit and preserved by oral transmission," was still entirely local at the time of the poem's composition. Stressing the "great capacity and efficiency of memory in an oral culture," she notes that legal knowledge was required in many social contexts, and that this knowledge, even when extensive, could have been learned orally. The legal profession, therefore, did not yet exist: "the whole community participated in judicial procedures, which were public, and decisions were oral." The poem's *sabidores* and *coñosçedores* (3005, 3070, 3137) were not lawyers in the modern sense, but simply "men who knew the law and whose responsibility it was to distinguish right from wrong." Webber suggests that legality in the *PMC* corresponds to what "an alert minstrel would have routinely acquired during the course of his wanderings." An educated poet, moreover, would have had great difficulty "studying customary law in all of its manifestations should he have so desired." Legal knowledge in the *PMC*, she concludes, derives not from anachronistic reference to written legal codes but from "matters of custom and precedent"—in other words, from the poet's oral background (Webber, "The *Cantar*" 85).

The notion of what constitutes a "lawyer" is crucial. Here, as in other aspects of social reality, specific vocabulary matters. Where there is no word for an action or function, the action or function may well not exist. Neither the word *abogado* nor the occupation of lawyer appear in the poem. Corominas (1: 2) notes that Berceo (a half century after the *PMC*) is the earliest witness in Castilian. If there is a discernible legal advocacy in the poem—in the sense of *abogar* as "defender en juicio"—it is exercised not by the *coñosçedores* cited by Colin Smith and others as "lawyers," but rather by the champions who defend the honor of the Cid and his daughters in judicial combat.

Webber's analysis of legality in the *PMC* is confirmed by Joseph J. Duggan, who disputes the position of all who defend, with variations, the "lawyerly" theory of the poem's authorship. Duggan also conceives of the poem's legality in "pre-legal" terms, pointing out the importance of oral transmission in customary law: "Intimate knowledge of the law, the customs, and the procedures of a specific region would by no means imply that the person possessing such knowledge was *culto* in the sense of being learned, or even literate." Roman law had barely begun to replace the dominant customary law of the Peninsula, so that "References to law [may be seen as those of] any intelligent and well-informed person of the period."[6]

Milija Pavlović and Roger Walker represent the most complete expression of the lawyerly approach to *PMC* authorship ("Money, Marriage and the Law" 199; "Roman Forensic Procedure" 99–101). Their legal study of the *PMC* is greatly expanded in two articles on the *rieptos* and the duels in the poem, which they contend are quite separate institutions. They counter the opinion of such scholars as Colin Smith (ed., 138, n to v. 3533) who, they argue, implies "that the poet feels obliged to follow the traditional epic pattern of vengeance through bloody combat, but that his heart is not really in it." They seek to demonstrate that the *rieptos* were "the culmination of the *cort* scene," rather than "an appendage to it, paving the way for the duels" ("Reappraisal of Closing Scenes I" 2–3). In a recent review, Pavlović criticizes Duggan's approach to legality in the poem with particular attention to the *rieptos*. It is incorrect,

Pavlović asserts, to invoke the concept of *judicium Dei* with regard to the *PMC*'s challenges and duels. The latter practices were quite distinct, with the challenge a prominent feature of noble society which did not invariably lead to a duel ("Oralist Vision and Neo-Traditionalist Revision" 873–74). I do not question the documentary erudition of these two authors, nor its general relevance to reading any medieval text, epic or otherwise. Their extensive citation of the *Partidas*, as if the poet were adhering to that law code, seems anachronistic. The *Partidas* are, as I have assumed throughout the present study, an indispensable source of information, ethnographic and sociological as well as legal. But they are useful because they, like the *PMC*, participate in the reciprocal mentality of revenge and vendetta. Revenge, as both material restitution and as eye-for-an-eye compensation, is clearly uppermost in the Cid's mind. In that sense, we may say that he, like the authors of the *Partidas* and of the Roman law that influenced them and other Peninsular codes, is legalistically primitive. Paradoxically, the *PMC*'s primitivism—the factor that would dispose its author and audience to adopt like-minded legal principles—is the very feature that renders such adoption redundant. This, in addition to the eccentricity of enforcement and discrepancies of vocabulary already mentioned, undermines the case for the *PMC*'s legality as a direct enforcement of any particular written code. Confrontation and redress as shown in the poem occur in many preliterate societies. Law, suggests Richard A. Posner, very probably "grows out of revenge and . . . many modern legal doctrines continue to reveal their traces of their origins in revenge." Feuds as the collective expression of revenge, as Posner observes (with particular reference to the *Iliad*), "can be far more destructive than the original aggression." Applying Posner's terminology, we note that the *PMC* poet is aware that "revenge is inimical to large-scale cooperation," but still retains a notion of revenge as "a primitive method of deterring wrongdoing and hence of maintaining a modicum of public order" (Posner 25, 29–30).

Above and beyond the question of specific custom and law, there is the problem of social cohesion as a principle. How does the poet conceive of rules and of the society to which rules are to be applied? The answer may first be sought in the passage describing the need for stringent sanctions against unauthorized departures from the group (1249–54). These sanctions include hanging and confiscation of booty. That there is little sense of delegated authority is seen from the very harshness of the threatened penalties. If the Cid's followers had any sense of consistent rules of conduct, such drastic measures would only be the extreme penalty in a code of escalating deterrents, rather than the code in its entirety. At the conclusion of the poem, when the Cid leaves for Valencia before the judicial combat, he mentions the urgent need to return to his newly captured kingdom. The insecurity of the Cid's power is revealed in his need to personally supervise operations in Valencia:

> "E yo fincaré en Valençia,  que mucho costádom' ha,
> grand locura serié  si la desenparás;
> yo fincaré en Valençia  ca la tengo por heredad.
>
> (1470–72)

This may well reflect a political reality. The Cid cannot command in the hierarchical sense we associate with a bureaucratized, stratified modern army. He may induce cooperation, but he cannot command obedience. That is why the way to discourage desertion is to emphasize the ritual vassalic relationship, to accentuate the promise, the oath, the word given, touching each vassal in his personal honor: "que ningún omne de los sos ques' le non spidiés,  o nol' besás la ma[no], / sil' pudiessen prender  o fuesse alcançado, / tomássenle el aver  e pusiéssenle en un palo" (1252–55).

Cooperation and consultation—not coercion and command— are the Cid's chief methods of leadership. Several speeches to his assembled followers eliciting suggestions for action confirm this: " 'grandes son los poderes  por con ellos lidiar, / dezidme, cavalleros,  cómmo vos plaze de far' " (669–70). The Cid feels his presence in Valencia is required because he cannot delegate leadership. Participation in a judicial combat can be entrusted to his champions because they can act as his surrogates. Leadership over a newly captured kingdom cannot be assigned to subordinates. At the same time, collective action must be channeled through the cooperative leadership of the Cid. These factors show that he operates without bureaucracy or administration. Where these are lacking, there is also no principle of hierarchized authority or chain of command. Authority in the world of the Cid leaves a great deal more leeway for improvisation and outright insubordination than in the modern state, where civil obedience depends on a thoroughly interiorized law of the land governing the behavior of most citizens and in which disobedience of that law constitutes criminality. In the epic environment, where feuds are endemic, the monarch cannot delegate authority, cannot issue peremptory commands, cannot induce or prevent action without, on the one hand, persuasion, and on the other, force or the threat of force. At the same time, when force is invoked there is no centralized sanctioning apparatus (i.e., no police). The king or ruler, therefore, must be sparing in the threat or use of coercion.

The Cid does appear to delegate authority to two of his lieutenants, Alvar Salvadórez and Galind Garcíaz de Aragón, upon his departure for the first *vistas* (1999–2001b): "a aquestos dos   mandó el Campeador / que curien a Valençia l   d'alma e de coraçón." He tells the rest of his men that these two act for him: "e todos los [*otros*]   que en poder d'éssos fossen." But this expedient has the same air of improvisation as the other kinds of "stand-in" replacements exhibited in the poem (most significantly, the judicial combats carried out by the Cid's champions). This is a substitution recognized as temporary, makeshift, short-term. Scenes involving emissaries and agents, involving a specific mission to be accomplished, likewise reflect the poem's very limited concept of delegation. A case in point is the scene depicting Minaya's return with the wife and daughters of his lord (1562–67): "Dozi[*en*]tos cavalleros   mandó exir privado / que rreçiban a Mianaya   e a las dueñas fijas d'algo." The poet immediately reminds us that the Cid cannot allow himself to leave his newly conquered kingdom: "él sedié en Valençia   curiando e guardando / ca bien sabe que Albar Fáñez   trahe tódo rrecabdo." Minaya is completely trustworthy, but again, job descriptions are ad hoc; there is little sense of plenipotentiary discretion when the Cid's vassals perform tasks for their lord. Supervision in the poem takes place in the somewhat abstract dimension of the range of obligations demanded by obedience to orders, implied or explicit. In other words, it requires subordination. But that subordination is personal and voluntary, rather than dispassionate and habitual. Scenes of command and prohibition abound. They are often marked by forms of the verbs *mandar* and *vedar*. It is the very frequency of their use and the specificity of their intent that remind us of the poem's vague sense of authority: "mandó ver sus yentes   Mio Çid el Campeador" (417); "Mandó partir   tod aqueste aver" (510); "Mesnadas de Mio Çid   exir quierén a la batalla, / el que en buen ora nasco   firme ge lo vedava" (662–63); "Todos los moros e las moras   de fuera los manda echar" (679). The Cid constantly commits the organizational faux pas of micromanagement (as in 689–91, 702–03):

> "e vós, Pero Vermúez,   la mi seña tomad,
> commo sodes muy bueno,   tener la edes sin art,
> mas non aguijedes con ella   si yo non vos lo mandar."

> "Quedas sed, me[s]nadas,   aquí en este logar,
> non derranche ninguno   fata que yo lo mande."

Pospisil has defined law as the concurrence of four criteria: (1) manifestation in a decision made by a political authority; (2) definition of the relationship between the two parties of the dispute (*obligatio*); (3) regularity of application (i.e., "the intention of universal application"); (4) the provision of a sanction. He further notes that law as so defined is found in all observed societies, although not always to the same degree of consistency nor on a global basis within a society. Subgroups within a society in which feuds are endemic, for example, may have law—"coexisting with feuds without incorporating them into the jural mechanism." A feud, as we have seen, implies both an intergroup fight and, frequently, defiance of a more general political authority by the feuding parties (who operate, nonetheless, "within a more inclusive, politically organized unit"). Law, on the other hand, refers to "intragroup settlement of disputes." When feuds are stopped by a higher authority, it is through application of laws expressive of the four above criteria (Pospisil 8). Indeed, the discontinuance of the perceived right to engage in feuds is one of the main features of the struggle between centralized, legalistic authority and primitive, traditional, kin-ordered segments of society. The triumph of the centralized legal system, moreover, is synergetically coterminous with the rise of the state. Even with the triumph of the state there are, as Reinhard Bendix observes, pockets of resistance to the statist enterprise who remain indifferent to, or even ignorant of, the momentous innovations of law codes and coercive enforcement systems (Bendix 307, 313–14). We recall in connection with such peripheral elements the remark of Brundage, who noted that innovations in marriage law went unnoticed for centuries by communities on the fringes of medieval European society.

Law in the *PMC* is primitive in that it does not enforce statutes; rather, it guarantees the right of feuding parties to prove their opponent wrong. This aspect of primitive law has been characterized in terms of a "systematization of retaliatory sanctions" designed to avert unchecked escalation of reprisals, leading to public disorder (Redfield 8). Justice in such circumstances is not an abstract quality dispensed by an impersonal agency: it is the case itself, upheld by the litigants (as most dramatically exemplified by judicial combat).

The Cid wants redress of the grievance occasioned by the "desondra" done him by the Infantes (2905–06). The hero's terminology, significantly, refers not to actions experienced as absolute wrongdoing, but rather as personal injuries; the focus is on the emotional response of the wronged party. Thus the Cid refers to his grievance in terms of "rrencura" (3203) or "rrencura mayor" (3254).

## Charisma

Despite the absence of strictly codified laws, and in spite of the poem's preoccupation with feud and a consequent notion of polity as a convenient method of settling personal grudges, the work does portray large-scale cooperative activities. The conquest of Valencia does not happen without some type of political endeavor. What is the poem's understanding of such collective accomplishments?

In the *PMC*, social inequality is not a condition to be endured but a resource to be managed. It is the leader who manages this resource. Work must be done; the collective perception of this and of the necessity for a division of labor is one stimulus for embarking on the construction of polity. This managerial aspect of patriarchal leadership is idealized according to the precepts of amity. The *PMC* is a portrait not of real social practice as exhibited by history, but of social ideals as conceived by the poet, and as frequently expressed in folklore and myth. The leader in this amicable scenario cannot be the lawgiver, he must be the guarantor of all that his men hold dear.

Max Weber's model of charisma, which sees leadership as a performative function rather than as an innate attribute of the master, provides a good descriptive apparatus. The charismatic function is, essentially, that of provider, in every sense. As Weber expresses it, charisma is the capacity for affording the good life as one's followers imagine it. The leader who does not play this nurturing role is deposed or otherwise removed. The belief in the leader's charismatic legitimacy springs from the needs and enthusiasms of the collectivity. Authority conceived in these terms cannot be based on any abstract notion of government. It must derive directly from the leadership ability of the leader, from authority directly and personally exercised by him. When the influence of a charismatic leader is consecrated by the community he leads and is confirmed by generalized and consistent compliance with his will, one may speak, asserts Weber, of the "routinization" of charismatic power. The habit of collective obedience to the leader may lead to an "institutionalization" of his power. Again, charisma is defined and confirmed by action: as long as the leader continues to satisfy his followers, they obey him; as long as they obey him, he is charismatic. The community led or founded by the leader can only become stable and enduring by means of a "traditionalization" of charismatic power. This occurs when the administrative personnel—an inner circle of adherents—have been confirmed as the legitimate successors of the leader, which is to say, when they have been approved by the collectivity. In any event, only a limited group of followers can continue to live from the "sporadic economic acquisition" (gifts, booty, contributions) of the group's early days. The majority of group members must see the group's daily activities as a reliable way of earning an everyday living. This pragmatic aspect of the charismatic succession is most risky, in terms of the group's survival: the original inner circle of intimates seeks to appropriate public functions and to monopolize the economic benefits that derive from them. At the same time, they institute criteria of recruitment for new members of the circle and of the community. The latter activities amount to a set of "proto-bureaucratic" practices that, in the leader's lifetime, establish a barrier of intermediaries between himself and his subjects. From this evolved state of affairs emerges what Weber calls the *Geschlecter-staat* ("familist state").[7]

The *PMC* perceives leadership from such a perspective. Charisma assures advancement, as conceived by those whose adherence and support define charisma in the first place: "Los que exieron de tierra   de rritad son abondados, / a todos les dio en Valençia casas,   e heredades l de que son pagados" (1245–47). This concept of charisma harmonizes readily with the patriarchal and amicable functions of agnatic ideology as explicated in the first chapter, and with the mild authority of the epic world, with its tolerance of improvisation and timely insubordination (recall Pero Vermúez's insubordinate defiance of the Cid's orders [707–10, 2355–57] and Bishop Jerome's similar disobedience [2375–80]). Where feuds are endemic, we have shown, the monarch cannot readily delegate authority or issue commands. Because his means are limited and his subjects unruly, he must husband his coercive resources. To induce compliance with either specific directives or behavioral models, the leader must rely on charismatic persuasion, his own heroic example, or the pressure of public opinion. His control or manipulation of that opinion represents an important aspect of leadership.

The leader manages the resource of inequality, as is suggested by the scenes in which the Cid is shown "acordando" his vassals (1712). The egalitarian nature of the Valencian society is revealed by the fact that no one shares the Cid's power, which is entirely the result of his personal charisma. Amity implies all for one, one for all. The Cid is the one; his vassals are the all. Solidarity, expressed in a "caretaker" concept of group membership and of partisan honor, envisions each vassal as both unique person and steward of group prestige. The implicit notion of esprit de corps as a stewardship of clanic prestige explains why Pero Vermúez rescues Fernando after the latter's cowardice in battle with the Moors, doing the other's work for him, then tacitly supporting him in his boasting (2338, and, presumably, in the lacuna of fifty or so verses preceding it; summarized by Pero in 3316–25).

Charisma as the principle of leadership explains one of the *PMC*'s central themes: the largesse of the epic hero. Discussed earlier in the present essay in connection with the beneficent aspect of paternal amity, the motif of the gift has been identified as an important aspect of the narrative's portrayal of "the gradual but certain vindication and ascension of Rodrigo," a pattern suggestive, argues Porter Conerly, of the *speculum principis* ("Largesse" 282). Duggan's analysis of reciprocal economic mentalities ("interested gift-giving") and of related predatory modes (extortion, banditry) illuminates the *PMC*'s portrayal of materialist voluntarism and regional pluralism as the chief factors in recruiting and retaining followers. The redistribution of plunder is integral to the poem's notion of leadership (804–06: "dio a partir estos dineros . . . / ¡Dios, qué bien pagó a todos sus vassallos!"). The Cid's liberality with regard to Alfonso, as we have seen, obliges the king to acquiesce, even as the hero's generosity toward his followers converts Rodrigo's riches "into an instrument of loyalty." Gift-giving is, then, the principal component in the Cid's political tool kit.[8]

Benefaction in the *PMC* may also be understood in terms of social patterns in the eleventh and twelfth centuries. There were other historical figures of that age who founded what might be termed "segmentary" kingdoms on the basis of charismatic leadership and interested gift-giving. The Normans, often acting in ways reminiscent of such segmentary peoples as the Nuer, submitted newly won territories to a systematic colonization, in order to secure their own political and economic situation. Eleanor Searle has portrayed the adventurism of the eleventh- and twelfth-century Normans as a protoimperialism operating as clanic power based on the "fulcrum" of political *bricolage*. The predatory economic conduct of the expansionist lineage was based on the collaboration of "nephews, cousins, brothers-in-law, [and] sons-in-law." This "segmental, family fighting force" strengthened itself by the same means employed by the Cid: "it built power only upon kinsmen, biological or artificial as might be," at the same time that it garnered wealth through predation and strategic marriages, which permitted it to reinforce its political and economic position. Thus was founded "a centralized political community, based not so much upon a principle of loyalty to a leader as upon one of cooperation . . . among all members of the community" (Searle 238–49).

The political and thematic perspectives on the *PMC*'s gift-giving, as exemplified by Duggan and Conerly, and as illuminated by suggestive parallels between the Spanish epic and the Norman society described by Searle, are valid approaches to the poem's understanding of generosity. But there is an additional and more central function of munificence. The giving and distribution of gifts are not merely virtues; they reveal a crucial function of heroic charisma and constitute the determining attribute of the leader of men who are drawn by the scent of material gain. "Mandó partir tod' aqueste aver," recounts the poet, in a typical scene (510). The leader owes his men a better life as they conceive it; his men owe him loyalty and gratitude. The poem consciously expresses the symbiotic reciprocity inherent to seigneurial charisma:

> A cavalleros e a peones fechos los ha rricos,
> en todos los sos non fallariedes un mesquino;
> qui a buen señor sirve siempre bive en deliçio.
>
> (848–50)

The poem conceives of charisma in terms of an implied pact between *caudillo* and followers. As long as the leader "delivers the goods," his men remain satisfied and loyal. Their commitment to the cause is perceived as an investment on which the redistributed booty is viewed as a return. The leader's reciprocal response to his follower's loyal service and hearty participation in campaigns is democratic. All are beneficiaries—"todos los sos," the poet insists—whether horsemen or footmen. The incentive that drives the Cid's recruiting campaign is material, its appeal universal:

> Sonando va[n] sus nuevas todas a todas partes,
> más le vienen a Mio Çid, sabet, que nos' le van.
>
> (1206–07)

The leader may aggrandize himself ("Creçiendo va en rriqueza Mio Çid el de Bivar" [1200]). His men do not resent this, since they can expect similar, if smaller, rewards that flow from the success of the group. The group's success, in turn, depends completely on the consistent loyalty and service of its members. The poem makes clear that the Cid is deferred to and obeyed because his men cheerfully recognize that he deserves deference and obedience. These are men who, of their own free will, acknowledge his superiority. They do so because, being men of good sense and canny recognition of their own best interests, they know a good thing when they see one: "vassallos tan buenos   por coraçón lo an, / mandado de so señor   todo lo han a far" (430–31).

Not only do the Cid's men show the exemplary teamwork discussed earlier—they outdo their chief in the studied nonchalance of their own discretionary liberality: "sos cavalleros   llegan con la ganançia, / déxanla a Mio Çid,   todo esto non preçia[n] nada" (474–75). Minaya, speaking for all the Cid's men, exemplifies this principle of reciprocal generosity, in which reciprocity, a spirit of potlatch, and the vassalic pact are all portrayed as elements of a single principle of symbiotic allegiance. The twenty-fourth *tirada* (493–505) presents a detailed portrait of this complex:

> "Mucho vos lo gradesco,   Campeador contado;
> d' aquesta quinta   que me avedes mand[ad]o
> pagar se ía d' ella   Alfonso el castellano.
> Yo vos la suelt*o*   e avello quitado;
> a Dios lo prometo,   a Aquel que está en alto,
> fata que yo me pague   sobre mio buen cavallo
> lidiando con moros   en el campo,
> que enpleye la lança   e al espada meta mano
> e por el cobdo ayuso   la sangre destellando
> ante Ruy Díaz   el lidiador contado,
> non prendré de vós   quanto vale un dinero malo.
> Pues que por mí ganaredes   quesquier que sea d'algo,
> todo lo otro   afélo en vuestra mano."

One possesses to give away, and one gives away so as to demonstrate that one is a giving person. In this sense, what the Cid's charisma guarantees is only secondarily materialistic. What it assures primarily is the opportunity of conspicuous prodigality for all those who join up. The Cid is truly first among equals: his charisma derives from the possibility he affords his men of imitating him in this fundamental dimension of manliness.

## Banditry and Redistributive Economy

There is more to lordly generosity in the poem than straightforward gift-giving. Donative practice may be seen as of two principal types: dyadic (between two persons or two groups) and redistributive. It is this latter type that is the more important in the career of the Cid. The concept of amity as kinship morality, we recall, implicitly separates the world into two opposed spheres of moral alignment and readily accommodates the notion of predation as a legitimate economic alternative. There is kinship and the familial domain, and there is non-kinship. The social universe is "polarized into a field in which the rule of amity prevails, and into its contrary, ultimately perceived as the outside world" (Fortes 232). The poem defines the Cid and his people as the in-group, governed by the moral principles— which are pragmatic, "team-spirit" imperatives—of amity. It readily classifies all outsiders as propitious victims. This ethnocentrism justifies the pillage, brigandage, banditry, and economic extortion engaged in by the Cid in order to obtain "pan e vino" for himself and his followers. The underlying pathology of the notion of the outsider as fair game facilitates a noteworthy psychological projection of compliance or cooperation onto the victims of pillage, as we see in the depiction of the Moors' response to the Cid's greatness: "los moros e las moras   bendiziéndol' están" (541).

In his treatment of the various towns and cities he besieges— some of them Christian, thereby forestalling any notion of a straightforwardly racial depredation—the hero is, in effect, a practitioner of what Angus MacKay has aptly termed "the protection racket" of the *parias* system (*Spain in the Middle Ages* 15–35). At the same time, like Robin Hood and other social bandits, the Cid regards moneylenders (Rachel and Vidas) as fair game, and abusers of political influence (*malos mestureros*) as his primary adversaries.[9] The Cid is a successful bandit in that he manages to attract and retain a large number of volunteers who will collaborate in such profitable projects as the sacking of towns or the defeating and stripping of enemy armies. Economy in the poem is a natural function of charismatic leadership: the lord who guarantees many and successful raids, as well as the conquest of an entire city with all that this represents in the way of economic rewards for his followers, is the charismatic savior of those followers. The Cid resembles Robin Hood and other social bandits because he "takes from the rich to give to the poor." Many who follow him into exile leave everything behind: "unos dexan casas e otros onores" (289). The redistributive aspect of the economic attitudes depicted is the chief mechanism of the voluntarist recruitment of the Cid's forces: his men join him above all by reason of "el sabor de la ganançia." They are not disappointed: "'Todos sodes pagados e ninguno por pagar'" (536). The Cid's motives, no less materialistic than those of his men, render his predicament all the more intelligible to an audience meant by the poet to identify with him in his declaration that losses in money and property—described in terms of "averes ... sobejanos" (2912)—were as offensive to him as the dishonor done to his daughters.

The equitable distribution of spoils fulfills the primary requirement of charismatic leadership in Weber's sense (which is plainly that of the poet): the assurance of a better life for one's followers. The betterment in question is viewed in exclusively materialistic terms, as we see from repeated references to winnings, property, and booty: "Estas ganançias allí eran iuntadas" (506); "Lo que dixo el Çid a todos los otros plaz. / Del castiello que prisieron todos rricos se parten" (539–40); "rrefechos son todos essos christianos con aquesta ganançia" (800); "el oro e la plata ¿quién vos lo podrié contar? / Todos eran rricos, quantos que allí ha" (1214–15).

Redistribution is defined by Polanyi, in a seminal article, as "appropriational movements toward a center and out of it again." Presupposing the existence of "an allocative center in the community," redistribution results from "institutional preconditions" that favor the establishment of such centers. Such preconditions, usually occurring in the absence of market economies, tend to involve reciprocity as well as redistribution as principles of social integration and organization, and to employ designated leaders as the personalized foci of reallocation.[10]

Fried provides modification of this basic redistributive model. Leadership in a redistributive context amounts primarily, he asserts, to an appropriate administration of the community's pooled resources. The locus of redistribution is "on the level of the village or even larger organizational unit." The correlation with Weber's model of charisma, although not mentioned by Fried, emerges from a consideration of his analysis of redistributive leadership: "the regularity of the role of village redistributor conveys prestige and bolsters political status." The position of "paramount redistributor" is a personal achievement "measured in cumulative instances of unbalanced reciprocity." Such ostentatious distribution of goods and gifts, designed to attain or to affirm the status of chief redistributor, is the cause of the frequently noted personal poverty of chiefs in such societies: "such persons were rich for what they dispensed and not for what they hoarded" (Fried, *Evolution of Political Society* 117–18).

The poem portrays the redistribution of booty as a sacred function of leadership. The satisfaction of the Cid's men is a clear endorsement of the redistributive principle and of the Cid himself as the ideal "paramount redistributor:" "Tan rricos son los sos que non saben qué se han" (1086). At the same time, in this world of brigandage, pillage, and border warfare, the tribute granted to the leader, in the form of a fifth of all captured wealth, is portrayed as an auspicious expression of collective appreciation. The Cid does not take this tribute—it is freely rendered to him by his men. The *quinta,* therefore, is, in its own way, as pronounced an example of interested gift-giving as the tribute sent by Rodrigo to win over his estranged lord. The *quinta* is, if I may be allowed the pun, the *quintessence* of pooled resources. Since the lord will presumably continue his giving ways, it is in no sense a hoarding by him to accept such tribute. The gifts received afford him a fund for maintaining his well-earned role as pinnacle of the (minimal) hierarchy, and as focus of the redistributive system. To grant him tribute is to insure the continuation of a system agreeable to all:

> Grant á el gozo Mio Çid con todos sos vassallos,
> dio a partir estos dineros e estos averes largos;
> en la su quinta al Çid caen *çiento* cavallos.
> ¡Dios, qué bien pagó a todos sus vassallos,
> a los peones e a los encavalgados!
> Bien lo aguisa el que en buen ora nasco,
> quantos él trae todos son pagados.

> (803–09)

Minaya, again the spokesman for all the Cid's vassals, expresses an all-for-one enthusiasm for the predatory enterprise and the loot that it affords, while frankly admitting the violence required by such operations:

> "De Castiella la gentil   exidos somos acá,
> si con moros non lidiáremos,   no nos darán del pan.
> Bien somos nós *seis*çientos,   algunos ay de más,
> en el no[*m*]bre del Criador,   que non passe por ál;
> vayámoslos ferir   en aquel día de cras."
>
> (672–76)

To which the Cid—ever the sagely appreciative recipient of counsel—replies in cognizance of his vassal's wisdom (677–78): "'A mi guisa fablastes; / ondrástesvos, Minaya,   ca aver vos lo iedes de far.'" Later, the violently predatory nature of the Cid's attitude is still more clearly expressed in his unflinching account of his occupation of the kingdom of Valencia, in which he readily acknowledges the right of his victims to resist his attack:

> "En sus tierras somos   e fémosles todo mal,
> bevemos so vino   e comemos el so pan;
> si nos çercar vienen,   con derecho lo fazen."
>
> (1103–05)

The brutal frankness of the Cid and his men as to the fitness of banditry as an economic alternative is expressed in the Cid's speech to the captured count of Barcelona. Here the Cid justifies the program of redistribution and the brigandage that supports it. He speaks in terms clearly analogous to those of the redistributive logic explicated by modern ethnographers and economists. Dire circumstance imposes the need for robbery and extortion, while amity within the group obliges the leader to become the provident shepherd of his flock. The leader, argues the Cid, has little choice:

> "mas quanto avedes perdido   e yo gané en canpo,
> sabet, non vos daré   a vós un dinero malo,
> ca huebos me lo he   e pora estos mios vassallos
> que comigo   andan lazrados.
> Prendiendo de vós e de otros   ir nos hemos pagando;
> abremos esta vida   mientra ploguiere al Padre sancto,
> commo que ira á de rrey   e de tierra es echado."
>
> (1041–48)

Charisma, to be effective, must never obstruct the impulse to vassalic initiative. The vassal must feel empowered, enfranchised, above all with regard to gift-giving as the vehicle of conspicuous personal honor. Thus *presentaia* means far more than "present," in the scene in which the Cid informs Jimena of the significance of the riches being brought to them by his vassals: " 'Riqueza es que nos acreçe   maravillosa e grand, / a poco que viniestes,   presend vos quieren dar, / por casar con vuestras fijas,   adúzenvos axuvar' " (1648–50). In this way, marriage articulates with both the gift-giving economy and economic predation. Even as his vassals render tribute to his family, the hero, on the occasion of his daughters' betrothal, distributes palfreys, mules, and garments: "conpeçó Mio Çid a dar   a quien quiere prender so don; / cada uno lo que pide   nadi nol' dize de no" (2115, 2117). The poet, as we have seen, highlights this distributive generosity and the impression made on its recipients: "Todos son pagados de las vistas,   quantos que í son" (2119). We recall that all things given away by the hero are funded by the allocative pool supported by the very population destined to become the principal beneficiary of Rodrigo's epic largesse. The Cid's assurance of more generosity to come on the occasion of the wedding is calculated to make a still greater impression: " 'qui quiere ir a las bodas   o rreçebir mi don, / d'aquend vaya comigo,   cuedo quel' avrá pro' " (2129–30). The fifteen days of the wedding afford the opportunity for further distribution of horses, mules, palfreys, rich garments, and cash gifts: "Qui aver quiere prender   bien era abastado" (2260). The departure of satisfied guests hints at the social impact of the Cid and his lucky confederates: "por pagados se parten   de Mio Çid e de sus vassallos" (2265).

## Social Mobility

The economy depicted in the *PMC* is a direct consequence of the limited economic circumstances "back home" and of the frontier conditions conducive to escape from those very conditions. The men who flock to the Cid's cause are motivated by "el sabor de la ganançia." They are, first of all, men with horses: "Veriedes cavalleros   venir de todas partes, / irse querie[n] a Valençia   a Mio Çid el de Bivar" (1415–16). The practical terms of the wealth to be won are simple. The poem clearly reveals, in the various battle scenes in which the hero's warriors capture riderless horses, the ready availability of the obvious primary prerequisite of the historically significant status of *caballero villano*. It is this status that was sought by the typical *vecino* poor enough and desperate enough to respond to promulgations such as those of the Cid, inviting all comers to participate in predatory campaigns. The recruiting announcements, designed to appeal to a wide spectrum of collaborators, are not limited to those prosperous enough to own a horse. Frequent mention of *peones*—who, along with the "encavalgados," are classed as "vassallos" of the Cid (806–07) and whose military contribution entitles them to a share of the booty (cf. 848: "A cavalleros e a peones   fechos los ha rricos")—confirms plurality of regional and social origins in the Cid's army. His men are immigrants in search of a better life. The motivation for joining up is expressed in exclusively economic terms: "Acógensele omnes   de todas partes me[n]guados" (134). Both the pluralism of the recruits, in terms of their multiregional origins, and their poverty, as suggested by their apparent socioeconomic standing and the straightforwardly economic nature of the incentives that motivate them, are expressed in repeated references to a recruiting campaign that, in conformity to the pattern of the charismatic leader, focuses on the promise of a better life:

> Por Aragón e por Navarra   pregón mandó echar,
> a tierras de Castiella   enbió sus mensaies:
> quien quiere perder cueta   e venir a rritad,
> viniesse a Mio Çid   que á sabor de cavalgar,
> çercar quiere a Valençia   por a christianos la dar:
> "Quien quiere ir comigo   çercar a Valençia,
> todos vengan de grado,   ninguno non ha premia."
> (1187–93)

The *PMC* dramatizes the Cid's attempted foundation of an independent kingdom in the captured Muslim city of Valencia. On this project converge the diverse forces mobilized by the hero. The incentives are plain: the chance to escape want ("perder cueta") and to garner riches ("venir a rritad"), the opportunity to elude oppression and to be one's own boss, by means of an open contract with a minimally authoritarian charismatic leader. Recruits are to join up of their own free will ("de grado"), and under no compulsion ("ninguno non ha premia"). The poet does not shrink from implied invidious comparisons with the kingdom left behind—the Cid's gain is clearly Alfonso's loss, since the latter's population represents, to a great extent, the pool from which the Cid gathers his forces. Thus the description of Minaya's arrival from Castile with fresh recruits, the king having given his permission to all his subjects who wish to join the Cid: " 'de todo mio rreino   los que lo quisieren far, / buenos e valientes   por a Mio Çid huyar, / suéltoles los cuerpos   e quítoles las heredades' " (891–93).

The social mobility sought and obtained in this poem does not, however, reveal the dysfunctional changes of residence, community, and status group membership that characterize social climbing in capitalist society. There is mobility in the poem, as this section demonstrates, but it is an entirely circumstantial improvement ideally designed to afford the ambitious man an opportunity of founding a lineage of his own. The Cid does not reveal that most conspicuous trait of the modern social climber, of which we may take Lazarillo de Tormes as a prominent literary example, namely, what Pitirim Sorokin called the dissociative syndrome. The socially mobile person, according to this concept, tends to exhibit, in his movement through the social spectrum, dysfunctional relationships with the persons he associates himself with along the way. His affiliations and friendships are necessarily transient. The Cid remains ever loyal to his followers as to his king.[11]

We may not, therefore, characterize the Cid as a "self-made man," a practitioner of "social climbing" in the modern sense. The poem's notion of social mobility is intimately connected with the Cid's redistributive generosity toward both "cavalleros" and "peones" (848). This division implies not "knights and commoners" but rather "horsemen and foot soldiers," a division recognizing economic advantage and handicap but not classes as self-aware interest groups in the Marxian sense. The often-quoted line 1213 seems to depict an opportunism we might readily correlate with social climbing: "Los que fueron de pie   cavalleros se fazen." But this is an example of that promotion from the ranks that is a well-known feature of frontier society in the era of the Reconquista. The chance of obtaining this type of pragmatic advancement is the whole point of joining up, from the perspective of the typical recruit.

The Cid's exultation at the magnitude of his achievement also conveys a sentiment of "getting somewhere" socially: " '¡Grado a Dios que del mundo es señor! / Antes fu minguado, agora rrico só, / que he aver e tierra e oro e onor / e son mios yernos ifantes de Carrión' " (2493–96). Then there are the famous verses on the second marriages of the Cid's daughters:

> Los primeros fueron grandes, mas aquéstos son miiores,
> a mayor ondra las casa que lo que primero fue.
> ¡Ved quál ondra creçe al que en buen ora naçió
> quando señoras son sus fijas de Navarra e de Aragón!
>
> (3720–23)

The Cid seems to be a parvenu on an epic scale. All the ingredients of the rags-to-riches story are here: property, land, riches, honor, and excellent marriages for both of the daughters. But we must be careful to define the poem's own notions of social mobility. While he does not use the term *social climber* to describe the hero of the poem, Menéndez Pidal seems implicitly to subscribe to a concept of the Cid as an *arriviste* when he accentuates "el espíritu democrático" of medieval Castile and the rise of "la clase de los caballeros" (*En torno* 211–12). In describing the Cid's social trajectory, it is important to distinguish the rise of an entire category of persons from the ascent of a single person. The *PMC* dramatizes not the triumph of all *infanzones* but rather that of a single, special *infanzón*.

Class structure implies individual social mobility. If one acquires the appropriate life-style and material attributes, one may aspire to move into the class of which they are the indicators (although fully recognized membership in the new class may accrue not to the social climber but to his or her descendants). Categories (i.e., levels) remain constant; it is their membership that changes. In a "birth-ascribed" system of ranking, by contrast, "one behaves and exhibits attributes in accord with his rank" (Berreman, "Race, Caste" 398–99). Class systems and what Gerald Berreman calls birth-ascribed ranking systems (such as the Indian caste system) may be contrasted in the following terms: in class systems, individual mobility is "legitimate," although usually difficult. In birth-ascribed systems, social mobility is "explicitly forbidden." Class systems, he argues, "prescribe the means to social mobility; systems of ascribed rank proscribe them." In birth-ascribed ranking systems, "the strata are named, publicly recognized, clearly bounded." In a class system, "individuals regard themselves as potentially able to change status legitimately within the system through fortune, misfortune, or individual and family efforts" ("Race, Caste" 398–99).

The reality of supposedly rigid "birth-ascribed" systems such as the Indian caste system is far more permissive of individual mobility than is usually assumed in the West. "Myths of stability," argues Berreman, are fostered by apologists of such systems, who, seeking to perpetuate them by justifying their inequalities, propagate the notion of people happy in their place. In reality, he argues, people are seldom "happy in their place," and even the most officially rigid stratification systems are characterized by chronic "mobility striving" ("Caste. The Concept" 338). Nor, it has been demonstrated, is mobility simply a matter, in the Indian caste system, of "vertical mobility only through movement by the whole corporate unit," rather than through "individual or familial movement" (the supposedly typical Western pattern). In reality, such individual mobility is frequent (Marriot and Inden 983, 986–87).

Nonetheless, some stratification systems are more rigid than others. As we have seen in our discussion of marriage, dowry and hypergamy appear to characterize systems that have not yet rigidified. In the absence of a verifiable consensus concerning the relative status of individuals and groups, there emerges a competition for status recognition. This sort of situation is suggested by the Cid's use of military achievements and high-reaching matrimonial schemes to upgrade his personal standing and the status of his lineage. This is not social mobility conceived in the recognizably modern terms of reclassification of personal or familial status. A commonplace of medieval Spanish and European social history, as Marc Bloch long ago pointed out, social mobility of the modern type is evidenced by the resistance of the European nobility of the twelfth and thirteenth centuries to admission into its ranks of the descendants of non-nobles. Bloch describes both the growing (and irresistible) numbers of those seeking noble status, and customary and legislative methods of regulating admission to knightly status, noting that "the evolution of legal opinion during the feudal period tended much less to impose a strict ban on new admissions than to subject them to rigorous control" (Marc Bloch 2: 322). For the Peninsular context, the findings of such social historians as Sánchez Albornoz, José María Lacarra, Carlé, and, more recently, Royer de Cardinal, and Powers, confirm that, from the early twelfth century on, social mobility (in the modern sense of individual social reclassification) became a prominent feature of Spanish society.[12]

The *PMC*, despite the historical patterns just described, does not endorse the historically frequent social mobility confirmed by the studies cited. We note in the career of the Cid a circumstantial mobility in terms of enhanced material prosperity, augmented political influence, and increased personal prestige. But there is as well a complete absence of real social mobility in terms of consciously pursued social reclassification. Precisely this self-conscious pursuit of social reclassification—in the form of attainment or even purchase of legally recognized titles such as *hidalgo* and *caballero*—characterized real-life medieval social climbers. The *Poema de Mio Cid,* however, is immune to, even unaware of, this historical trend.

Referring to the special conditions of early medieval Spanish frontier society, Guglielmi speaks of an almost exclusive tendency toward "movilidad vertical ascencional." This trend does not preclude the poetic Cid's modest refusal to change his status. Thus the hero attains "una posición eminente, un encumbramiento que lo aleja de su primitivo status, aunque no lo modifique." Even as he amplifies his status in this way, the Cid remains "el primitivo hidalgo," retaining his position within "el grado más humilde de la jerarquía nobiliaria." Thus, prestige and wealth are augmented, without thereby guaranteeing "el cambio de status" (Guglielmi, "Cambio y movilidad social" 53n44). The poem's notion of personal advancement, firmly anchored in economic incentives and expedient battlefield promotions, implies a limited framework of expectations. Advancement within the Cid's forces is also contingent on the availability of the means of accomplishing the duties of the *caballero*. Thus the "los que fueron de pie" who are converted to "cavalleros" in 1213 are not "commoners transformed into knights," but merely the beneficiaries of an entirely pragmatic and fortuitous occupational mobility, dictated by the fortunes of war and the exigencies of military circumstance on the Peninsular frontiers. They are foot soldiers promoted to soldiers on horseback. Their promotion is rendered all the more expeditious by the numerous stray horses present after every battle: "tantos buenos cavallos [veriedes] sin sos dueños andar" (730); "non pudieron ellos saber la cuenta de todos los cavallos / que andan arrad[í]os e non ha qui tomallos" (1777–78); "[veriedes] cavallos sin dueños salir a todas partes" (2406).

The perpetual warfare of the frontier, points out María Eugenia Lacarra, readily allowed for this limited, expedient social mobility. At the same time, she observes, this circumstantial improvement does not extend to reclassification of one's "estamento jurídico." In her view, the primary characteristic of the poem's social mobility

> . . . es que . . . la adquisición de bienes por medio del esfuerzo propio es la base de la movilidad social, sin que se altere la condición jurídica de los estamentos. En la [sociedad] de Alfonso, por el contrario, hay una resistencia a la movilidad expresada por una minoría de nobles poderosos que se oponen al cambio por méritos personales.[13]

Social mobility in the fullest sense only occurs when there is a change of recognized class membership (in the sense both of recognized social standing and of group membership). This change, as both Guglielmi and Lacarra accurately observe, does not appear in the *PMC*. The Cid shows spectacular improvement in power, wealth, and personal prestige (cf., " 'si venciéremos la batalla, creçremos en rrictad' " [688]; " '¡Maravilla es del Çid que su ondra creçe tanto!' " [1861]). But at the end of the poem, as Menéndez Pidal points out, the Cid remains an *infanzón* and aspires to nothing more. Indeed, at every opportunity he reconfirms his role as vassal and his status as *infanzón*. This modesty is emphasized in the scene in which the Cid pointedly declines Alfonso's invitation to sit in the royal chair (3115, 3118). This sense of propriety, even as it sets a good example of vassalic humility for the hero's own men, is compatible with a social order in which prestige accrues to the individual through the good marriage of his offspring, but also—and more importantly—to the kinship group of whose honor he is the steward. The often-cited line 3724 ("Oy los rreyes d'España sos parientes son") depicts a long-term, intergenerational mobility (vicarious from the viewpoint of the instigator) suggestive of the patterns of clan-oriented ambition outlined in the first chapter.[14] At the same time, the kings referred to are themselves members of a lineage exalted by the exploits of an illustrious ancestor. Menéndez Pidal points out that the Cid does not seek a marital alliance with a family of the higher nobility, nor does he himself aspire to membership in "la nobleza de linaje." The poet makes it clear, affirms Menéndez Pidal, that "No le puede honrar el emparentar con reyes; los que se honran son los reyes (v. 3725)" (*En torno* 212–13).

Weber has pointed out "the rigorous reactions against the claims of property *per se*" on the part of "privileged status groups" for whom "economic labor" is a "status disqualifier." It is far more often the descendants of the parvenu, schooled in the requisite life-styles and attitudes, who are accepted into social elites. The descendants of the founder of a lineage, in other words, are steeped in the "conventions of their status group and . . . have never besmirched its honor by their own economic labor" ("Class, Status, and Party" 192). Edward Shils also points out that wealth by itself elicits only "a qualified deference." The wealthy must acquire "an appropriate style of life and associations" in order to be accepted by "those whom they equal or exceed in wealth and who already have a high deference position." In agreement with Weber, he notes the well-known disdain for the *nouveau riche* and observes that "it often takes a generation for wealth to acquire the appropriate education, religion, occupation and style of life . . . necessary for assimilation into a higher deference-stratum" ("Deference" 423).

The modern social climber, avidly seeking admission to a new status group, and therefore alert to the nuances of convention and decorum, would avoid reference to the hard work needed to reach the platform of material wealth required to gain admittance to the desired in-group. Accentuating the effort of the climb, in fact, characterizes the outsider. The Cid, ignorant or disdainful of such considerations, proudly emphasizes both the depth of his hardship and the struggle it has taken to gain what he has: "'yo fincaré en Valençia, que mucho costádom' ha'" (1470); "'Echado fu de tierra, é tollida la onor, / con grand afán gané lo que he yo'" (1934–35).

Despite its references to categories of persons (e.g., *condes, infanzones*) the poem shows little sense of class solidarity as a principle of social action. For example, the scene (vv. 3495–504) in which the Cid embraces Count Anrrich and Count Remond, inviting them and his other supporters at court to take as much as they like of his riches, suggests a man-to-man, rather than a class-structured, comprehension of society. This dyadic bias, along with the demonstrated tendency toward feuds, expresses an ignorance or a disavowal of class ideology. In a class-stratified environment, economic categories cut across kinship lines (hence the phenomenon of the poor relation shunned by his rich relatives). In the kin-ordered environment, dyadic relationships cut across economic strata (hence the phenomenon of the penniless retainer who will fight to the death in service to his lord). This explains the discrepancies of power, wealth, and social prestige among the members of a single clan defined by a common name and a common ancestor, and the agnatic solidarity that such disparities paradoxically implied. In the Basque country and in Castile, suggests Heers, the confrontation and alliances of *bandos* correspond to those between and among the clans of other regions. The closest approximation to class structure were the federations of lineages, organized into the pseudo-clanic groupings, the *bandos,* which were the principal units of conflict and alliance in the factional strife so typical of medieval times.[15]

When the characters in the poem show a sense of communalization they are most conscious of such clanic affiliations. Such allegiances, allowing for inequality within the group, are compatible with the thoroughly apolitical or pre-political individualism of the poet and, presumably, his audience. As Heers demonstrates, modern class theory occasions an anachronistic interpretation if applied too readily to clanic society. While the societal model of the three orders (clergy, nobility, third estate) offers perhaps a more reliable criterion for social analysis, since this system was known to people of the time and exerted some influence on social life and institutions, "it is," observes Heers, "far from certain that this classification was felt by the men of the age, or indeed that it regulated all social relationships" (Heers 6). He argues that the real social groups, the authentic "frameworks . . . of individuals' social lives," were based on social bonds deriving from the "ever present heritage of primitive societies which had a tribal, more or less communalistic character." Groupings based on this and other factors (Roman traditions such as the concept of the *gens;* professional and religious brotherhoods) "counterbalanced the weakness of the state." The impotence of royal authority, the inefficacy of urban administration, "caused the formation of natural or artificial social groups and increased the strength of those already in being." It was in fact for that very reason that conflict over many centuries centered on the confrontation between such groups and monarchical prerogatives: "to institute a solid royal administration was to attack these groups' power." At the same time, both civic and ecclesiastical authorities, each for separate but often intersecting motives, "strove to reduce the power of family clans, to forbid private conflicts and to assert peace and order" (Heers 7). The poem's depiction of group interactions seems to conform to Heers's model of clan-based group sensibility and to confirm María Eugenia Lacarra's contention that the poem expresses not antipathy toward nobles as a class, but only hostility toward a certain group: the Beni-Gómez family and its descendants (María Eugenia Lacarra 134–201).

In its glorification of amity, of dyadic relations, and of achieved status, and in its concentration on issues of clan and lineage, the *PMC* expresses a pointed denial of class reality. One cannot, at the same time, denounce that which is completely alien. Shils speaks of the "disposition to defer and the performance of acts of deference" as depending on the perception of "deference-entitling properties or entitlements." It is possible, we may infer, to determine the degree of class structuration by the extent to which "judgements of deference" are aroused by "deference-entitlements" based on such group-defined factors as occupation, wealth, life-style, educational level, political and corporate influence, "proximity to persons or roles exercising political or corporate power." Additional elements in "judgements of deference" include kinship connections and ethnicity, and—perhaps most significantly—"the possession of 'objective acknowledgements' of deference such as titles or ranks" ("Deference" 422).

Deference as thus defined lies beyond the face-to-face dimension of small-scale societies. It is determined by the perception and "simultaneous assessment" of one's own and of others' deference-entitlements, with reference to the "cognitive map" of one's society. Such a map, whose existence may be taken as an indication, if not a definition, of polity, "locates the primary or corporate groups of which (human beings) are active members and the larger society which includes these groups, but with which they have little contact." The society so plotted is not merely "an ecological fact or an environment," but rather "a significant cosmos from which members derive some of their significance to themselves and to others" (Shils, "Deference" 422–23).

The social universe depicted within the *PMC* reveals awareness of a greater society outside the context of the Cid's family. It is this greater domain that determines the arbitration and judicial resolution at the end of the poem's central feud. Feuds, as we have seen, are defined as conflicts between groups, but within a recognized system of reprisal, arbitration, and compensation. At the same time, there can be no doubt that Jimena and her daughters show deference to the Cid not because he is a great war leader but because he is husband and father. In kin-ordered societies, deferential behavior is performed on the basis of kin-defined inequalities. We may assume, therefore, that all fathers and husbands within the society of the *PMC* are granted the same treatment by their wives and children. It is the kin-defined deference that determines the grammar of deference in the extrafamilial sphere, especially in situations that are clearly those of fictive kinship, as in the case of vassalic relationships. It is useful to recall Eric Wolf's account of "the escalation of kinship from a set of interpersonal relations to the political order." In the *PMC*, "kinship becomes a governing ideological element in the allocation of political power." The ideology of kinship, in other words, is the basis for political convictions in societies that organize the political sphere not around centralized administrative and judiciary bureaucracies but around kinship and pseudo-kinship networks (Wolf, *Europe* 93).

## Pluralism, Polity, and the Emerging State

Kinship predominates as the political ideology of the *PMC*. The opposite situation, in which the political realm determines the idiom of the familial, would indicate that the escalation of interpersonal relations suggested by Wolf had proceeded some considerable distance along its trajectory—in short, that power within the political order had ceased to be allocated according to kinship and its surrogate forms. The essential element of this political realm is an acceptance, however reluctant, of societal pluralism. This factor accounts for much of the tension at the heart of the *PMC*. The poem extols old-fashioned, patriarchal, familial unity in the face of a political dimension, overseen by Alfonso, that represents the need to manage an inescapable diversity of interests. The king's power, such as it is, is based on arbitration and influence more than on personal charisma as we have defined that phenomenon. This is what makes the poet see the king as weak—it is the weak leader who does not commit himself. The poet refuses to see that political as opposed to patriarchal leadership requires a concept of administrative neutrality. At the same time, prestige and influence within the pluralistic domain are largely based on what German historians call *Königsnähe*—proximity, whether physical or genealogical, to the royal person. Hence the power of *mestureros* to undo even the bravest and most loyal vassal; hence the social leverage of characters like the Infantes, who, though personally worthless, receive consideration merely because " 'an part an la cort' " (1938).[16]

Here we have the notion of city and country, of court and hinterland. The Cid of the poem is clearly from "up-country." He is the gruff, old-fashioned man's man, intolerant of the fancy ways of courtiers, still conceiving of authority and organization in terms of dyadic, "direct-access" relationships between leader and men. The Cid's foundation of a new kingdom in Valencia is an expression of the poet's utopic fantasy. The new kingdom represents an idealized tradition. The paradoxical contradiction inherent to this narrative development is that the Cid of the poem thinks of his project as segmentary—as the foundation of a new household in the old-fashioned mold. Few of the Cid's men are either kin or vassals, in any traditional sense. Yet, they are the only materials available: he must make use of them. Seeking to fashion a traditional, uncluttered familial unity, the Cid instead founds a pluralistic political regime. In trying to re-create the old, he forges the new. Seeking to create a new segment of the old clanic reality, he brings into being the very type of polity he thinks to escape.

Pluralism is seen in the composition of the Cid's forces: "por los de la frontera   piensan de enviar, / non lo detienen,   vienen de todas partes" (647–48). This is, perhaps, how the poet conceives of recruitment in all contexts, as we see from his description of the armies of the Moorish leaders Fáriz and Galve:

> Por todas essas tierras   los pregones dan,
> gentes se aiuntaron   sobeianas de grandes
> con aquestos dos rreyes   que dizen Fáriz e Galve.
>
> (652–54)

Polity, however, is not simply a matter of pluralistic composition or demographic dimensions. The Cid's forces can be quite numerous, while showing little inclination to organize themselves politically. But polity implies a more inclusive set-theory of group relations than kinship. Polity thinks in terms of inclusive associations, where amity thinks in terms of exclusive groups. Viewed from the perspective of a small-scale or traditional society that is in the process of fabricating a polity on the foundation of the kin-ordered world, the old ways of amity, emphasizing person-to-person rights and responsibilities, appear to be sacrificed at every turn. The more they are sacrificed, the more political the community becomes. Once polity exists, however, sectors of the community may still retain their attachment to kin-ordered tradition. These sectors, rejecting the viewpoint of the society at large, and the notions of political action and class confrontation, persistently construe social issues as dyadic problems. This refusal to envision societal questions and social change in terms of impersonal forces and group interactions may well be termed reactionary. The *PMC* exhibits just such a lingering commitment to the concept of rugged individualism, to the notions of honor and virtue as strictly personal or familial issues. All of this corresponds to the vision of social order as fundamentally the settlement of man-to-man altercations. For the *PMC* poet, the new-fangled order of polity signifies organization, fractious controversy and chronic disputes, rules, litigation, mediated arbitration, stratification, multiplicity of social categories, delegated authority. The Cid's world, by contrast, embodies deferential relations, harmonious unanimity, purposeful cooperation, dyadic intimacy, egalitarian participation. Both worlds show inequality, but that of Alfonso's court is ascribed and arbitrary; that of the Cid's kingdom, achieved and meritorious.

Polity emerges from the spontaneous collective effort to fabricate a system encompassing groups, not all of them based on kinship. This is suggested, among other things, by the presence of a communal assembly, and of an emerging differentiation between the public and private dimensions. M. I. Finley points out, for example, that the assembly convened by Telemachus at the end of Book 2 of the *Odyssey* reveals just such a distinction between public and private business. The suitors and their behavior are the affair of Odysseus and his *oikos;* the prolonged absence of Odysseus as king is the problem of every *oikos* collectively. The assembly, observes Finley, implies "the imposition upon kinship of some territorial superstructure." It requires from the associated kin groups "a partial surrender of autonomy." In such a context a distinction is made between the private dimension, "within the sole authority of the *oikos* or kinship groups," and the public, "in which the decision [is] for the heads of all the separate groups to make, consulting together" (Finley 83).

The many scenes in the *PMC* involving *vistas* (1899, 1911, 1948, and many more) or the more uncommon and exceptional institution of the *cortes* (2733, 2914, 3147, 3255, etc.) suggest the council and assembly scenes of Homeric narrative, as explicated by Finley. But where Finley adopts an analytical, detached perspective, the *PMC,* in the thick of the action, as it were, views *vistas* and *cortes* as if they existed for the sole convenience of the hero. The *PMC* resists surrender of the kin-related prerogatives mentioned by Finley. The poet, that is to say, picks sides, as if assuming that the audience was of the Cid's *bando.*

Finley emphasizes the informality of the political arrangement depicted in the *Odyssey.* The assembly did not vote or decide: its functions were "to mobilize the arguments pro and con," and to "show the king or field commander how sentiment lay." The assembly did not meet at regular times, but only when called. Its opinions were expressed by "less orderly forms" of acclamation (e.g., shouting down an unpopular opinion). The assembly's opinions were not binding on the monarch. But the king who chooses to ignore public opinion, custom, tradition, or *mores,* as expressed in the assembly, runs various risks, as the case of Agamemnon shows. The prepolitical nature of the situation is underscored by the fact that Achilles and Agamemnon spoke directly to each other, "like two men wrangling in the privacy of their homes." Kings are not obeyed unthinkingly. This is not the world of bureaucratic compliance, of internalized law and order observed by a citizenry schooled to proper behavior (Finley 88–89).

Here again is a useful model to be extended to the *PMC*'s portrayal of meetings and assemblies. Informality is indeed used by the king or commander in such a situation. Alfonso, we see, takes heed of public opinion at the assemblies he calls, while the wrangling as if in private mentioned by Finley is a very adequate description of the confrontations dramatized at the end of the poem (e.g., the exchange between the Cid and García Ordóñez [3270–90]).

In state-centralized society, the individual is largely defined by group membership and group psychology. He is of this or that class, this or that status group, this or that vocational or bureaucratic category, and he tends to identify himself primarily as a member of one or more non-kinship groupings, such as a class or professional group, and secondarily as the member of a family. Identity is verified in this state-stratified context by the typical questions, "What is your name?" followed by the more crucial "What do you do?" The latter interrogative is designed to reveal all manner of ancillary information, placing the answerer within a network of (often intersecting) social categories. Traditional society tends to ask: "Who are your parents? Who are your people?" The contradiction is that while the state exalts the individual and his rights, so that the functions of society and of the state are expressed in terms of their support or suppression of the individual, the singular ego is depersonalized by its isolation from all support systems save those imposed or approved by the state.

In what we may take as a definition of the partially formed polity, with strong continued influence of kinship, Finley notes that "the superimposition of a community, the territorial unit under a king, upon the household-kinship system merely weakened the dominant position of the latter, but only in part and only in certain respects." This is as good a description of the kin-ordered society in epic context as I have come across. Finley points out that the same verb, *anassein,* "to be lord," "to rule," is used "with almost complete indifference" for the primary activity of both a king (*basileus*) and the head of household (*oikos*). To rule, moreover, is often qualified by the adverb *iphi,* "by might." This does not mean by means of tyrannical power. It means rather, "possessed of the appropriate amount of strength required to rule." It means, argues Finley, "that a weak king was not a king, that a king either had the might to rule or did not rule at all" (Finley 90–91).

The *PMC* insists on just this notion of the personal character of governance. The household, as defined in an earlier chapter, is the model of society. There is little sense of a ruler's having better things to do than to facilitate the settlement of personal quarrels. Hence the wishful thinking by poet and audience when Alfonso is made to cut off García Ordóñez in his tirade against the Cid: " 'Dexad essa rrazón, / que en todas guisas miior me sirve que vós' " (1348–49). The king is shown choosing sides, discovering the error of his ways, seeing the light as to who his real friends are.

Finley suggests that in a modern war novel such as *The Red Badge of Courage,* the confusion of battle is itself part of the story; in Homer it is "merely an unavoidable condition of heroic poetry." The story for Homer is in the individual hero's tale, not in the confrontation of groups (80). Finley comments that when Homer's protagonists act together, as in battle,

> the confusion is indescribable. No one commands or gives orders. Men enter the battle and leave at their own pleasure; they select their individual opponents; they group and regroup for purely personal reasons. (80)

This aspect of the epic as a literary genre reflects at once the dyadism and the political disorder of the pre-state society. Thus we are not surprised, in the *Chanson de Roland,* to hear Charlemagne's irate response (in the midst of furious hand-to-hand combat) to the Saracen emir's arrogant offer ("Deven mes home . . . Ven mei servir . . .") of Spain as fief if Charlemagne will surrender. " 'Mult grant viltét me sembl[et],' " cries the Christian emperor, "Pais ne amor ne dei a paien rendre." He counters Baligant's demand by telling him to convert to Christianity; to this the Saracen replies, " 'Malvais sermun cumences!' " (Whitehead 3595–600). The Cid's challenge to Búcar is expressed in similarly man-to-man terms: " '¡Acá torna, Búcar! . . . ver te as con el Çid . . . saludar nos hemos amos e taiaremos amistad.' " To which the Moor replies: " '¡Cofonda Dios tal amistad!' " (2409–12).

While the modern reader may deduce within the text the presence of groups in confrontation, analyzing the portrayed situation according to sociological criteria, the poet's chief concern remains the man-to-man relationship. This, contends Finley, may be explained in terms of a pervasive "kinship thinking," which insured that "even the relatively new, non-kinship institutions of the community were shaped as much as possible in the image of the household and the family." The hallmark of this transitional state of affairs was "the metaphor of the king as father" (90).

Political issues arise in all societies. A poet's disregard for or rejection of such problems situates him politically. Elman R. Service points out that a society's "gravest problems . . . are political, and all societies must be able to solve them in order to perpetuate themselves." Some societies "have found political-cultural solutions that not only have preserved the community but also have enabled it to grow to ever-greater size and complexity." He speaks of "the watershed in the evolution of human culture" that lies between primitive and civilized society. Primitive societies are "segmented into kin groups [that are] egalitarian in their relations to each other." From this egalitarian coexistence of kin groups there eventually emerges a new state of affairs, in which some of these groups become "hierarchical, controlled and directed by a central authoritative power—a power instituted as a government" (Service 3–4).

The *PMC* seems to present the crisis of a society at the very moment when stratification is being introduced into an "egalitarian coexistence of kin groups." The poet hates the Infantes and portrays them with the cruel disdain that he does because they represent the introduction of unjustified inequality and the perpetuation of ascribed disparities of status among groups that should be viewed as naturally equal. In this sense, the poet's class consciousness is shrewdly expressed. However, in failing to understand that "authorized power instituted by government" comes from the very interventions one invites for private purposes, the poem shows itself naïve.

"Social structures," writes Reinhard Bendix, "may be distinguished by the magnitude and psychological implications of the solidarities they achieve." Solidarity in traditional societies is achieved through "relatively small groups that tend to be isolated from one another." The participants in such small groups enjoy "an intensity of emotional attachment and rejection which modern men find hard to appreciate and which they would probably find personally intolerable." Modern societies, by contrast, rely for the creation of solidarity not on small groups but rather on two factors "which hardly exist in the traditional society," namely, the nuclear family and "the national, patriotic community" (Bendix 302).

The *PMC* is on the verge, perhaps, of emphasizing the nuclear family, while retaining a powerful commitment to cousinship. But there is no sense of a larger national community. The consequent absence of anything remotely approaching patriotism is matched by an apparent indifference to religious fervor as a principle of collective action. References to "christiandat" (770, 1116, 1199) or to "moros e christianos" (107, 566, 731) express ethnic identity rather than confessional adherence. It should be remembered as well that one of the Cid's best friends (Abengalbón) is a Moor, while the hero's worst enemies (the Infantes and their clan) are Christians.

The antecedents of contemporary debates on tradition and modernity may be found, affirms Bendix, among social philosophers of the seventeenth through nineteenth centuries. Conservatives among these writers, he argues, tended to entertain a romantic nostalgia for a past society "characterized by a rank-order of privilege and subordination based on land and the rights associated with landownership." This conservatism emphasizes the supposed stability and harmony of a traditional society "associated . . . not only with the benevolence of paternalistic rule but also with the warmth of personal relations and the sense of personal belonging made possible by a closely knit, hierarchic community" (Bendix 279).

On this point the *PMC* reveals its own ideology of nostalgically exalted paternalism. Its utopically re-created intimacy of amicable relationships represents perhaps the earliest expression, in Spanish vernacular literature, of the topical contrast between country and city. The poem's expression of this topos conveys the contrast between *urbanitas* and *rusticitas* from the biased viewpoint of an inhabitant of the latter dimension who feels threatened by the encroachments of the former. More learned expressions, emanating from the culture of urbanity, represent their affinity with the country in terms of bucolic nostalgia; they yearn for something lost. The *PMC* does not long for primal reality; it seeks to protect a reality perceived to be endangered.

Caro Baroja discusses the ancient contrast, commonplace since Plato, of primitive innocence living on alongside evolving civilization, while the latter mode "affected artifice and corruption." The peasant, in later formulations of this classical model of social evolution, tended to be placed "midway between an hypothetical state of primitive anarchy . . . and the state of corruption associated always with the life of ports and towns." This, argues Baroja, is the origin of the age-old view of the rural community as the bastion of virtue and social harmony, and of the city as the den of injustice, immorality, and disorder. The tradition's voices would include Antonio de Guevara—to cite but one Spanish example—and such theoretical sociologists as Tönnies (*Gemeinschaft* vs. *Gesellschaft*) and Durkheim (mechanical vs. organic solidarity).[17]

If we subscribe to a "before-and-after" model of societal transformation, argues Bendix, we run the risk of "mistaking ideal types for accurate descriptions," thus falling into the trap of assuming that "clusters of attributes [are] actually and not just hypothetically correlated." He cites as an example an attribute of Western modernization over the past several centuries: "the decline of kinship ties and the concomitant rise of individualism." Although this is a verifiable historical trend, we have learned, he notes, "how many meanings and exceptions were . . . compatible with this overall tendency." We may not, therefore, maintain that modernization cannot occur unless kinship ties also decline. To do so would be to disregard "the exaggerations and simplifications which went into the formulation of the ideal type in the first place." To do so actually impedes comprehension of the role of kinship in modernizing Europe. Linking kinship deterioration with modernization may also prevent our understanding of "the possible ways in which kinship ties and collectivism might be . . . compatible with the modernization of other areas" (Bendix 296–97).

Bendix remarks that the plausible notion that the state emerges as an agenda that encroaches on kinship, gradually replacing it, largely derives from Weber's life-long project to demonstrate how traditional kinship is replaced by the state and by capitalism, with the aid of such ideological instruments as Christian doctrine (we recall Goody's thesis) and revived Roman law. On the other hand, Bendix argues, kinship is not only frequently compatible with the modernizing trends supposedly inimical to it, but is itself undeniably used to further so-called modernizing trends (Bendix 297, 308). Similarly, Giddens speaks of the tendency toward characterizing the advanced societies by simplistic comparisons of "traditional" vs. "modern" societies. Such a contrast, he argues, is necessarily expressed by means of "abstract typologies" ("ideal-typical" in Bendix's terms, borrowed from Weber) such as that of feudalism vs. capitalism, or the distinction between *Gemeinschaft/Gesellschaft* proposed by Tönnies. Not, Giddens clarifies, that such typologies are completely inadmissible— they can be useful and legitimate for certain purposes—but that they are too often conducive of certain suppositions or correlatives ("latent rather than explicit"), namely, that societies are characterized by their level of technological or economic development, and that the more economically advanced societies offer to other societies "an image of their future" (*Central Problems* 229).

Allowing that the model of phases and transitions may impede understanding of the place of the literary text in history, how may we approach the text of a work like the *PMC*? The story is undeniably about resistance to something that threatens the poet and his audience. The menace is change, innovation, perceived as nefarious. At the same time, the protagonist and his loved ones are doomed, in their defense of cherished tradition, to bring about the very transformation they fear. They are in the process of becoming that which they hate.

Some aspects of modernization theory are of unavoidable utility in the interpretation of the *PMC*'s angst concerning these

matters. We must, however, be careful to select those consonant with the poet's apprehension concerning impending or
actual social change. Of particular importance is the emergence
of the state. We see in the *PMC* a snapshot, as it were, taken
from the viewpoint of the poet, of a moment in social time. The
contents of the picture's frame suggest the emergence of the
state. How does the poem see the state? There are two levels of
social perception to be addressed. The first, that of the poet's
conscious understanding. The second, that of our own perception of a deducible background reality.

Some minimal aspects of the state, notes Morton Fried, are
"organized police powers, defined spatial boundaries . . . a formal judiciary." Noting the complex "relationship of the state
to the existence of socioeconomic classes," he reminds us of
"the philological interdependence of state, estate, and status"
(due to their common origin in the Lat. *status*). Evolutionist
approaches to the state focus on the "conditions and processes
whereby states are precipitated." Functionalist (i.e., division-
of-labor) approaches "tend to eliminate 'state' as a term, equat-
ing 'state' with 'political organization.'" Other, so-called
operationalist theories, concentrating on "the study of clearly
separable parts of the political process and their interactions,"
view the state as "a variable congeries of complex institutions"
(Fried, "State" 143–44).

The poet sees the state as, on the one hand, an array of forces
and interests predisposed to meddle in local, private affairs. It
is a project into which the poet and his audience feel they might
be lured, cajoled. The temptation is to be feared precisely because—the other side of the anti-state perspective—the state is
something that can prove useful in dealing with one's enemies
and in aiding one's friends. We can speculate, bearing this outlook in mind, about the king behind the poetic image of the
weak monarch misled by the conniving courtiers whom the poet
blames for all the hero's troubles. The ruler behind the image, as
well as the persons and groups consciously aligning themselves
with the court, supports the statist project. Contemporary documents convey the elements of the collective undertaking, whose
most natural collaborators are well known to history: self-made
men of humble origin; courtiers and climbers of every stripe;
the merchant class. The historical Alfonso VI, a well-known practitioner of monarchical statecraft, would have had more things

on his mind than the settlement of petty quarrels between squabbling barons, even as he accepted the need and the utility of mediating such quarrels in terms of dividing to conquer. The Cid of our poem, meanwhile, is one of the divided parties too focused on the dispute to realize that this very preoccupation will insure the demise of the tradition he seeks to defend.

Although state defies conclusive definition, one must include some concept of territoriality, argues Fried. Contrasting the state with a "kinship society" occupying and being identified with a certain territory, Fried observes that a state will reveal "loci from which regular sanctions emanate," and

> a formally organized, territorially demarcated, elaborately coordinated society, composed of members whose only bonds are those of participation in the same social system or even in overlapping but largely discrete segments of a complex system. (Fried, "State" 145)

Sovereignty, or the "identification and monopoly of paramount control in a society," is likewise a significant aspect of state identity. Indeed, Fried considers "paramountcy of control" one of the diagnostic features of the state. One of the characteristics of sovereignty as an issue is conflict between levels of a bureaucracy or administrative corps. When we find a higher level of authority unable to "apply its force to every issue and trouble spot," being instead obliged to "husband" that force, the state may be considered weak, may even be destroyed due to "the gap between the claims of sovereignty and the availability of force." We also note, he points out, that the same terms apply to situations in which the state has only partially succeeded in imposing itself, or to circumstances in which the state has never appeared at all.[18]

Another historically frequent aspect of states is the use of law to promote universalist criteria. Such "goals of universality," affirms Fried, involve the incorporation of elements common to all traditions in a multisecular territory. These universalist trends are exemplified by the Roman *jus gentium*. This concept, like many other state-sponsored ideological programs, tends to express "fictions of commonality," and to foster "selectively distilled myths" of national identity ("State" 149).

"The state," summarizes Frederick Watkins, "is a geographically delimited segment of human society united by a common obedience to a single sovereign." The concept of sovereignty thus involves the notion of a society "united under a determinate rule of law ... backed by effective sanctions." The state may thus be further defined as "a territory in which a single authority exercises sovereign powers both *de jure* and *de facto*." Historically, the modern state emerged in the form of a "gradual increase in the power of territorial princes at the expense of all other authorities." Fourteenth-century France, the paradigm for other European monarchical states, shows the typical techniques of "reducing the independent powers of the church and ... controlling the feudal magnates." Although in less extreme terms than those proposed by Fried and others, Watkins contrasts the state and smaller, more intimate polities which function as "a close-knit community of citizens." The modern state, by contrast, "often appears as an external agency of control, ruling over a more or less random and heterogeneous collection of subjects." The distinctive agenda of the state is its "attempt to monopolize coercive power within its own territory" (Watkins 150, 151, 155).

Charles Tilly presents a list of events and processes that occur "over and over" in the history of European state formation. While presenting the "epitaph" of the ideas he dismisses as "pernicious postulates," including that of social evolution, he enunciates a set of conditions whose recurrence nonetheless implies an evolutionary mechanism of some sort. The statist trends he describes are universalist in the sense that they subvert localized, particularist—and presumably traditionalist—countertendencies. These recurrent elements include: "the early uncertainty as to the location of the government"; "intense campaigns of kings ... to tear down castle walls, disarm the lords, diminish the private use of armed force" (as in dueling, banditry, private armies); the creation of "government-controlled police forces"; the use of this police power "to impose taxation [and] military conscription"; the definition and suppression of smuggling; the control of criminal and civil justice systems; the systematic "registration and surveillance" of the population; the regulation of "all other organizations" (*Big Structures* 59).

Measured by this inventory of statist features, the *PMC* is decidedly pre-state. It sets little store by the establishment of a locus of political power; there is no reference to any coherent campaign against local sovereignty; there are no police; extortion and tribute prevail, rather than a rational system of taxation; there is no evidence of a written code of criminal or civil justice; surveillance or regulation of the population are completely alien to the poem's outlook. These perspectives help us to understand the disparity between the poem and the social world of its time. In that world there were a number of emerging states, in the Peninsula and in Europe, if we may define "emergence" in the terms suggested by the social scientists cited here.[19] The very fact of the disparity between the *PMC*'s outlook and the facts of on-going statist trends contemporary to its composition obliges us to see the author and his audience in terms of their distance from the sociopolitical epicenters of emerging governments and the attendant social repercussions. The disjunction is to be correlated with discrepancies noted previously: the poem's ignorance of or indifference to marital consent and divorce; the emphasis on kinship as opposed to other principles of social cohesion; the obsession with economic redistribution. The incongruities in question, all of which suggest a decided primitivism, lead us to postulate not an earlier date of composition, but a cultural discontinuity. Everything about the poem's social outlook implies the marginal, the peripheral, the provincial. The notion of the backwater or the fringe as the social context of the poem's composition leads us to view the poet and his audience as unaware of or impervious to the various social phenomena that, for the sake of convenience, we may group under the heading of modernization. Whether the poet knowingly dissembles, or is genuinely naïve, his work must view such things as stratification, territorial unification, and legalism through a traditionalizing prism.

Tilly, focusing on the formation of the state from a pan-European perspective, analyzes the tendency, among the nascent European states (for example, the Habsburg Empire), to persist as a diffuse and fragmented coalition of counties and principates "weakly subordinated to the imperial center." In the first phases of European nation-state formation, and until well into the period of true nationalism as an expression of collective consciousness, the "peasant base," dominated economically by the landowner class, maintains its own cultural identity and shows a "tenacious resistance" to the expansion of the state and to "nationalist enterprises" ("Reflections" 13). Although we must speak of social change—over time and over a broad territorial range—there are, Bendix maintains, no grounds for speaking of change as singular in cause or effect. Discontinuity, contradiction, and coexistence are thus useful concepts in the analysis of social transformations:

> Kinship ties, religious beliefs, linguistic affiliations, territorial communalism, and others are typical forms of association in a traditional social order. None of these ties or associations have disappeared even in the most highly industrialized societies; to this day the relative decline of "traditional" and relative ascendance of "modern" solidarities remain or recur as social and political issues. (Bendix 307)

The Cid's status as "Spanish national hero," chiefly propounded by Menéndez Pidal, in an influential body of work, has prevented us from understanding many aspects of both the literary and the historical figure.[20] The predatory and violent nature of his campaigns while in exile suggests a distinct parallelism with similar practices shown by so-called predatory or bandit cultures (like the Arabian and North African Bedouin) and, more especially, by the social bandit and primitive rebel described by Hobsbawm and other social historians. The legitimation of economic predation as a way of life suggests comparison to such bandit and gangster figures as Robin Hood, Jesse James, Al Capone, the Sicilian bandit Giuliano, the Brazilian Lampião, and many others. All of these are outsiders whose folkloric appeal is to the oppressed or marginal elements of the regions or countries in which their tales are told. Such folkloric parallels to the *PMC*, although perhaps seeming far-fetched, are difficult to avoid. They illuminate some of the work's darker social perceptions, its unsavory economic practices, and, very possibly, its implied audience. The poem's notions of money, exchange, gift-giving, property, and redistribution, in conjunction with its endorsement of pillage, tribute, and "protection rackets," are clear signs of a precapitalist economy. At the same time, the poem's concepts of kinship and vassalic relations, of marriage and divorce, of legality and social organization, are all thoroughly prepolitical, kin-ordered, and, very possibly, preliterate.

The "folk" at whom such a folkloric text was aimed were primitive not in terms of historical chronology, but rather in terms of deficient participation in the project of modernization that makes for nationality. The present essay constitutes a meditation, therefore, on the fact that the epic masterpiece of Spanish literature is "pre-Spanish" in its origins. This study is an attempt to get around one of the salient difficulties of reading a work that might well have been composed according to genuinely oral-traditional techniques. Rather than cite written texts—literary, legal, chronistic, or otherwise—in order to test the orality of the *PMC*, I have chiefly looked to non-literary contexts for points of comparison. To test for illiteracy, you have to look at illiteracy—and this cannot be done, by definition, by comparing the text to be scrutinized with written texts. Acting on the assumption that no work, even a possibly completely oral one, is composed in a vacuum, I have assumed throughout that the poem speaks for itself, if we only train our ear to listen.

# Chapter Five

# Conclusion

Deference and Inequality

Adrian Montoro contends that the *PMC* expresses the three primordial social functions delineated by Georges Dumézil. These Montoro summarizes as, first, the sacred function, comprising the realms of magic, religion, knowledge, and political authority and administration in their divinely guided aspect; second, the "warrior function," encompassing "la fuerza física, brutal, y . . . los usos de la fuerza; and the third function, including fecundity (human, animal, and vegetable), as well as health, peace, sensuality and eroticism, economy, and wealth. Montoro argues that this "trifunctional structure" is manifest throughout the *PMC*. The first instance, he suggests, occurs in the Corte de Toledo (3145–507), where the hero demands that the Infantes return his swords and his *averes*, and that King Alfonso preside over a judicial combat. "Salta a la vista," affirms Montoro, "que las reclamaciones corresponden, respectivamente, a la segunda, tercera y primera funciones." That the functions are presented in the order indicated results from the "astutas consideraciones tácticas" of the Cid, who leaves his principal concern, the "rrencura mayor," for last (v. 3254). But the Cid's claims entail the "orden canónico" of the traditional three functions, with the *judicium Dei* representing divine justice; the swords, "la fuerza viril y la proeza bélica"; and the monetary assets, "la riqueza, la abundancia de bienes." To this functional cluster is opposed a mirror-image set of attributes presented by the Infantes. Their greed (cf. 1371) corresponds to the third function; their cowardice, as in the episodes of the lion and the battle with King Búcar (2278–310, 2315–537), embodies "el vicio opuesto a la virtud guerrera"; and finally, their treacherous behavior toward Abengalbón and their sadistic treatment of their wives (2647–88, 2689–760) present them as "violadores de las normas que rigen las relaciones entre los hombres bajo la sanción de Dios y del rey" (Montoro 554–55, 556, 558, 559).

Dumézil records illustrations of the tripartite program throughout the Indo-European world, noting that outside that domain the system is limited to regions historically colonized or influenced by Indo-Europeans. Some regional variants present difficulties in the application of the model. India, for example, shows a quadripartite organization, involving a fourth category, the Shudras ("servants," "have-nots"). This is accounted for in Dumézil's analysis by explaining this fourth classification as a socioeconomic appendage to the original three divisions. Because the Shudras, he argues, are essentially "cut off from the other three, and . . . by nature irremediably sullied," they are virtually peripheral to the tripartite society that is the traditional core of Indian culture (Dumézil 7).[1]

Without calling into question the encyclopedic range and rigorous documentation of Dumézil's monumental project, we may note the ever-present danger in applying elegant theory to chaotic social reality. One does not want to fit the evidence to the theory. At the same, the inhabitants of the societies studied by historians and ethnographers theorize about their own social reality; such indigenous autodefinition has no greater claim to accuracy than the conjectures of outsiders. This must be recalled when considering that most conspicuous example of the trifunctional theory, the Indian system of the *varnas* (literally, "colors"), which arranges society into categories comparable to the medieval European estates. The Brahmins (priests = *oratores*) are followed by the Kshatriyas (warriors = *bellatores*), then by the Vaishyas (farmers = *laboratores*). Each division is contingent upon subclassifications theoretically marked by standards of membership based on heredity, marriage rules, and stern codes of proscription and interdiction. Louis Dumont observes that the system of *varnas* (a word he translates as "estates"; Fr. *état*) has a multifarious correlation with the *jāti,* the castes proper. The latter divisions are distinguished by three primary properties: separation (indicated by interdictions on intercaste marriage or personal contact), division of labor (vocations or trades are assigned to each group, "in theory or by tradition"), and hierarchy (categories are invidiously ordered "as relatively superior or inferior to one another"). The *varna* system, in other words, emphasizes function over both inheritance and stratification. The caste system, by contrast, is predicated on inherited status rather than on function. For Dumont, the Indian concept of society and polity is an attempt to reconcile the incompatible factors of honorific status and sociopolitical power: ". . . for pure hierarchy to develop without hindrance it was . . . necessary that power should be absolutely inferior to status." Hierarchical purity is determined by adherence to the perceived moral truth of the transcendent superiority of the spiritual over the material.[2]

Some historians and literary critics assert that the European system of the three estates (*oratores, bellatores, laboratores*) constitutes an explanation of social reality, using literature to explain society, rather than the other way around. Contemporary social historiography would consider such an attempt chimerical. The ideology of any community, in Georges Duby's phrase, "is not a reflection of life, but a project for acting on it." This includes the trifunctional postulate in its later European manifestations, which emanated from the same learned culture that promulgated law codes. This functionalist or "division-of-labor" approach to societal structure postulates an ostensibly egalitarian harmony. However, to the degree that medieval estates categories justify social inequality, they are transformed from a social theory with utopian overtones into status-defensive functionalist thought—becoming, argues Duby, "the sacralized basis of oppression." The medieval European estates system, in its very consistency and elegance, therefore constitutes not a description of a stable hierarchical social reality, but rather the utopic image of a society whose inhabitants are happy in their respective functions, regardless of disparities in status, wealth, and power. Estates theory purveys, in other words, a myth of social stability and permanence. Its very coherence as theory implies a circumambient reality that is anything but secure (Duby, *Three Orders* 7, 74).

We noted in the conclusion of the previous chapter that contemporary discussions of tradition and modernity inherit a vocabulary bequeathed by conservative social philosophers of the seventeenth through nineteenth centuries. These authors contemplated social change as a romantic nostalgia for an orderly past society distinguished (according to conservative models) by a decorous and orderly distribution of power and privilege. Paternalistic landownership presided over a community that was more intimate, more closely knit, precisely because it was hierarchic. There arises, in conjunction with such nostalgic models, a temporal version of the city/country dichotomy, expressed as the vision of a Golden Age of societal harmony and traditional morality inevitably contrasted with the disorder and depravity of the present day. Raymond Williams notes the varied and continual recurrence of this pastoral fantasy of "what seems an old order, a 'traditional society' . . . against which contemporary change can be measured." Such images represent, he argues, "an idealization of feudal and immediately post-feudal values: of an order based on settled and reciprocal social and economic relations of an avowedly total kind" (Williams, *Country and City* 35).

It is in light of this utopic nostalgia that we must understand such tripartite expressions as that expressed in the *Partidas*, which depict society in terms of "los que ruegan a Dios por el pueblo," who are called *oradores*; those who "labran la tierra," called *labradores*; and those who "an a defender a todos," who are termed *defensores* (II.xxi.Intro.). The social elitism of the *Partidas* emerges in their reference to "caballeria" as "la compaña de los nobles homes, que fueron puestos para defender las tierras." This elite fellowship is called *caballería* not merely because its members ride on horseback, but because "los que son escogidos para ser caualleros, son mas honrrados que todos los otros defensores" (II.21.1).

Trifunctionality is as much a philological as a sociological phenomenon. Dumézil traces functions not as analytically discernible behavioral attributes, but rather as named categories. The essential thing about trifunctional systems, particularly as they manifest themselves in estates theory and its congeners (such as the Indian *varna* system), is that the categories are named and their functions strictly separate. What is vital, from the viewpoint of their proponents, is the underlying functionalism, which is subverted by any blurring of categories. The fiction is of a division of labor, whether or not this concept is adorned with an egalitarian overlay. At the core of trifunctionality—an ideology, not a way of life—is a notion of strict division of social functions and the rewards that accrue to them. The logic of social relationships in the *PMC*, however, is resolutely non-functionalist. Inequality is accepted, as we have seen, but there is no territoriality to the observed social functions. Categories are not autonomous or distinct. Jealous observance of one's own functions and a scrupulous avoidance of the functions of other categories, particularly those deemed inferior—these traits, significantly, are absent.

It is therefore with some skepticism that we must view Montoro's assertion that the Cid's entire career is a virtual calque on the tripartite pattern: "parte de la segunda función para alzarse . . . hasta la primera (majestad soberana), no sin mantener siempre conexiones explícitas con la tercera (riqueza, fecundidad)." True, all these functions are represented. The Cid reveals "un estilo de acción claramente *mayestático*," characterized by "sabiduría, mesura, serenidad, alto sentido de la justicia y del derecho." Other characters, by contrast, represent the other functions. Thus, the spirited Minaya, avid for battle (cf. 779–80), personifies the warrior function, while Martín Antolínez is chiefly associated (as in vv. 65–69) with such "actividades de tercera función" as the provisioning of the Cid's band (Montoro 555, 561). However, there is a constant blurring of definitions as representatives of one supposed category perform tasks from another. The Cid, a warrior, engages—as we have seen—in economic activity, Montoro's third category. Minaya is a diplomat and advisor as well as a warrior (871–80, 1245–54); Martín Antolínez challenges and fights the Infante Diego (3361–72, 3646–70), thus expressing the sacramental function. Bishop Jerome mixes the two dominant estates, in one scene saying mass (1702), and in another showing himself the equal in bellicosity of any of the Cid's men: "quando es farto de lidiar con amas las sus manos, / non tiene en cuenta los moros que ha matados" (1794–95). He, like Turpin in the *Chanson de Roland*, is a folkloric figure on a par with Friar Tuck of the Robin Hood legends. *Cavalleros* and *peones*, meanwhile, are not rigid membership categories, but are treated almost as mere descriptive labels.

The estates, significantly, are not named in the *PMC*. Whether in India or medieval Europe, the essence of the estates systems, as Dumézil, Duby, Dumont, and others have demonstrated, is the naming of divisions. There is, moreover, no doctrine of communal service, no sense of functionalist justification. The Cid is in it for the money, the power, the glory. So are his men. The men are treated with egalitarian disregard for differences of station. The Cid's immediate entourage constitutes not an elite or a nobility or an upper class, but rather a retinue of intimates who are all kinsmen or *criados* (what amounts to foster kin).

Deference and social inequality in the *Poema de Mio Cid* are of the essence, but their special style, emanating from the kin-orderedness of the poet's worldview, are not of the restrictive type envisioned by theories of estates. The principal conflict in the *Poema de Mio Cid* occurs between two clans, that of the Cid and that of the Infantes de Carrión. On the surface, the dispute is about a case of spousal abuse. The Infantes are wife beaters brought to justice. But on a deeper level, the story is about a dispute over the relative status of the two clans. The triumph of the Cid's champions over the two Infantes and their brother Assur González vindicates the Cid's clan, while humiliating the Infantes and their *bando*. The victory embodies more than such well known medieval judicial concepts as the "arbitrament of the sword," described by Henry Charles Lea as an "appeal to the highest court" (Lea 234). This practice, the so-called *judicium Dei*, was founded on a concept characterized by R. Howard Bloch as "a belief in the immanence of supernatural powers within the natural sphere." The underlying postulate assumed that the incontrovertible fact of victory demonstrated the rightness of the winner's cause (*Medieval French Literature and Law* 19).

Such doctrines explain the poem's finale as a judicial outcome. However, more is demonstrated by the judicial combats than the legal rectitude of the Cid's case; more is vindicated than the honor of his daughters and his family. The Cid's ethical position is based on a social philosophy, a system of thought for which he stands. It is an ideological program that accounts for his military achievement, his political following, his economic accomplishment. The Cid's faction epitomizes, in conformity with the very conscious sociological intention of the poet, a style of leadership and allegiance that is dramatized and vindicated by the poem as much as are the character and personality of the hero himself.

The Cid's group, as we saw in our chapter on amity, is distinguished by spontaneous cooperation, by egalitarian teamwork: "Todos los de Mio Çid   tan bien son acordados" (2217); "Los vassallos de Mio Çid   assí son acordados" (2258); "Assí lo fazen todos,   ca eran acordados" (2488). The *bando* of the Infantes and their *parientes*, by contrast, schemes and deliberates: "Prenden so conseio   assí parientes commo son" (2988; also 2996, 3539). The Infantes are given to sequestered connivance (3161: "Essora salién aparte   iffantes de Carrión"), while the Cid and his men achieve consensus openly and simply. Their vassalic unanimity is unplanned and unaffected: "Respondieron todos:   'Nós esso queremos, señor'" (3082).

The *PMC* reveals what Berreman describes as "egalitarian" and "kin/role ranked" systems. In these, "differential prestige" depends on age, sex, familial roles, and either "personal characteristics" (the egalitarian) or "position in the kin system" (the "kin/role ranked"). In small-scale, face-to-face egalitarian societies, he writes, "interpersonal dominance arises out of interaction occurring in response to particular situations and is sustained as a result of personal characteristics and circumstances." In the egalitarian economy typical of such small, so-called stateless societies, generosity and reciprocity—rather than accumulation of property—are the principal "criteria for esteem and high status." Dominance in such a context is a matter not of ascribed status but of achieved performance: in such societies, "status tends to be individual or situational rather than categorical," while "prestige is more competed for than power and wealth" (Berreman, "Social Inequality" 8–9).

Honor in the *PMC* is primarily a matter of personal achievement rather than ascription, reflecting a mentality described by J. G. Peristiany as typical of "small scale, exclusive societies where face to face personal, as opposed to anonymous, relations are of paramount importance." In such an environment, he notes, actions speak louder than words; one therefore observes an "insecurity and instability of the honour-shame ranking." Even inherited honor must, in this context, be "asserted and vindicated," in that "an aspersion on [one's] honour is an aspersion on the honour of [one's] group." The individual, then, "is forcibly cast in the role of his group's protagonist."[3]

Relatively simple "pre-state" or "stateless" societies emphasize this more conditional status, while complex, territorially centralized, bureaucratic societies stratify themselves not according to person-to-person contrasts, but rather in terms of membership in hierarchized categories that are, as Berreman phrases it, "differentially powerful, esteemed, and rewarded." These systems of "collective social ranking" possess various sorts of "ideological support systems" and show great variety in the "distinctiveness, number and size of the ranked categories." In both egalitarian and role-ranked societies, argues Berreman, economic exploitation—"the concept of inequality as it implies disadvantage or degradation"—is largely absent. Productive roles in such circumstances coincide with family roles, since kin-based relationships imply "mutuality, shared commitment, shared effort, shared responsibility . . . and shared rewards." In such societies, therefore, one's kin "constitute the social and political as well as the economic unit." Kinship is thus "the idiom for virtually *all* relations in nonstratified societies," while "kin organization" is "their defining characteristic" ("Race, Caste" 385–86).[4]

An evolutionist typology emerging from the supposed contrast between state and stateless societies, it has been suggested, leads to a generalized assumption that the absence of organized authority and of divisions according to wealth, status, or rank mean that a society is, as James Flanagan phrases it, " 'egalitarian' by default." He cites Morton Fried's definition of egalitarian societies as those in which "there are as many positions of prestige in any given age-sex grade as there are persons capable of filling them," with the added qualification that such societies have "as many people of paramount prestige as can display the qualities necessary." Flanagan points out what Fried overlooks: that "the [theoretical] focus is on the ideal characteristics of the role—not on its performance" (245–46).[5]

One might establish a polarity with the truly egalitarian society at one extreme and the thoroughly stratified society on the other. Real societies, such a model implies, may be situated on this spectrum according to their degree of stratification. Yet the possibility must be considered, observes Flanagan, that truly egalitarian societies do not exist. There are always at least "minimal stratification criteria." He cites the list proposed by Marshall Sahlins: "age, sex, and personal characteristics." Flanagan points out that stratification is a more complex phenomenon than hierarchy. The latter phenomenon, explains Flanagan, involves relations of face-to-face inequality. The participants in the system focus on their connections with specific persons perceived as just above, equal, or just below. Stratification implies, on the other hand, "division into institutionalized categories of persons." Whether these classifications be "groups, classes or castes," Flanagan argues, it is their complexity and the intricacy of their interactions that makes for this difference (248). He cites Claude Meillassoux's observation that class comes not from mere categories (e.g., elders, juniors), but from "the dominance of entire, organically constituted communities which endow *all* their members, irrespective of age or sex, with prerogatives and privileges over *all* the members of the dominated communities" (Meillassoux, *Maidens* 81). From this contrast between hierarchy and stratification derives yet another distinction, between ideologies "which may mask inequalities in the ability to achieve desired ends" and practices that are authentically egalitarian. An ideology of equal opportunity may exhibit "enormous inequalities in both material resources and access to power—such inequalities being attributed to differential aptitudes or abilities." This leads, in turn, to an attribution of "differential merit" as the source of disparate ranking.[6]

The perception and management of inequality directly bear upon a society's political organization. In a study that examines status discrepancies in terms of situations and behavioral styles, Lloyd Fallers confirms that in pre-state contexts, "thought and action about inequality center . . . upon interpersonal relations of superiority and inferiority" (*Inequality* 29). A variation of this dyadic hypothesis is enunciated by Elman R. Service, in terms of a "watershed" between primitive and civilized society. What characterizes the primitive in this model of a "great divide" is the segmentation of society "into kin groups that [are] egalitarian in their relations to each other." Civilization arises when some lineages become "hierarchical, controlled and directed by a central authoritative power . . . instituted as a government" (Service 3–4).

Sahlins remarks that the truly egalitarian society must be one in which "rank allocation" is based on the universals earlier referred to (age, sex, personal characteristics), and that, in such

circumstances, "every individual has an equal chance to suc-
ceed to whatever statuses may open" (*Social Stratification* 2).
While societies adhering strictly to such an ideal would be very
rare, some do indeed show an absence of institutionalized
dominance or authority. Flanagan cites the Eskimo head of
household, who is not empowered "to make binding decisions
even in his own household." Such "assertively egalitarian" societies thwart control over means of production, emphasize
sharing, and avoid "personal accumulation." Although it may
be, concludes Flanagan, that there are no absolutely egalitarian
or simple societies, "there are egalitarian contexts, or scenes,
or situations" that are "as much constitutive of social structure
as the hierarchical relationships we have privileged up to now"
(249–50, 260–61).

The broad question of whether or not truly egalitarian and
stateless societies exist is beyond the scope of the present essay.
What is of interest is that the poet portrays the society founded
by the Cid in exile as a community approximating the egalitarian society, and that the poet's perception of hierarchy is resolutely dyadic and kin-ordered. The work's portrayal of social
inequality is based, that is, on such fundamental factors as age,
sex, and personal characteristics. In addition, the *PMC* endorses
the negotiated or circumstantial status defined by Gerald
Berreman and John Peristiany. This accounts for the characters'
jockeying for prestige and orients our social reading of the
poem. Wealth and power serve as the basis for enhanced prestige, rather than the other way round. The subjects of a king or
lord in the *PMC* view themselves as members of a macrofamily
grounded in extended pseudo-kinship, in which each person
enjoys a one-to-one relationship with the patriarchal ruler.
Conflict between the hero and his enemies is thus psychologi-
cally more akin to sibling rivalry than to class struggle. The
relationships of subject to king and vassal to lord represent, in
this context, an idealization of the concept of *paterfamilias*.
Age is the criterion of inequality: Alfonso and the Cid are, in
effect, elders in the community. Social inequality is experienced not in terms of a pyramidal layer-cake of class groupings, but rather in those of a multitude of person-to-person
relationships. Each member of the Cid's army enjoys a one-
on-one vassalic relationship with his lord. Each and every

man who leaves the army, for instance, must kiss the Cid's hand (1252) in leave-taking. Vassalic respect is expressed by all, and not just by any special category of persons (i.e., by a "nobility").

The dyadic nature of the poem's vassalage is conveyed by such phrases as "Alegre era Mio Çid e todos sos vassallos" (1739). A pervasive esprit de corps—the sentimental aspect of that same principle of sharing that inspires economic redistribution—insures that the Cid and his men experience joys and sorrows as a team. This moral and emotional synchrony characterizes a vassalic pact that includes all *cavalleros* and *peones* who join the hero's campaign. *Las peonadas*, it is true, are opposed to *cavalleros*: "dozientos con él, que todos çinen espadas, / non son en cuenta, sabet, las peonadas" (917–18). The inequality of the two categories does not mean that those with horses possess an inherited status: they simply engage in a mode of combat considered enviable, more glamorous, but in no way inherent to its practitioner. Foot soldiers contribute greatly to the group's operations: the poet speaks of "las peonadas e omnes valientes que son" (418). There is unequal sharing of booty, to be sure, but this is accepted as one of the facts of life on campaign:

> Mandó partir tod aqueste aver,
> sos quiñoneros que ge los diessen por carta.
> Sos cavalleros í an arribança,
> a cada uno d' ellos caen *çiento* marcos de plata
> e a los peones la meatad sin falla,
> toda la quinta a Mio Çid fincava.
>
> (510–15)

The difference between *peones* and *cavalleros* seems to be one of function. Cavalry is more important than infantry in the frontier raiding parties depicted. Any man equipped with horse and armor is allowed to partake of the perquisites of the horseman. Moreover, there is equality of opportunity of becoming a horseman: "Los que fueron de pie cavalleros se fazen" (1213).

The Cid, for whom kinship terms have not yet escalated into political metaphors, takes things personally. The man-to-man nature of rivalry is underscored by such personal confrontations as the clash between the Cid and the Moorish king Búcar

(2408–26), or the exchange between the Cid and García Ordóñez (3270–90). Such confrontations are characterized by what Walter Ong calls the "agonistic tone," chiefly typified by face-to-face verbal sparring, taunting, bragging, and "reciprocal name-calling." Agonistic language is a common feature of epic (Ong mentions the *Iliad*, *Beowulf*, and the African *Mwindo Epic*), and indeed of oral culture everywhere (Ong 43–44). The dyadic sensibility of our poem is expressed, therefore, through its agonistic perception of relationships.

Given the foregoing features of agonistic tone and dyadic relationships, it is not surprising that the poem reveals no institutionalized, system-wide acceptance of stratification by group. Deference consistently expressed toward high-status persons is lacking. Thus the Cid's reluctance to form an alliance with the family of the Infantes (2082–110) and his contemptuous treatment of Count García Ordóñez (3281–90).[7] Status in the *PMC* is the responsibility of the individual. The Cid experiences this responsibility as part of a coherent system of behavioral rules, in which all acts are meaningful endorsements or subversions of the ethical code that binds all to all. Indeed, the poem regards status as an attribute whose worth is measured by one's commitment to its public defense. This corresponds to a pattern observed in small-scale societies, in which, notes Pierre Bourdieu, "the ethos of honour is but the transfigured expression of . . . economic and political facts." A man makes himself respected in such an environment by never overlooking a challenge to his own standing or to that of his line: "only the punctilious, active vigilance of the *point of honour*" can guard the innermost values of the family. Bourdieu characterizes these values as a man's true assets, as his "symbolic capital." In such circumstances, "poverty, far from contradicting or prohibiting respectability, makes doubly meritorious the man who, though particularly exposed to outrage, nonetheless manages to win respect." The brave defense of things deemed worthy of defending enriches a man before the world; the very act of will required to accomplish this feat generates additional symbolic capital. "The point of honour," states Bourdieu, "has a meaning and a function only in a man for whom there exist things worthy of being defended" (Bourdieu, *Outline* 61). Because every man is responsible for his own *ondra*, to be unable to defend *ondra* in the face of public blame is to incur shame, as demonstrated in Alfonso's admonition to the Infantes before their combat with the Cid's champions:

> "Si del campo bien salides,   grand ondra avredes vós,
> e si fuére[*de*]s vençidos,   non rrebtedes a nós,
> ca todos lo saben   que lo buscastes vós."
>
> (3565–67)

The Infantes, like the Cid, view the conflict mainly as a confrontation between the two clans, as we can see from their collaboration with their *parientes* and other members of their *bando* (2988, 2996, 3162, 3538–41). At the same time, the Infantes show a marked contempt for the Cid and his family: " 'De natura somos,' " Diego arrogantly declares, " 'de los condes más li[*m*]pios' " (3354). The point of honor defended by the Cid has been keenly analyzed by Duggan. Addressing the themes of social status, legitimacy, and inherited worth, he demonstrates, basing his argument on detailed references to the *romancero* and chronicle traditions, that Assur's challenge (" 'Fuesse . . .   los molinos picar / e prender maquilas' " [3379–80]) alludes to a legend, well known at the time of the *PMC*'s composition and for centuries afterward, of the hero's illegitimate birth to a miller's wife or daughter. It is thus the implicit "disabling quality of bastardy in legal actions" that underlies Assur's innuendo (Duggan, *The "Cantar"* 48–52, 53, 54–55).

In his challenge to Fernando, Pero Vermúez declares, while calling the former "malo" and "traidor," that the Infantes have, through their abuse and abandonment of the Cid's daughters, lost both face and honor. Pero's speech expresses a judgment based on gender role—the daughters, although women, are more worthy than the unmanly ruffians who have abused them:

> "por quanto las dexastes   menos valedes vós;
> ellas son mugieres   e vós sodes varones,
> en todas guisas   más valen que vós."
>
> (3346–48)

The centrality of the feminine, from the viewpoint of the males of the offended clan, derives from several elements.

Leaving aside the obvious Freudian aspect (of suppressed desire for females forbidden by rules of incest and endogamy), we may concentrate on the implications of uxorifocality for the daughters' extended clan. Through the metonymic logic of kinship, they symbolize lineal honor. Injury to them hurts the clan in its most sacred, most vulnerable core of identity. Precisely because of this cultural element—presumably taken for granted by the audience—a subtle utilization of them occurs in the poem, in terms of narrative strategy. The daughters are, on a metanarratological level, the lure that entices the Infantes into the trap. When the Infantes take the bait, they provide, through the Afrenta de Corpes, a pretext for degradation, bringing on themselves the inevitable, grinding humiliation of the climactic judicial duels. Foredoomed to ignominy by the poet's inarticulate class hatred (inarticulate because couched in terms of denial of class structure), the Infantes are "set up" so as to afford the poem's audience the delicious pleasure of witnessing a well-deserved thrashing of loathsome *señoritos*. It is in this light that we must understand the narrator's partisan declaration:

> Grant es la biltança  de ifantes de Carrión:
> qui buena dueña escarneçe  e la dexa después
> atal le contesca  o siquier peor.
>
> (3705–07)

The role of the "buena dueña" in the *PMC* suggests sexual stratification, in that the "good woman"—in conformity with a well-known Mediterranean pattern—is principally viewed as the conduit of patrilineal integrity. The Cid's wife and daughters are not consulted concerning the marriages. After the match to the Infantes has been arranged, the Cid conveys the news first to his wife (2187–88: " '¡Grado al Criador,  vengo, mugier ondrada! / Yernos vos adugo  de que avremos ondrança' "), then to his daughters (2189: " '¡gradídmelo, mis fijas,  ca bien vos he casadas!' "). The marriages, indeed, are depicted as deals between the Cid and his king, and between the Cid and his sons-in-law. Thus the king thanks his vassal for conceding the matchmaking function to him:

> "Grado e graçias . . .
> quem' dades vuestras fijas  pora los ifantes de Carrión.

D'aquí las prendo por mis manos   don Elvira e doña Sol
e dolas por veladas   a los ifantes de Carrión.
Yo las caso a vuestras fijas   con vuestro amor."

(2095–99)

Shortly thereafter, when the king has placed the Infantes under
the Cid's authority (2101, 2103–04), the hero reminds his lord:
"'Vós casades mis fijas   ca non ge las do yo,'" (2110). Later
the Cid's consent—again, not that of the wife or daughters—is
sought by Alfonso, on the occasion of the second nuptials:
"'que plega a vós,   e atorgar lo he yo, / este casamiento   oy se
otorgue en esta cort'" (3411–12). This disregard of the wife's
prerogatives in marital consent goes against a pattern upheld
by many *fueros*, of "participation of mothers together with fathers" in the arrangement of marriages (Dillard 42). Jimena and
her daughters may thus be said to show both deference toward
the Cid—and, by extension, toward his lord—and a recognition of the daughters as patriarchal property. "'Fém' ante vós,'"
declares Jimena, "'yo e vuestras fijas'" (269). Paternity, therefore, determines existence, while the wife's role is to facilitate
patrilineal continuity. "'Vós nos engendrastes,'" the daughters
tell their father, "'nuestra madre nos parió'" (2595). The
poem's conclusion confirms matrimonial alliance as the principal motive of the hero: "Oy los rreyes d'España   sos parientes
son" (3724).

This depiction of marriage arrangements reflects the syndrome critiqued by Luce Irigaray in her analysis of exchange
and commodification of women, as practiced by men in real-
world patriarchal society, and as theoretically formulated by
anthropologists like Lévi-Strauss. Irigaray observes that in ethnographic theory and in phallocentric practice, "women always
pass from one man to another, from one group of men to another." Man, in this pattern, "begets man as his own likeness,"
while "wives, daughters, and sisters have value only in that they
serve as the possibility of, and potential benefit in, relations
among men." In this system, the "use of and traffic in women"
insures that "men make commerce *of* them, but they do not
enter into any exchanges *with* them" (Irigaray 171–72, 193).

Laurel Bossen also criticizes transactional terminology: men
are transactors, women are transacted. On the other hand,
it may be "certain types of rights in women (labor, sexual,

reproductive) [that] are what are being transacted, not the women themselves." In fact, Bossen suggests, the oversimplicity of the transactive model overlooks the fact that "women often reject, veto, or nullify the agreements made between men, making men scramble to restore economic order when women disrupt their arrangements." Two questions that must be asked are: "why women permit themselves to be transacted," and "whether men are transacted."[8] Bossen's assessment would imply that Irigaray, in taking patriliny at its word, is herself guilty of admitting certain patriarchal axioms. Irigaray's critique of marital exchange and commodification assumes that the official goals of patrilineal matchmaking are in all cases implemented with rigorous efficiency—that is, with the invariable compliance of women. It is perhaps true that in patrilineal exchange systems, as Meillassoux suggests, women "*are dispossessed of their children* to the benefit of men," and are thereby "subjected to conjugality which dominates their kinship relations, [so that] what they produce enters the domestic sphere through the mediation of a man" (Meillassoux, *Maidens* 77; emphasis in original). At the same time, in societies lacking economic diversity and the profusion of vocational and bureaucratic roles that make possible social mobility and sexual liberation, both men and women are imprisoned in the narrow range of possible roles implied by kin-ordered society. Both sexes are constrained to participate in team efforts that reproduce a status quo that is deemed to be right and proper. Cooperative incentives are perceived to exist, even by those who are objectively exploited.

Matrimonial strategies, observes Bourdieu, are "directed towards the conservation or expansion of the material and symbolic capital jointly possessed by a more or less extended group," and thus pertain to a system of "reproductive strategies." These, in turn, may be defined as "the sum total of strategies" employed by individuals and groups "to reproduce or improve their position in the social structure" (*Outline* 70). Such a system in no way precludes the active participation of all family members—of both sexes, and on both bride's and groom's sides—at every stage of matchmaking negotiations. The publicized outcome of these necessarily presents to the community an official image of decorous clanic consensus. Such harmony often camouflages acrimony and dissension.

The *PMC* presents an image of clanic unity. At the same time, although their cooperation is exemplary, the Cid's daughters are not mere commodities. They are, in the absence of brothers, primary heirs, in adherence to a historical pattern explicated by Julian Pitt-Rivers: "a Spanish woman of high birth is able to transmit her patrilineal status to her children" ("Honour and Social Status" 69). It is instead the Infantes who are commodified, from the viewpoint of the Cid's lineage. In addition to contributing their familial prestige, the Infantes enable the Cid's agnatic lineage to perpetuate itself. This pattern corresponds to the so-called *epiclerate*, discussed in the chapter on marriage. Often viewed in terms of a "strategy of heirship" designed to recruit sons-in-law into the lineage as if they were adopted sons, thereby transforming daughters into surrogate male heirs, this practice is evident in the *PMC*: " 'los yernos e las fijas   todos vuestros fijos son,' " declares Alfonso to the Cid (2106); later he reminds his vassal of the Infantes' new status: " 'Evad aquí vuestros fijos,   quando vuestros yernos son' " (2123). Still later the Cid again confirms the filial status of these sons-in-law: " '¡Venides, mios yernos,   mios fijos sodes amos!' " (2443).[9]

The size and importance of the hero's household, suggested by numerous references to the *dueñas* attendant upon Jimena and her daughters, hints at the daughters' incentive to marry. The foundation of a household of one's own constitutes, we recall, a significant enhancement of status in the kin-ordered world. The ladies in attendance serve mother and daughters, as shown in the Cid's commending them to the care of Abbot Sancho: " 'a ella e a sus dueñas   sirvádeslas est año' " (254). The members of this entourage are not merely numerous, but high born: "de pro," "buenas" (239, 1412). The prestige of the Cid's household is enhanced by the quality of those who serve in it. The mention of service by the *dueñas* does not, however, necessarily indicate the institutionalized categorical distinctions that Meillassoux mentions as signs of emergent class structure. The inequality implied could simply reflect the kin-based notion of *criados(as)*, persons fostered in the household of a lord or prominent kinsman, such as those "muchos   que crió el Campeador" mentioned in line 2514. Herlihy, we recall, reports a pattern prevalent everywhere throughout the Middle Ages, of rich households as "bigger, and presumably more complex, than the poor." Young people, moreover, tended to circulate among wealthy households before they married. This pattern suggests a "movement . . . across wealth categories, and up and down the social scale" (*Medieval Households* 153, 155–56).

Inequality centers chiefly on personal characteristics. These are understood in terms of public opinion. The Cid's concern for this factor is seen in his plea at the *vistas*: "que lo oyan quantos aquí son" (2032b). Service points out that "powerful forces of social control [that] inhere in small face-to-face societies" empower public opinion, so that "people [are] extraordinarily sensitive to the reactions of the group to any social action." In Colin Turnbull's formulation, such traits as "kindness, generosity, consideration, affection, honesty, hospitality, compassion, charity" constitute the all-important societal bond of small-scale society. To behave otherwise is to be inhuman, deserving of expulsion.[10] Where status differences are expressed in dyadic, agonistic terms, the criterion of status is not group membership but performance. The audience that judges the performance is the community. Honor is applause; shame is derision. Generally defined as an "external sanction," shame involves not "fear of active punishment by superiors," but rather "social expulsion, like ostracism" (Piers and Singer 29, 64). Caro Baroja further explicates shame as the antonym of *prestige*, a concept expressed in medieval Spanish by *más valer*, whose implicit antonym—*menos valer*—plays an important part in the poem's contentious discourse (as in 3268, 3300, 3334, 3346). Such notions, according to Baroja, are based on a notion of honor "which is not individual but collective." The community at large attributes honor and shame through approval or disapproval of clans and their members, with each member standing for his lineage ("Honour and Shame" 89, 92–93).

The poet, no less a theoretician of social laws than the ethnographers just cited, presents just such a face-to-face society. The Infantes' lack of remorse at their sadistic treatment of the Cid's daughters shows a complete absence of the internal sanction represented by guilt. They are unrepentant, even exultant (2757–62), so long as they are not discovered. Their attitude amounts to perversion, from the moral viewpoint of the poet: they do not consider themselves answerable to public opinion. Their notion of *ondra* as an innate manifestation of (elite-)group membership is reaffirmed by García Ordóñez, as he denies any wrongdoing by the Infantes in the Afrenta de Corpes:

> "Los de Carrión   son de natura tal
> non ge las devién querer   sus fijas por varraganas,
> o ¿quién ge las diera   por pareias o por veladas?"
>
> (3275–77)

The status of legitimate wife is denied to the Cid's daughters. This is the rhetorical correlative of the Afrenta—the insult added to injury. Only a cad, a villain, could think such a thing, given that, since moral performance legitimates, the *buena dueña* is entitled to legitimate status precisely because she is a good woman. Law in the statutory sense is thus not uppermost in the mind of the poet—it is the humiliation, the *biltança* (as in 3705) of the abusive adversary that matters. This outcome has another aspect besides the obvious disgrace to which the Infantes are subjected. With the Cid's departure for Valencia on the eve of judicial combat (3507), the story presents a hero who is not even an eyewitness to the vindication of his clan and the humiliation of his enemies. The king initially declares that the combat will be the day after the audience and the challenge: "'Cras sea la lid,   quando saliere el sol, / d'estos *tres* por tres   que rrebtaron en la cort'" (3465–66). However, the Infantes ask for and are granted a delay so that they may retire to Carrión to obtain arms and equipment for the combat (3468–70). The king offers the Cid the right of choosing the site for the encounter (3472), to which the Cid replies, with significant contrast to the geographical loci of the rival lineages: "'No lo faré, señor; / más quiero a Valençia   que tierras de Carrión'" (3473–74). The king then offers to take the Cid's three champions under his personal protection: "'que non prendan fuerça   de conde nin de ifançon'" (3479), while granting the Infantes a delay of three weeks, with the site of battle to be, again significantly, the "begas de Carrión" (3480–81). As he departs for Valencia, the Cid declares to his king:

> "Estos mis tres cavalleros   en vuestra mano son,
> d'aquí vos los acomiendo   como a rrey e a señor;
> ellos son adobados   pora cumplir todo lo so,
> ¡ondrados me los enbiad a Valençia,   por amor del Criador!"
>
> (3487–90)

We have, then, a narrative climax in which not only is the hero physically absent, but the humiliation of his enemies takes place in their own territory, presumably in front of their own family and their entire *bando*. What would seem an oddly antidramatic ingredient in a revenge scenario is deciphered by the poem's insistence on the Cid's "having it done for him." For the mark of the true leader is the *mesnada* of vassals eager to execute the will of their lord. The Cid's absence thus underscores the insignificance of the Infantes: he cannot be troubled to witness their defeat (which is, of course, a foregone conclusion). The Cid's absentee, surrogated humiliation of the Infantes reminds us that in the shame-oriented society, loss of face is tantamount to social hellfire. For shame implies the presence of a scrutinizing, evaluating community that exercises control. Shame *is* the imposition of a judgmental sanction, in the form of ridicule, blame, or vilification. Margaret Mead defines such sanctions as "mechanisms by which conformity is obtained, by which desired behavior is induced and undesired behavior prevented." If personal standards obviate outside enforcement, the sanction is internal. Behavioral conformity achieved solely as a response to "forces which must be set in motion by others" makes for external sanctions. We have seen that the Infantes are exclusively motivated by external sanctions—as long as they are not caught, they feel no compunction.[11]

Because all relationships are considered dyadic in the small-scale world, and because the community imposes a constant scrutiny, no man is an island entire to himself. This insures that a leader, first among equals, cannot make things happen—he must let them happen. The lord is he who can see to it that people do things for him because they want to. He seeks to touch them in their honor (as when the Cid encourages, rather than commands, the defense of his family honor by Pero and the other two champions). This voluntary recognition of leadership is expressed through a mutual generosity, a reciprocal circulation of affection, in the form of deferential acts. These constitute a grammar of beneficent deportment, designed to compromise both parties in the exchange.

Deference is marked by "acts of appreciation or derogation" involving a "clear intimation of a person who defers." There is, on one side, an expressed desire to receive deference (involving a belief that one is "entitled to it through the possession of the qualities which are conventionally accepted as the grounds on which deference is elicited or granted") and, on the other, a desire "to grant or accord deference," which involves "a need to live in a social world implanted with worthiness" and "to acknowledge the embodiments of that worth and to derogate those who are unworthy." The bilateral behavior described appears in all societies (Shils, "Deference" 420).

In the *PMC*, deference granted and received is yet another aspect of the reciprocity, the "interested gift-giving," pointed out by Duggan. Just as the hero's persistent generosity toward Alfonso compels the king to relent, redistributive generosity toward his men transforms Rodrigo's wealth "into an instrument of loyalty" (Duggan 30, 33, 36). Deference, a kind of giving, allows obedience to be dressed up as a gift. When the Cid overcomes his misgivings concerning the marriage between his daughters and these young men who are "mucho urgullosos" and who "an part en la cort" (1938), he declares that he will enter into marriage negotiations in deference to his lord: "mas pues lo conseja. el que más vale que nós / fablemos en ello, en la poridad seamos nós" (1940–41). Deference is itself an act of generosity that compromises the accepter as surely as the grantor; submission solicits a counterdeference, in the long or short term. Deference is, then, the grammar of compliance and cooperation in a pre-legal or pre-bureaucratic network, which, like that of Alfonso, relies on the voluntary collaboration, the resourceful teamwork, of the participants. Hence, to mention another example, the attitude of conspicuous acquiescence in the Cid's agreement to attend the *vistas*:

> "Non era maravilla si quisiesse el rrey Alfonso;
> fasta dó lo fallássemos buscarlo ir[i]emos nós,
> por darle grand ondra commo a rrey de tierra.
> Mas lo que él quisiere esso queramos nós.
> Sobre Taio, que es una agua cabdal,
> ayamos vistas quando lo quiere mio señor."
>
> (1950–55)

Deference, to be an effectively binding instrument of social cohesion, must consecrate a bilateral involvement. Deference is therefore expressed by vassal to lord and lord to vassal.

Alfonso thus defers to the Infantes (1893: " 'pues bós lo queredes'"), while showing himself eager to leave the choice of site for the *vistas* to the Cid, likewise his vassal. The king's act of meeting the Cid—of going to him—is in itself a significant prestation: " 'dó él dixiere í sea el moión. / Andarle quiero a Mio Çid en toda pro' " (1912–13); " 'sean las vistas d'estas *tres* semanas; / s[i] yo bivo só, allí iré sin falla'" (1962–63). The poem depicts a similarly bilateral deference between the Cid and his men, as when the hero goes out to meet his new followers:

> Quando lo sopo Mio Çid el de Bivar
> quel' creçe conpaña por que más valdrá,
> apriessa cavalga, rreçebirlos salié,
> . . . . . tornós' a sonrrisar;
> lléganle todos, la mánol' ban besar.
>
> (295–98b)

The poet expresses a notion of interdependence of lord and vassal. The Cid goes forth to meet the newcomers, whose "conpaña" assures him, literally, a "greater worth" ("por que más valdrá"). His recognition of their contribution, like the deferential consideration shown to him by Alfonso, constitutes a kind of prestation. He *lends himself* to the arrival of the new men, thus enabling them to render a covenantal counter-prestation of their own ("lléganle todos, la mánol' ban besar").

Each inhabitant of this society is enmeshed in a network of potentially deferent relationships. The degree and number of such connections result from a multiplicity of what Shils calls "judgements of deference." These, he suggests, are aroused by such "deference-entitlements" as social or familial roles, "socially recognized accomplishments," "wealth," and "political power [and] proximity to persons or roles exercising power." In addition, deference is granted or expected on the basis of "objective acknowledgements," such as titles or ranks (Shils, "Deference" 421). In the small-scale, dyadic society, where the entitlements cited by Shils are less in evidence—where, in fact, their scarcity or deficiency are an important element of the definition of "small-scale"—the leader must operate without police power and systematic law. The leader who seeks to exact unilateral deference risks the alienation of the vassals upon whom he depends. Collective action must therefore be exhorted or adjured; it cannot be mandated or coerced. At the same time, some principle of consolidation is required to insure participation while showing a continued regard for the personal sovereignty of participants.

A notable passage is the one in which the Cid prescribes the penalties of hanging and confiscation of booty as punishment for neglecting the protocol of leave-taking. The scene is introduced by a passage describing the rewards provided by an extravagantly munificent hero: "El amor de Mio Çid ya lo ivan provando, / los que fueron con él e los de después todos son pagados" (1247b–48). Patriarchal bounty rewards all vassals alike, whether they are of the original band or among the waves of late arrivals. There follows, however, a startling contrast to this fatherly generosity:

> véelo Mio Çid que con los averes que avién tomados
> que sis' pudiessen ir fer lo ien de grado.
> Esto mandó Mio Çid, Minaya lo ovo conseiado,
> que ningún omne de los sos ques' le non spidiés, o
>                         [nol' besás la ma[no],
> sil' pudiessen prender o fuesse alcançado,
> tomássenle el aver e pusiéssenle en un palo.
>
>                               (1249–54)

The unstinting love of the benign *paterfamilias* on the one hand; the severe retribution of the tyrant on the other. How does the poet reconcile these extremes? How did he expect his audience to accept them in his hero? Ian Michael footnotes the scene thus: "El castigo tenía que ser bastante disuasorio para poder asegurar el mantenimiento de un ejército capaz de retener Valencia" (167n). This is, of course, plausible, given that, like bandits everywhere, the Cid's men would tend to go home with their booty after a successful battle or campaign.[12] It is significant, however, that the Cid is not chiefly concerned with the desertion of his men. It is their deference toward their lord that matters—what we would consider the etiquette of their leave-taking. The *besamanos* as the formal observance of leave-taking is later seen in the case of the king's vassals: "Veriedes cavalleros que bien andantes son / besar las manos [e] espedirse del rrey Alfonso" (2158–59). Deference affirms vassalage, which in turn guarantees cooperative action. Vassal-age is only real when constantly maintained by deference. Thus, the men may leave, but they will do so less readily if obliged to do so ceremonially. If they do leave, the vassalic relationship continues, rendering more likely their return at a later time.

The severity of the penalties prescribed would constitute heinous atrocity in a community for which discourtesy, how-ever flagrant, is only a breach of decorum. In the precarious world of the Cid, however, infraction of etiquette transcends the venial transgression of bad manners—it is *the* mortal sin in the deferential system. The unstable nature of vassalage, as the poem depicts it, requires a penalty that emphasizes the vassal's perdurable honor, not his transitory presence. Vassalage is shown to be a fragile, ephemeral relationship, maintained from day to day. Instances of insubordination, already mentioned in connection with avuncular indulgence, confirm this. When the Cid orders his men to stay in ranks, Pero Vermúez, unable to restrain himself, ignores his uncle's orders (704: "Aquel Pero Vermúez non lo pudo endurar"). When the Cid tries to dis-suade him (709: "¡Non sea, por caridad!"), Pero replies: " '¡Non rrastará por ál!' " (710). Pero again shows himself insubordi-nate in the scene where the Cid charges him with looking after the Infantes in the upcoming battle: " 'oy los ifantes a mí por amo non abrán; / cúrielos qui quier, ca d'ellos poco m'incal' " (2356–57). Bishop Jerome's demand to strike the first blow (2379), referred to earlier in the discussion of small-scale so-ciety, shows the unruliness underlying bellicose cooperation in the pre-state context.

The free will of the vassal is the all-important factor in a society where individual morality is regulated by honor and shame. "An oath which is not made freely," notes Pitt-Rivers, "is not binding, nor is a word of honour which is not intended as such." Attempting to force a man by ritual means to "com-mit" his honor is impossible, "since his honour is what he wills and the attempt to oblige him to do so invites him to 'cross his fingers.' "[13] In line with this logic, one of the principal induce-ments of the Cid's recruitment campaign is to assure voluntarism and personal latitude: "todos vengan de grado, ninguno non ha premia" (1193). The number and regional pluralism of the recruits are stressed (395: "grandes yentes se le acoien  essa noch de todas partes"; also 403), as is their poverty (134: "omnes  de todas partes me[n]guados"), and the naked materialism of the recruiting incentives: "quien quiere perder cueta  e venir a rritad" (1189).

This situation recalls the primitive feudalism of Carolingian times rather than the more codified system of classical feudalism, with its proliferation of subvassals and consequent conflicts of obligation. In the beginnings of feudalism, F. L. Ganshof points out, any free man could aspire to become a *vassus* of the king. Royal vassals in the early feudal centuries were often of inferior social condition. Only gradually did those of higher social standing become vassals, with a growing interposition of lords between their own vassals and the king.[14]

What makes the society of the poem egalitarian is not the absence of authority but the short range of its distribution. On the one hand, the Cid represents an authoritarian singularity. On the other, his vassals, an egalitarian multiplicity. No one has authority but the Cid. To be sure, he does appear to delegate authority to two of his lieutenants, Alvar Salvadórez and Galind Garcíaz de Aragón, upon his departure for the first *vistas*: "a aquestos dos  mandó el Campeador / que curien a Valençia I  d'alma e de coraçón / e todos los [*otros*]  que en poder d'éssos fossen" (1999–2001b). As noted in the previous chapter, the poem shows a limited concept of delegation, so that plenipotentiary delegation—an indicator of structured hierarchical authority—is conspicuous by its absence. The Cid, therefore, is insecure in his control of Valencia: " 'yo fincaré en Valençia,  que mucho costádom' ha, / grand locura serié  si la desenparás' " (1470–71).

The Cid's managerial system—the incentives and penalties offered or imposed—must be understood in conjunction with the other elements in his vassalic program. One of these is the constant example he sets. In the observance of vassalic duties toward his own lord, the Cid goes far beyond the requirements of custom, tradition, and law, in that he remains loyal even though his lord has unjustly severed the vassalic bond. Repeatedly, and with unwavering observance of vassalic etiquette, the Cid reaffirms this vassalage. His commitment is dramatized in the scene in which Alfonso seeks to honor him:

> El rrey dixo al Cid: "Venid acá ser, Campeador,
> en aqueste escaño quem' diestes vós en don;
> maguer que [*a*] algunos pesa, mejor sodes que nós."
> Essora dixo muchas merçedes el que Valençia gañó:
> "Sed en vuestro escaño commo rrey e señor,
> acá posaré con todos aquestos míos."
>
> (3114–19)

The king attempts to show extraordinary deference, inviting the vassal to sit beside him, but the Cid shows dignity even as he displays an exemplary humility. The poet portrays the Cid in this light so that the hero's humility stands in sympathetic contrast to the arrogance of the Infantes. There is also the pragmatic shrewdness of modesty as public policy. Alejandro Mosley ("De Vivar a Valencia") has astutely remarked that the Cid must maintain a "poker face," presenting to the world "la cara sufrida de un súbdito devoto y abnegado." He must, Job-like, suffer "pacientemente los embustes del demonio y ser por dentro un hombre muy astuto." He thereby highlights the scandalous nature of the Afrenta de Corpes, and accomplishes an ethical blackmail of his lord, shaming Alfonso into conciliatory behavior. And, finally, he models appropriate vassalic behavior for his men, exhibiting a seemly reserve in the most public and dramatic manner.

There is no such thing, in this delicately balanced world of keenly perceptive public opinion and consequent propensity for shame, as mere protocol. Infractions against the code of behavior directly threaten the cohesion of the body politic. Deference is a crucial component of inequality, and is concomitant to the man-to-man nature of relationships in the poem. A key to the work's sense of deference is its frequent depiction of the cere-mony of the *besamanos*. Michael (ed., n to 2039–40, p. 214), glosses the handkiss as "el beso de la fidelidad," noting both its antiquity in Hispanic feudal usage, and references to it in such works as the *Partidas* (IV.xxvi.2). Observing that the simple handkiss does not correspond to European feudal usage, he suggests that the Cid's kneeling down to kiss Alfonso's hand (2039: "Inoios fitos las manos le besó") may be attributed to "un exceso de meticulosidad, como si el Cid desease hacer absolutamente firme su nueva condición de vasallo." Michael compares this instance of the *besamanos* to other acts of deference, such as the Cid's prostration before the king, on hands and knees, when he eats "las yerbas del campo" (2021–22), or the hero's kiss delivered to his king (2040: "levós' en pie e en la bócal' saludó"), which provokes the approval of all witnesses (2041: "Todos los demás d'esto avién sabor").

The symbolic significance of the handkiss must be understood in association with other acts of deference. Jacques Le Goff interprets vassalic ceremony not on an "element-by-element" basis, but rather as an entire symbolic system, no part of which is intelligible without reference to the whole. He describes the "symbolic categories" that inform the performance of the ritual of vassalage ("speech, gesture, and objects") and attempts to explicate their connection to the three stages of entry into vassalage ("homage, faith, investiture of the fief"). French vassalic ritual included the *osculum* (kiss on the mouth), the *immixtio manuum* (interlacing of hands), and various symbolic objects, particularly the *festuca* (a stick, symbolizing authority). Le Goff points out that "medieval documents provide no symbolic interpretation of vassalage" and "offer few detailed descriptions of such rites." For this reason he takes an ethnographic approach, referring to documents and studies from a wide variety of periods and cultures ("Symbolic Ritual" 248–59).

Le Goff emphasizes the public nature of the vassalic rituals of feudalism. Such rites mark the relationship between two men, but as rites they are designed to verify the relationship before the world. In the observances portrayed in the *PMC*, however, it is both the man-to-man relationship and its exhibition before the world that matter. The *besamanos* and other symbolic acts of deference were, as Le Goff and many others have pointed out, extensions of kinship-oriented acts of deference. In kin-ordered societies, in other words, deferential behavior is performed on the basis of kin-defined inequalities. Vassalage takes its cue from family, and not the other way around ("Symbolic Ritual" 256–61). That is why, in the *PMC*, both wife and daughters perform the *besamanos*. The daughters, indeed, show deference to their father and mother: "Al padre a la madre las manos les besavan" (2607); "Besaron las manos las fijas al padre" (2895). But Jimena and her daughters show deference to the Cid not as to a lord or a great war leader, but rather as to a husband and father. We may assume that all fathers and husbands within the society of the *PMC* are granted the same treatment by their wives and children: this is deference expressed toward the holder of an ascriptive kinship status (i.e., father and husband). When the Infantes first approach the Cid, their respect is thus couched in terms of abject deference: " '¡Omillámosnos, Çid, en buen ora nasquiestes vós!' " (2053), while their subsequent association is marked by the *besamanos*: "ban besar las manos al que en ora buena naçió" (2092). Thus the Infantes show a filial rather than a vassalic deference to the Cid and his wife after the marriage: "a Mio Çid e a su mugier van besar la mano" (2235).

The Cid's vassals, on the other hand, express deference precisely because the Cid earns his patriarchal status. Since it is the kin-defined deference that determines the grammar of deference in the extrafamilial sphere—the more so in clear situations of fictive kinship, as in the case of vassalic relationships—kissing, especially handkissing, is the chief expression of vassalic deference in the poem. Indeed, there is scarcely an instance of kissing in the *PMC* that may be termed merely or uniquely affectionate. Familial affection is to be seen among the members of the hero's immediate family: "Mio Çid a sus fijas ívalas abraçar, / besándolas a amas, tornós' de sonrrisar" [2888–89]). But kissing is more frequently an adroit and purposeful manipulation of social situations. Thus, Alfonso, embarrassed by the Cid's abject prostration, sets limits on the degree of deference he exacts or will accept (thus implying degrees of deferentiality, of suitability of deference, always recalling that acceptance of deference compromises the person deferred to): " 'Levantados en pie, ya Çid Campeador, / besad las manos ca los pies no[n]; / si esto non feches, non avredes mi amor' " (2027–29). The Cid, remaining on his knees, uses exaggerated deferentiality in an aggressive way: "Inoios fitos sedié el Campeador: / 'Merçed vos pido a vós, mio natural señor, / assí estando, dédesme vuestra amor, / que lo oyan quantos aquí son' " (2030–32b). The Cid is careful to maintain a deferential attitude until after the public pardon is exacted (2033–35), allowing him to kiss the king publicly (2040). Later, the Cid's acceptance of Alfonso's offer of hospitality is accompanied by the handkiss: "Besóle la mano, Mio Çid lo otorgó" (2051). Following this, the Cid beseeches Alfonso to accept a gift, with the implication, conveyed through the formulaic assurance of handkissing, that deference will be granted in exchange for acceptance of the gift: " 'tomad aquesto e beso vuestras manos' " (2146).

The prevalence and multifarious utility of the *besamanos* are evident from a brief survey of examples. The Cid greets the king upon arriving at the final *vistas*: "besóle la mano e después le saludó" (3034); "Mio Çid la mano besó al rrey e en pie se levantó" (3145); "Reçibió [*el Çid*] las espadas, las manos le besó" (3180); "Levantós' Mio Çid, al rrey las manos le besó" (3414); "Mio Çid al rrey las manos le besó" (3486); "beso vuestras manos con vuestra graçia, señor" (3506); "Mio Çid en el cavallo adelant se llegó, / fue besar la mano a Alfonso so señor" (3511–12). Martín Antolínez, upon his acceptance of the sword Colada from the Cid's hands: "Besóle la mano, el espada tomó e rreçibió" (3198). The three champions of the Cid's cause salute Alfonso: "Besámosvos las manos commo a rrey e a señor" (3574). The emissaries of the princes of Navarre and Aragon, arriving at court to sue for the hand of the Cid's daughters, also show deference by handkissing: "Besan las manos al rrey don Alfonso" (3397); "besaron las manos del rrey don Alfonso" (3423). The Infantes' humiliation is accentuated by Minaya's expression of an envisioned deference, after the daughters have been betrothed to the heirs of Navarre and Aragon: "agora besaredes sus manos e llamar las hedes señoras" (3450).

The handkiss expresses greeting, gratitude, respect, supplication. The variety of contexts represented by the above examples shows how family and vassalage provide behavioral models for the greater set of social relations. The handkiss is, as it were, the currency of the exchange system embodied by deference. Deference may therefore be surrogated by means of a handkiss performed in the deferring person's stead, as when the Cid charges Muño Gustioz with bearing a message to the king: " 'Lieves el mandado a Castiella al rrey Alfonso, / por mí bésale la mano d'alma e de coraçón' " (2903–04). The Cid's vassal outdoes himself, just as his lord has already done. Kneeling before the king, Muño kisses the monarch's feet (2935), declaring: " 'Los pies e las manos vos besa el Campeador / ele es vuestro vassallo e vós sodes so señor' " (2937–38).

This example of surrogated deference includes a formula of salutation, a kind of rhetorical potlatch acknowledging the power and prestige of the monarch and renewing the vassalic bond between the Cid and Alfonso. Muño prefixes the request for justice, the primary content of his message, by reiterating verbally the deferential observance: " 'Por esto vos besa las manos  commo vassallo a señor' " (2948). Other examples of surrogated deference occur in the passage in which the Cid sends greetings ahead to the king (3016–17: "[*a*] Alvar Fáñez adelántel' enbió / que besasse las manos  al rrey so señor") and in the scene in which the Cid himself conveys the respects of his wife and daughters: " 'Mi mugier dona Ximena,  dueña es de pro, / bésavos las manos,  e mis fijas amas a dos' " (3039–40).

Hilda Grassotti has pointed out both the peculiarly Spanish nature of the vassalic *besamanos* and its extreme importance in epic poetry, law codes, and chronicles. Obscure in origin, the practice may have originated in Visigothic monastic ritual (involving the kissing of hands and feet), as exemplified by the phrase accompanying a description of an eighth-century king's donation of land for a monastery: "qui a nobis pedes osculaverunt." On the other hand, it is quite possible that the widespread use of deferential handkissing among the Arabs of Spain may have given rise to imitation and assimilation in Christian territory. Whatever its culture of origin, the practice, starting as a "fórmula de agradecimiento y de homenaje amistoso," became an indication of "humilde reconocimiento de la jerarquía superior de quien lo recibía." As a "práctica de habitual cortesía," it came gradually to signify the entrance into vassalage. Its function in this sense is illustrated by the scene already cited (298b), in which newcomers kiss the Cid's hand to indicate their entrance into a vassalic relationship with him (*Las instituciones feudo-vasalláticas* 1: 141–51).

Le Goff, commenting on the contrast between the Spanish *osculatio manuum* and the ceremonies of vassalage in the French style, notes that in the Spanish rite "the vassal's gesture of humility is much more pronounced." At the same time, he points out, in possible Arabic models or analogues, the importance of the reciprocity of the gesture ("Symbolic Ritual" 242, 359n16). The pronounced humility he remarks in the Spanish *besamanos* has, as we have seen, everything to do with the gesture's reciprocal nature. The humble submission, making for an offer that cannot be ignored, solicits a counterdeference, above all in a society in which modesty is so obviously valued.

In addition, the Spanish *besamanos*, while occasionally marking public entry into the lord-vassal relationship, is primarily reiterative and intermittent in its observation, and frequently occurs in private. In such cases it cannot be construed as a rite of "renewal" of vassalage, since its performance is invariable and circumstantial—in fact, formulaic, as etiquette is formulaic, rather than dramatic, as ritual is dramatic. What is more, persons clearly excluded from the vassalic category as defined in standard feudalism are allowed to perform the *besamanos*. Thus, in addition to the women of the Cid's family, already mentioned, we see the *besamanos* conferred upon the Cid by the Jewish moneylenders Rachel and Vidas (153, 159).

What we might be tempted to call the ethnographic primitivism of this poem—i.e., its prestratified "kin-orderedness," its commitment to the rule of amity—is not an unconscious expression of primordial mentality. Dyadism and its correlative conditions are endorsed; they are not simply depicted. The *PMC* presents the Cid's community as one of harmony, cooperation, altruism, generosity. The glorification of dyadism may well express nostalgia for a tradition utopically imagined. Leadership in such a vision is a symbiotic relationship: men in this poem are shown as wanting to defer and to obey because they think it proper to do so. The insubordination of Pero and of Bishop Jerome exemplifies the negative option open to every man in the simple and manly universe of amity. Forgoing the refractory alternative constitutes a deliberate act of cooperative generosity by each individual follower or family member.

The voluntarism underlying recruitment, vassalage, teamwork, and economic redistribution is incompatible with the coercion associated with social modernity. Constraint in the amicable universe is unenforceable—and impolite—because it adulterates the spontaneity of the follower's gift of fidelity. The *PMC* experiences social inequality as a resource to be managed rather than as a condition to be endured. The Cid is great because he commands loyalty without compulsion or intimidation. In this the *PMC* reveals its author, and presumably its original audience, to be conservative—even reactionary—in their support of idealized asymmetrical political and economic relationships. Power and privilege in this traditionalist schema are not inherent attributes of a ruling class, but trophies earned through individual heroic performance. To assume that social standing is ascribed rather than achieved, as do the Infantes de Carrión, is to partake of the degeneracy of such effete personages. The daughters' second marriages thus comprise not only the final humiliation of the villains of the piece, but also, in their preference of true royalty over counterfeit nobility, the repudiation of a way of life and of a social philosophy. At the same time, the invocation of a transcendent power to put the competing clan in its place facilitates the division-for-conquest which is the essence of the state.

# Notes

## Introduction

**1.** Antecedent to his chapter on "Historical, Literary, and Other Sources and Motives" (*Making* 137–79), perhaps the most thorough and reasonable survey of these topics in recent Cid scholarship, Colin Smith devotes chapters to the "Twelfth-Century Background" (9–48) and "The Cid in Legend and Literature of the Twelfth Century" (49–72). A very detailed and complete profile of the historical Cid is that of Jules Horrent in *Historia y poesía en torno al «Cantar del Cid»* (9–89). It is an indispensable tool for both the historicist scholar and—perhaps even especially—the antihistoricist determined to confirm the poet's departures from history.

**2.** The neotraditionalist position is summarized and eloquently defended by Samuel G. Armistead, "The *Mocedades de Rodrigo* and Neo-Individualist Theory." This is ably rebutted by Colin Smith, "Epics and Chronicles: A Reply to Armistead." The identification, based on a supposed common individualist orientation, of various British scholars—of whom Smith, Ian Michael, and Alan Deyermond are prominent examples—as a British "school" of Cidian criticism, has been rejected by the scholars so classified. There can be no question, they have pointed out (in places too numerous to cite here), of a critical school composed of such disparate perspectives.

**3.** John S. Miletich persuasively explicates the relevance of the Parry-Lord theory to Peninsular epic: "Medieval Spanish Epic and European Narrative Traditions" and "Folk Literature, Related Forms, and the Making of the *Poema de Mio Cid*." For a recent bibliographic survey of Parry-Lord studies relevant to medieval Spanish epic, see Ruth House Webber, "Hispanic Oral Literature: Accomplishments and Perspectives."

**4.** For Lord's original formulation of the theories of formula and theme (the latter term was *motif* in Parry's system), see his *Singer of Tales*, chs. 3 and 4.

**5.** The siglum *PMC* refers throughout the present study to the *Poema de Mio Cid*. All quotations, unless otherwise indicated, are from the edition of Ian Michael. Italics are as in this edition.

**6.** The Montgomery analysis in question is "The *Poema de Mio Cid*: Oral Art in Transition."

**7.** María Eugenia Lacarra 134–57; Catalán 811, 813–19.

**8.** For a more complete discussion of class structure and mentalities, with references to a number of critics who have written on these topics as they bear on the poem, see my "Class Conflict" 174–83.

**9.** The generalization concerning cross-cultural patterns of status emulation derives from research discussed in my "Estates Theory and Status Anxiety in the *Libro de los estados* and Other Medieval Spanish Texts," esp. pp. 15–20.

**10.** "Class Conflict" 206–17; also in "Movilidad social" 85–96.

**11.** See relevant entries in *History of the Family and Kinship* (Soliday et al.); also the seminal article by Peter Laslett, "The History of the Family."

**12.** Garci-Gómez's own recent work, such as "The Economy of Mio Cid," would seem to belie his expectations for a "pure" reading of the poem.

## Chapter One
## Kinship

**1.** Meyer Fortes notes the widespread adoption of Morgan's contrastive approach to kinship and descent, expressed by Morgan in terms of "kindred and gens." See Fortes 38.

**2.** Goody reproduces Isidore's genealogical schema (*Development* 143) from the saint's *Etymologiae* IX.vi.29.

**3.** Scheffler uses the term *ego-centric* throughout his discussion of the contrasts between kinship and descent ("Kinship" 756–65); in my own discussion I prefer to use the somewhat more specific *ego-centered*, because it is not, like *ego-centric*, a synonym of *self-centered*.

**4.** Much of the present discussion is concerned with the simultaneity of two or more apparently contradictory principles of descent. The bilateral kinship evident in the *PMC* must be understood from the perspective of studies done on so-called double descent systems, a topic that informs the present essay's discussion, but that is too ample a subject to treat of in detail here. See Goody, "The Classification of Double Descent Systems"; Daryll Forde, "Double Descent Among the Yakö"; Robin Fox 135–39.

**5.** Leyser's article is a reply to D. A. Bullough's "Early Medieval Social Groupings: The Terminology of Kinship," a study we will refer to in a later chapter, in connection with the meaning of *friend* in the medieval context. See also Leyser's "The German Aristocracy from the Ninth to the Early Twelfth Century."

**6.** See also Scheffler ("Kinship" 761), who discusses how bilateral kindreds readily lend themselves to the improvisation of impermanent "ad hoc 'action groups.'"

**7.** Marc Bloch discusses special traits of Peninsular feudalism (1: 186–89), a topic we will address more completely in our discussion of fictive kinship in the poem.

**8.** My statements on the historical or fictional nature of characters in the poem are based on Michael's onomastic index to his editon of the *PMC*. They are also drawn from Chalon 35–45. The latter provides such interesting details as the existence of the historical Cid's son Diego.

**9.** See also, for further literary examples of the avunculate in Germanic and Indo-European tradition, Bell 105–64.

**10.** Bremmer 68. See also Beekes 47.

**11.** Farnsworth's outmoded assumption of the primacy of "mother's-rights" as a primordial phase in societal development does not diminish the utility of his work as a survey of this theme in French epic.

**12.** See also, for additional relevant discussion of uncle-nephew relationships in matrilineal societies, Schneider and Gough 427, 169–70, 348–51, 600.

**13.** For a more extended discussion of patrilineal origins and structure, see Herlihy, *Medieval Households* 82–88.

**14.** Barlau 101, 104–06, 107, 118–21, 126–27.

**15.** Meinhard 6–12. Murray (22), in essential agreement with Meinhard, documents the long-standing predominance of the "Sippe-theory" (i.e., of primordial agnation in ancient Germanic kinship), characterizing "the patrilineal clan theory" as "a formalized, and even extreme aspect of German historiography."

**16.** The concept of simultaneity of kinship modes is supported by Goody, *Development* 224; also by Herlihy, *Medieval Households* 83.

**17.** Guichard 19; cited by Glick 141n15.

**18.** See also chs. 738 and 743 of *Primera Crónica General* (*Reliquias* 183.18–21, 192.17–22); also from *Crónica de 1344* (*Reliquias* 199.29–200.3, 213.7–214.17). The passages identifying the Moorish lover of Gonzalo as Zenla, the sister of Almanzor, are reconstructed by Menéndez Pidal, *Reliquias* (213–14, vv. 160–82).

**19.** *Reliquias* (*Siete Infantes*) 217, vv. 195–96; (*Crónica*) 217.3–20; (*Tercera crónica*) 217–18.

**20.** For an expanded discussion of class structure, from a different perspective than that conveyed by Anthony Giddens (cited in our Introduction), see Stanislav Ossowski, *Class Structure in the Social Consciousness* 72–73. See also my "Class Conflict" 175–83).

**21.** Herlihy, "Making" 124; *Medieval Households* 82. See also Duby, *Medieval Marriage* 11; Goody, *Development* 228–29.

## Chapter Two
## Amity

**1.** See also Shmuel N. Eisenstadt, "Ritualized Personal Relations"; George M. Foster, "Cofradía and Compadrazgo."

**2.** *Partidas* IV.vii.7, where the law clearly recognizes the function of adoption as a means of providing men with heirs; also, in greater detail, IV.xvi.1–10. Goody's generalization on the revival of adoption is found in *Development* 73. The *Partidas* also recognize godparenthood and tutelage (IV.vii.1–5; VI.xvi.1–21). Co- and godparenthood, as well as tutelage, figure in a wide range of institutionalized pseudo-kinship relationships. The practices so established tend to be adaptable to changing social and economic conditions, although, according to Sidney W. Mintz and Eric R. Wolf, in a much quoted study, with a pronounced bias, in many areas, toward facilitating "vertical" or cliental relations between families of disparate classes, as well as toward the solidification of "social relationships horizontally among members of the same rural neighborhood." See Mintz and Wolf 341, 347–49. The same broad array of amicable practices has been studied by Joseph H. Lynch, with specific focus on the European Middle Ages, as expressions of what he calls the "sponsorship complex," incorporating sponsorship, spiritual kinship of various kinds, and a number of other practices, including adoption. See Lynch 59–60, as well as Stephen Gudeman, *"Compadrazgo* as a Reflection,"* commended by Lynch (59, 62–63) as a revision of the hypothesis of Mintz and Wolf, which Lynch criticizes for its questionable secondary sources, and a historical introduction that "telescopes" legislative and anecdotal sources from many times and regions, thus conveying a view of the Middle Ages as "an undifferentiated whole" (Lynch 65). Seeking to correct Mintz and Wolf, who "retrojected" Latin American findings into medieval contexts, Lynch points out that (66–67), in contrast to the Latin American emphasis on relationships among co-parents, the European Middle Ages tended always and everywhere to emphasize *padrinazgo*—the relationship between godparent and godchild.

3. Marc Bloch 1: 123–24; Bullough 12; Heers 73; Hinojosa, "La fraternidad artificial" 259.

4. Pitt-Rivers, "Pseudo-Kinship" 410.

5. Heers 169–201, 215–21.

6. Colin Smith, *Poema* App. 1, p. 167.

7. *Mesnada(s)* referring to the Cid's forces: 487, 662, 745, 837, 1083, 1115, 1601, 1674, 1736, 2294; to those of Alfonso: 509, 528, 1980, 1982, 2038, 3128. Another time it is used by the Cid to indicate, somewhat dismissively, the forces of Count Remont of Barcelona, as he tells his men that a disparity of numbers in the count's favor should be of no concern: " 'çiento cavalleros   devemos vençer aquellas mesnadas' " (995).

8. Sahlins, "Ideology and Composition" 104–07; cited and discussed by Maurice Bloch 76.

9. Duggan 30–36. See also Porter Conerly, "Largesse of the Epic Hero as a Thematic Pattern in the *Cantar de Mio Cid.*" The redistributive economy, including the ethical and political implications of charismatic largesse, will be discussed in greater detail, with reference to such theoreticians as Mauss and Polanyi, in our chapter on polity.

10. Mayer, "Significance of Quasi-Groups" 112, 117–18; see also his *Caste and Kinship* 4.

11. Pitt-Rivers, "Kith and the Kin" 98. Prestation (*OED* 12: 425) comes from Lat. *præstationem* (v. *præstare,* "to give, to render"), the "action of lending, tendering." In modern anthropological usage, it is the "gift, payment, or service that forms part of some traditional function in a society, given or due either to specific persons or to the group." The counterprestation responds to and is prompted by an initial prestation; it may be

different in kind from the prestation (thus service in response to material gift, symbolic gesture as reply to service, etc.).

**12.** The economic implications of societal commitment to redistribution are discussed by Polanyi, "Economy as Instituted Process" 243–50.

## Chapter Three
## Marriage

**1.** Colin Smith, *Making* 74–86, esp. pp. 78 and 228–29n9; Hinojosa, "El derecho" 571–72. García González points out the legal discrepancy— indicating a depiction of reality which must be characterized as "poco exacta"—of the *PMC*'s oversight in regard to consultation of the wife (541–42).

**2.** García González (537, 539) emphasizes that Alfonso's matchmaking must be seen as an "acto amistoso, sin especial significación jurídica." The family of the Infantes is not a factor because the consent of males was not deemed essential. On the other hand, Alfonso apparently exercises *potestad* over the Infantes, which he transmits to the Cid (vv. 2101, 2121, 2125). The Infantes are very probably the king's *vasallos de criazón;* he is therefore, in effect, their foster father.

**3.** Derek W. Lomax argues ("The Date") that the year mentioned in the PMC's colophon (1207) may indeed refer to the date of composition, a possibility disregarded by many scholars, most notably Menéndez Pidal. Lomax's appraisal of various theories is informed by a healthy skepticism: for instance, the "sacred date" of 1140, accepted for many years, is "merely a whim of Menéndez Pidal, reinforced by the literary historians' insatiable thirst for exact dates and their reluctance to believe that sometimes these may not be ascertainable" (76). Lomax comes to the reasonable conclusion that "we simply do not know when the poem was written," although such evidence as there is, both historical and linguistic, suggests the work was composed "in the reign, and probably in the kingdom of, Alfonso VIII." Meanwhile, 1207 "has at least the authority of the only manuscript" (81).

**4.** Goody, *Development* 46–47, 151–53. Goody's very powerful theory has been variously criticized as too programmatic, too voluntarist, too "economistic." See Herlihy, *Medieval Households* 13; Brundage 606–07; Davis 149–50; and Verdery 265–68.

**5.** Dillard points out that the ecclesiastical innovators did not all pose an equal threat to lineal prerogatives: "[the view] of Gratian, who advised parental guidance, represented a less serious threat to secular custom than did Lombard's and not all customs were out of step with Gratian's assumption that fathers did and should arrange their children's marriages, especially those of their daughters" (41).

**6.** The foregoing discussion is the distillate of readings—with an eye to the *PMC*—from Bourdieu's discussion of "officializing strategies"

(38–43), "collective beliefs and white lies" (43–52), and above all, "matrimonial strategies and social reproduction" (58–71).

7. The statistical preponderance of the word *fija* in the poem first came to my attention through the insight of Sally Stokes, "Language of Kinship" 39–41.

8. Hallet 64–65, 66–67, 90, 205, 291.

9. Goody, "Bridewealth and Dowry" 17–18; Goody, "Strategies of Heirship" 10–13.

10. Menéndez Pidal, *España del Cid* 1: 219; Chalon 25.

11. Menéndez Pidal, *En torno* 212.

12. Guichard 19, 41–47; Patai 258–62.

13. Klass 98–100; Mayer, *Caste and Kinship* 205–06.

14. Duby, *Medieval Marriage* 68; also his *Knight, Lady, Priest* 94.

15. Duby, *Knight, Lady, Priest* 144; "Le Mariage dans la société du haut Moyen Age" 29–30; "Dans la France du Nord-Ouest" 216, 219. See also, on the question of heiress-hunting by young nobles, Verkauteren, "A Kindred in Northern France" 96–100.

16. Hinojosa, "El derecho" 578; García González 562–63, 564; Pavlović and Walker, "Money, Marriage and the Law" 204–05.

17. Goody, "Bridewealth and Dowry" 6. Herlihy notes Tacitus's conflation of the concepts of *bridewealth* and *reverse dowry*, citing *Germania* 18: "among the Germans the groom brings a dowry to the bride, not the bride to the groom." Herlihy notes further: that "this reverse dowry or bridewealth is the universal rule of marriage throughout the early Middle Ages" (*Medieval Households* 50).

18. Merêa, "Sobre a palavra «arras»" 140–41; Herlihy, *Medieval Households* 7.

19. Hughes, "From Brideprice to Dowry" 263–64; see also Levy, 140–41.

20. Merêa, "O dote nos documentos" 61. The betrothal document he cites is reprinted from Menéndez Pidal, *España del Cid* 2: 96–99. "Et dono tibi," the document pledges, "istas villas que sunt suprascriptas pro ipsas villas que michi saccarunt Albaro Faniz et Albaro Albariz, sobrinis meis, propter ipsas dono tibi istas que superius diximus ab omni integritate, terras, vineas, arbores, seu pomiferis, pasquis, seu padulibus aquis aquarum, defesas et in molinarum sive exitus etiam et regressus."

21. Harrel and Dickey 108–09; Lisón-Tolosana 158.

22. Dillard 27; see also 227n36 for references to the extensive number of *fueros* supporting this generalization.

# Chapter Four
## Polity

1. Weber, "Class, Status, and Party" 180; also, in the same collection, "Structures of Power" 159–62, 172–79; "Bureaucracy" 196–98, 204–09, 212–14, 221–35.

**2.** Walker 260. See also Hinojosa, "El derecho" 544, and Hart, "Hierarchical Patterns" 162–64. María Eugenia Lacarra (115–16, 160–63), disputing Menéndez Pidal's "democratic" vision of the *PMC*'s social world, suggests that the Valencian society founded by the Cid is at least as hierarchical as that of Castile and León.

**3.** Alejandro Mosley, in an unpublished ms. ("De Vivar a Valencia: el ascenso épico del que en buena hora nació"), presents an ingenious analysis of the Cid's pragmatic political motives in his apparent humility. As a leader of unruly followers, argues Mosley, Rodrigo must act the part of the respectful, obedient, self-deprecating vassal; otherwise he risks encouraging his own men to violate their own vassalic obligations toward him.

**4.** Finley 83–84. I cite his work not as social science, but as a meditation on society as portrayed in epics. Precisely because he never mentions medieval epic, parallels that emerge from correlation of his analysis of Homer with my own examination of the *PMC* are suggestive of very deep narrative structures grounded in social context.

**5.** Pospisil 3–7; Wright 90 (quoted by Pospisil 3).

**6.** Duggan 64, 66–67. María Eugenia Lacarra 65–101, 255; Colin Smith, *Making* 75–86.

**7.** Weber, "Nature of Charismatic Authority" 52. See also Eisenstadt, Introduction to *Max Weber* xlii–xliii.

**8.** Duggan 5, 17, 20–26, 30, 33, 34, 36.

**9.** See also Maddicott 294–95; Keen, "Robin Hood—Peasant or Gentleman?" 9–10, and *Outlaws of Medieval Legend* 147–50. The definitive explication of banditry and its implications is that of Hobsbawm, *Bandits* chs. 1 and 2; the relevance of his studies to *PMC* scholarship is covered in my "Class Conflict" 206–17.

**10.** Polanyi, "Economy as Instituted Process" 250–54. He cites as examples of a redistributive phase of economic development (again, characterized by "collecting into, and distributing from, a center"): "the Central African *kraal*, the Hebrew patriarchal household, the Greek estate of Aristotle's time, the Roman *familia*, the medieval manor, or the typical large peasant household before the general marketing of grain" (254). It is this redistributive common denominator, as defined by Polanyi, that, I believe, permits us to compare the *PMC* with such apparently disparate contexts as the legends of Robin Hood and Shaka Zulu, and the modern urban folklore devoted to such gangsters as Al Capone. See my "Movilidad social" 89–97.

**11.** Sorokin 522–25; see also Ellis and Lane 538. The only study specifically devoted to the topic of social mobility in the *PMC* remains Guglielmi, "Cambio y movilidad social en el *Cantar de Mio Cid*." However, see also my "Class Conflict" 194–203.

**12.** See, concerning European patterns, Perroy 26–30; Runciman 3–8, 26–30. For the Spanish context, see José María Lacarra 48–53; Carlé,

"Caminos del ascenso" 250–74; Royer de Cardinal 277–328; Powers 162–87. For cross-cultural discussions, see Matras 401–08; Cancian 237–40; Raymond T. Smith, "Anthropology and the Concept of Social Class" 470–89.

**13.** María Eugenia Lacarra 163. See also Sánchez Albornoz 2: 77 ff.; Pescador, "La caballería popular" (1961): 126–47; also MacKay, *Spain in Middle Ages* 47–50; Glick 154–60.

**14.** See Pearson, "Aspects of Social Mobility" 155–59.

**15.** Heers 25. See also MacKay, "Lesser Nobility" 171–75.

**16.** For the practical social implications of *Königsnähe*, see Schmid, "Structure of Nobility" 38–39.

**17.** Caro Baroja, "City and Country" 29–30, 34. See also Stock 26–28 for a detailed meditation on the rhetorical and philosophical impact of the city/country topos on medieval literary culture.

**18.** Fried, "State" 145–46. Bernard Crick defines the concept as a theory that "in every system of government there must be some absolute power of final decision exercised by some person or body recognized both as competent to decide and as able to enforce the decision." The rise of the theory of sovereignty is coterminous with the emergence of national states, and is an integral element of their rationale and their propaganda: "Sovereignty sees the world in the light of survival alone and is most appropriate as a theory when the world of settled expectations seems urgently threatened." The idea originated "as an expression of the search for a purely secular basis for authority amid the new state organizations in Europe of the sixteenth and seventeenth centuries" (Crick 77).

**19.** Joseph P. Strayer summarizes the features of the nascent states of twelfth- and thirteenth-century Europe in terms very similar to the general theoretical descriptions of Fried, Watkins, and Tilly (Strayer 32–35).

**20.** Menéndez Pidal, *España del Cid* 1: 29–45; 65–66, 78, 88–89.

## Chapter Five
## Conclusion: Deference and Inequality

**1.** For another perspective on functional tripartition in Indo-European society, see Benveniste (2: 279–92). He suggests that this functional division was not the effective basis of social organization among early Indo-European peoples; rather, political and social structures were forged by means of the extensive vocabulary centering on family, lineage, clan, house, tribe, and territory (2: 293–319).

**2.** I summarize here from Dumont's extensive discussion of tripartite structures in *Homo Hierarchicus* 21, 66–67, 69, 71–74, 74–75. For views of caste and social functionality that examine aspects of these phenomena other than the hierarchical, see Marriot and Inden (982–85, 989–91) and Raheja (24–36, 212–47).

**3.** Peristiany, Introduction 11. Joan Ramon Resina points out the significance of the Cid's honor from the viewpoint of what we might call his constituents: "Los valores que le elevan a la categoría de modelo son los del pueblo que se siente ratificado, y en cierta manera representado por su héroe" (419).

**4.** Berreman suggests a three-stage development, with an intermediate phase he characterizes as one of "kin/role ranking." In such a context "ranking depends on position in the kin system," as well as on religious or military roles ("Social Inequality" 9–10).

**5.** For statements of the earlier theories, Flanagan critiques: Fortes and Evans-Pritchard, Introduction, *African Political Systems* 5; Lawrence Krader 11–28; Southall, "Stateless Society"; Service 47–102; Fried, *Evolution of Political Society* 33–79; see as well, Hatch 342–45, 350–53.

**6.** Flanagan 248. With regard to minimal stratification, he cites Sahlins, *Social Stratification in Polynesia* 1.

**7.** Shils, "Deference" 421.

**8.** Bossen 133, 142. Both Irigaray and Bossen are cited by Flanagan, who summarizes the recent feminist polemic concerning the "androcentric bias" of Lévi-Strauss's model of the circulation and exchange of women (251–52).

**9.** For the *epiclerate* in general ethnographic terms, see studies cited in Chapter Three, esp. Pitt-Rivers, "Pseudo-Kinship" 408–09; Goody, "Bridewealth and Dowry " 17–18, and his "Strategies of Heirship."

**10.** Service 83; Turnbull 31.

**11.** Mead, *Cooperation and Competition* 493–505; cited and discussed in Piers and Singer 64–65.

**12.** Concerning the predatory economics of raiding warfare in medieval Spain, see Powers (162–87). For banditry and raiding as a way of life, see Hobsbawm (*Bandits* 30–40, 83–97), as well as Patai (36, 79, 208, 264) and Cole (85–88, 120, 139). The latter two discuss raiding warfare as an element in a vanishing way of life.

**13.** Pitt-Rivers, "Honour and Social Status" 34.

**14.** Ganshof 39–43, 46–48, 77–78. See also García de Valdeavellano's appendix to Ganshof, "Las instituciones feudales en España" 233, 253–63.

# Bibliography

Aberle, David F. "Navaho." Schneider and Gough 96–201.

Ake, Claude. "Charismatic Legitimation and Political Integration." *CSSH* 9 (1966): 1–13.

Alfonso X, el Sabio. *Siete Partidas del rey don Alfonso el Sabio.* Real Academia de la Historia. Nueva ed. 5 vols. Paris: Librería de Rosa y Bouret, 1861. Rpt. of 1807 ed. 3 vols. Madrid: Imprenta Real.

Alonso, Amado. "¡Dios, qué buen vasallo! ¡Sí oviesse buen señore!" *RFH* 6 (1944): 187–91.

Apter, David E. "Government." *IESS* 6: 214–30.

Ardant, Gabriel. "Financial Policy and Economic Infrastructure of Modern States and Nations." Tilly, *Formation* 164–242.

Armistead, Samuel G. "The *Mocedades de Rodrigo* and Neo-Individualist Theory." *HR* 46 (1978): 313–27.

Banton, Michael, ed. *The Social Anthropology of Complex Societies.* Association of Social Anthropologists of the Commonwealth, Monographs 4. London: Tavistock, 1966.

Barbero, Abilio, and Marcelo Vigil. *La formación del feudalismo en la Península Ibérica.* Barcelona: Editorial Crítica, 1978.

——. *Sobre los orígenes sociales de la Reconquista.* Barcelona: Ariel, 1974.

Barbero, Alessandro. "Lignaggio, famiglia ed entourage signorile nel *Cantar de Mio Cid." Annali della Scuola Normale Superiore di Pisa: Classe di Lettere e Filosofia* 14.1 (1984): 45–117.

Barlau, Stephen B. "Germanic Kinship." *JIES* 4 (1976): 97–129.

Barth, Frederic. "Descent and Marriage Reconsidered." Goody, *Character* 3–19.

Bartlett, Robert. "Colonial Aristocracies of the High Middle Ages." Bartlett and MacKay 23–47.

Bartlett, Robert, and Angus MacKay, eds. *Medieval Frontier Societies.* Oxford: Clarendon, 1989.

Basehart, Harry W. "Ashanti." Schneider and Gough 270–97.

Beattie, J. H. M., and R. G. Lienhardt, eds. *Studies in Social Anthropology: Essays in Memory of E. E. Evans-Pritchard by His Former Oxford Colleagues.* Oxford: Clarendon, 1975.

Beekes, Robert S. P. "Uncle and Nephew." *JIES* 4 (1976): 43–63.

Beidelmann, T. O., ed. *The Translation of Culture.* London: Tavistock, 1971.

Bell, Claire H. *Sister's Son in the Medieval Epic*. University of California Publications in Modern Philology 10. Berkeley: U of California P, 1922.

Bellini, Giuseppe, ed. *Aspetti e problemi delle letterature iberiche: Studi offerti a Franco Meregalli*. Rome: Bulzoni, 1981.

Benabou, Marcel. "Pratique matrimoniale et représentation philosophique: Le Crépuscule des stratégies." *AESC* 42 (1987): 1255–66.

Bendix, Reinhard. "Tradition and Modernity Reconsidered." *Essays in Comparative Social Stratification*. Ed. Leonard Plotnicov and Arthur Tuden. Pittsburgh: U of Pittsburgh P, 1970. 273–336.

Bendix, Reinhard, and Seymour M. Lipset, eds. *Class, Status, and Power*. 2nd ed. New York: Free, 1966.

Benedict, Burton. "Societies, Small." *IESS* 14: 572–77.

Benveniste, Emile. *Le Vocabulaire des institutions indo-européenes*. 2 vols. Paris: Editions de Minuit, 1969.

Berman, Harold J. "Legal Reasoning." *IESS* 9: 197–204.

Bermejo Cabrero, José Luis. "Sobre nobleza, señoríos y mayorazgos." *AHDE* 55 (1985): 253–305.

Berreman, Gerald D. "Caste. The Concept of Caste." *IESS* 2: 337–38.

——. "Race, Caste, and Other Invidious Distinctions in Social Classification." *Race* 13 (1972): 385–414.

——, ed. *Social Inequality: Comparative and Developmental Approaches*. New York: Academic, 1981.

——. "Social Inequality: A Cross-Cultural Analysis." Berreman, *Social Inequality* 3–40.

Blanco Aguinaga, Carlos, Julio Rodríguez Puértolas, and Iris M. Zavala. "Edad Media." *Historia social de la literatura española*. 2nd ed. 3 vols. Madrid: Castalia, 1986. 1: 51–219.

Bloch, Marc. *Feudal Society*. Trans. L. A. Manyon. 2 vols. Chicago: U of Chicago P, 1961.

Bloch, Maurice. "The Long Term and the Short Term: The Economic and Political Significance of the Morality of Kinship." Goody, *Character* 75–87.

Bloch, R. Howard. *Etymologies and Genealogies: A Literary Anthropology of the French Middle Ages*. Chicago: U of Chicago P, 1983.

——. *Medieval French Literature and Law*. Berkeley: U of California P, 1977.

Blok, Anton. *The Mafia of a Sicilian Village, 1860–1960*. Oxford: Blackwell, 1974.

———. "The Peasant and the Brigand: Social Banditry Reconsidered." *CSSH* 14 (1972): 494–503.

Bluestine, Carolyn. "The Role of Women in the *Poema de Mio Cid*." *Romance Notes* 18 (1978): 404–09.

Bohannan, Paul, ed. *Law and Warfare: Studies in the Anthropology of Conflict*. Austin: U of Texas P, 1967.

———. "Law: Law and Legal Institutions." *IESS* 9: 75–78.

Bohannan, Paul, and John Middleton, eds. *Kinship and Social Organization*. Garden City: Natural History, 1968.

———, eds. *Marriage, Family and Residence*. Garden City: Natural History, 1968.

Bossen, Laurel. "Toward a Theory of Marriage: The Economic Anthropology of Marriage Transactions." *Ethnology* 27 (1988): 127–44.

Bouchard, Constance R. "Consanguinity and Noble Marriages in the Tenth and Eleventh Centuries." *Speculum* 56 (1981): 268–87.

Bourdieu, Pierre. *Outline of a Theory of Practice*. Trans. Richard Nice. Cambridge Studies in Social Anthropology 16. Cambridge: Cambridge UP, 1977.

Bremmer, Jan. "Avunculate and Fosterage." *JIES* 4 (1976): 65–75.

Brenner, Robert. "Agrarian Class Structure and Economic Development in Pre-industrial Europe." *P&P* 70 (1976): 30–75.

Brooke, Christopher N. L. *The Medieval Idea of Marriage*. Oxford: Oxford UP, 1989.

Brooks, Peter. *Reading for the Plot*. New York: Vintage, 1985.

Brown, Elizabeth. "The Tyranny of a Construct: Feudalism and Historians of Medieval Europe." *American Historical Review* 79 (1974): 1063–88.

Brundage, James A. *Law, Sex and Christian Society in Medieval Europe*. Chicago: U of Chicago P, 1987.

Bullough, D. A. "Early Medieval Social Groupings: The Terminology of Kinship." *P&P* 45 (1969): 3–18.

Burdeau, G. "Delegation of Powers." *IESS* 4: 72–74.

Burns, Norman T., and Christopher Reagan, eds. *Concepts of the Hero in the Middle Ages and the Renaissance*. Albany: State U of New York P, 1975; London: Hodder and Stoughton, 1976.

Burns, Robert I., S.J. "The Significance of the Frontier in the Middle Ages." Bartlett and MacKay 307–30.

Campbell, J. K. *Honour, Family and Patronage*. New York and Oxford: Oxford UP, 1964.

Cancian, Frank. "Social Stratification." *ARA* 5 (1976): 227–48.

Carlé, María del Carmen. "Caminos del ascenso en la Castilla bajo-medieval." *CHE* 65–66 (1981): 207–76.

———. "Infanzones e hidalgos." *CHE* 33–34 (1961): 56–100.

Caro Baroja, Julio. "The City and the Country: Reflexions on Some Ancient Commonplaces." Pitt-Rivers, *Mediterranean Countrymen* 27–40.

———. "Honour and Shame." Peristiany, *Honour and Shame* 81–137.

Catalán, Diego. "El *Mio Cid*: nueva lectura de su intencionalidad política." Melena 807–19.

Chalon, Louis. *L'Histoire et l'épopée castillane du Moyen Age: Le Cycle du Cid, le Cycle des comtes de Castille.* Paris: Champion, 1976.

Chasca, Edmund de. *El arte juglaresco en el "Cantar de Mio Cid."* 2nd ed. Madrid: Gredos, 1972.

———. "The King-Vassal Relationship in the *Poema de Mio Cid.*" *HR* 21 (1953): 183–92.

Cheyette, Frederic L., ed. *Lordship and Community in Medieval Europe.* Selected Readings. New York: Holt, 1968.

Claessen, Henri J. M., and Peter Skalník, eds. *The Study of the State.* The Hague: Mouton, 1981.

Cohen, Ronald, and John Middleton, eds. *Comparative Political Systems.* Garden City: Natural History, 1967.

Cole, Donald Powell. *Nomads of the Nomads.* Arlington Heights, IL: Davidson, 1975.

Collier, Jane Fishburne. *Marriage and Inequality in Classless Societies.* Stanford: Stanford UP, 1988.

Collomp, Alain. "Ménage et famille: Études comparatives sur la dimension et la structure du groupe domestique (note critique)." *AESC* 29 (1974): 777–86.

Comaroff, John L. "Bridewealth and the Control of Ambiguity." Comaroff, *Meaning* 160–96.

———. Introduction. Comaroff, *Meaning* 1–47.

———, ed. *The Meaning of Marriage Payments.* New York: Academic, 1980.

Conerly, Porter. "Largesse of the Epic Hero as a Thematic Pattern in the *Cantar de Mio Cid.*" *Kentucky Romance Quarterly* 31 (1984): 281–89.

Corbier, Mireille. "Les Comportements familiaux de l'aristocratie ro-
maine (IIᵉ siècle avant J.-C.—IIIᵉ siècle après J.-C.)." *AESC* 42
(1987): 1267–85.

Corfis, Ivy A. "The Count of Barcelona Episode and French Customary
Law in the *Poema de Mio Cid*." *La Corónica* 12 (1984): 169–74.

Coriden, James A., Thomas J. Green, and Donald E. Heintschal, eds. *The
Canon Law: A Text and Commentary*. New York: Paulist, 1985.

Corominas, Joan, and José A. Pascual, eds. *Diccionario crítico
etimológico castellano e hispánico*. 6 vols. Madrid: Gredos,
1980–91.

Correa, Gustavo. "El tema de la honra en el *Poema del Cid*." *HR* 20
(1952): 185–99.

Critchley, John. *Feudalism*. London: Allen, 1978.

Crick, Bernard. "Sovereignty." *IESS* 15: 77–82.

Dahrendorf, Ralf. "On the Origin of Inequality Among Men." Laumann
et al. 3–30. Rpt. from *Essays in the Theory of Society*. Stanford:
Stanford UP, 1968. 151–78.

Dalton, George, ed. *Tribal and Peasant Economies*. Austin: U of Texas
P, 1981. Rpt. from Natural History Press ed., New York:
Doubleday, 1967.

Davis, Natalie. Rev. of Goody's *Development of the Family and Marriage
in Europe*. *American Ethnologist* 12 (1985): 149–51.

Day, John. *The Medieval Market Economy*. Oxford: Blackwell, 1987.

De Heusch, L. "The Debt of the Maternal Uncle." *Man* 9 (1974): 609–16.

Deyermond, Alan. *El «Cantar de Mio Cid» y la épica medieval española*.
Biblioteca General 2. Madrid: Sirmio, 1987.

——, ed. *Medieval Hispanic Studies Presented to Rita Hamilton*. London: Tamesis, 1976.

——. "Medieval Spanish Epic Cycles: Observations on Their Formulation and Development." *Kentucky Romance Quarterly* 23
(1976): 281–303.

——, ed. *"Mio Cid" Studies*. London: Tamesis, 1977.

——. "A Monument for Per Abad: Colin Smith on the Making of the
*Poema de Mio Cid*." *BHS* 62 (1985): 120–26.

——. "La sexualidad en la épica medieval española." *NRFH* 36 (1988):
767–86.

——. "Tendencies in 'Mio Cid' Scholarship, 1943–73." Deyermond,
*"Mio Cid"* 13–47.

Deyermond, Alan, and Margaret Chaplin. "Folk Motifs in the Medieval Spanish Epic." *Philological Quarterly* 51 (1972): 36–53.

Diamond, Arthur S. *Primitive Law, Past and Present.* London: Methuen, 1971.

Diamond, Stanley, ed. *Culture in History.* New York: Columbia UP, 1960.

Dick, Ernst S. "Bridesman in Indo-European Tradition: Ritual and Myth in Marriage Ceremonies." *Journal of American Folklore* 79 (1966): 338–47.

Dillard, Heath. *Daughters of the Reconquest.* Cambridge: Cambridge UP, 1984.

Dixon, Suzanne. "The Marriage Alliance in the Roman Elite." *JFH* 10 (1985): 353–78.

Donahue, Charles, Jr. "The Canon Law in the Formation of Marriage and Social Practice in the Later Middle Ages." *JFH* 8 (1983): 144–58.

Dore, Ronald P. "Modernization. The Bourgeoisie in Modernizing Societies." *IESS* 10: 402–09.

Douglass, William A. "Iberian Family History." *JFH* 13 (1988): 1–12.

Doyle, Thomas P., S.P. Intro. and comment. to Title VII, "Marriage," cc. 1055–1165. Coriden et al. 737–833.

Dozy, Reinhart. *Recherches sur l'histoire et la littérature de l'Espagne pendant le moyen âge.* 3rd ed. 2 vols. Leyden: Brill, 1881.

Duby, Georges. "Dans la France du Nord-Ouest au XIIᵉ siècle: Les 'Jeunes' dans la société aristocratique." Duby, *Hommes et structures* 213–25.

——. "The Diffusion of Cultural Patterns in Feudal Society." *P&P* 39 (1968): 3–10.

——. *The Early Growth of the European Economy.* Trans. Howard B. Clarke. London: Weidenfeld, 1974.

——. *Hommes et structures du Moyen Age.* Paris: Mouton, 1973.

——. *The Knight, the Lady and the Priest.* Trans. Barbara Bray. New York: Pantheon, 1983.

——. "Lineage, Nobility, and Chivalry in the Region of Mâcon during the Twelfth Century." Forster and Ranum 16–40.

——. "Manorial Economy." *IESS* 9: 562–65.

——. "Le Mariage dans la société du haut Moyen Age." *Matrimonio Società altomedievale* 2: 15–39.

——. *Medieval Marriage: Two Models from 12th-Century France.* Trans. Elborg Forster. Baltimore: Johns Hopkins UP, 1978.

———. "Structures de parenté et noblesse dans la France du Nord aux XIᵉ et XIIᵉ siècles." Duby, *Hommes et structures* 267–85.

———. *The Three Orders: Feudal Society Imagined*. Trans. Arthur Goldhammer. Chicago: U of Chicago P, 1980.

Duby, Georges, and Jacques Le Goff, eds. *Famille et parenté dans l'occident médiéval*. Rome: Ecole Française de Rome, 1977.

Dufourcq, C. E., and J. Gautier-Dalché. "Les Royaumes chrétiens en Espagne au temps de la 'Reconquista,' d'après les recherches récentes." *RH* 248 (1972): 367–402.

———. "Economies, sociétés, institutions de l'Espagne Chrétienne du moyen âge." *RH* 79 (1973): 73–122; 285–319.

Duggan, Joseph J. *The "Cantar de Mio Cid": Poetic Creation in Its Economic and Social Contexts*. Cambridge: Cambridge UP, 1989.

Dumézil, Georges. *L'Idéologie tripartie des Indo-Européens* Brussels: Latomus, Revue d'Etudes Latines, 1958.

Dumont, Louis. *Homo Hierarchicus: The Caste System and Its Implications*. Rev. Eng. ed. Trans. Mark Sainsbury, Louis Dumont, Basia Gulati. Chicago: U of Chicago P, 1980. Orig. publ. 1970.

Dundes, Alan, ed. *The Study of Folklore*. Englewood Cliffs: Prentice, 1965.

Eggan, Fred. "Kinship. Introduction." *IESS* 8: 390–401.

Eisenstadt, Shmuel N. Introduction. Eisenstadt, *On Charisma* i–lvi.

———, ed. *Max Weber: On Charisma and Institution Building*. Chicago: U of Chicago P, 1968.

———. "Ritualized Personal Relations." *Man* 56 (1956): 90–95.

Ellis, Robert A., and W. Clayton Lane. "Social Mobility and Social Isolation: A Test of Sorokin's Dissociative Hypothesis." Lopreato and Lewis 523–39.

England, John, ed. *Hispanic Studies in Honour of Frank Pierce Presented by Former and Present Members of the Department of Hispanic Studies in the University of Sheffield*. Sheffield: Dept. of Hispanic Studies, U of Sheffield, 1980.

*Espagnes Médiévales: Aspects économiques et sociaux: Mélanges offerts à Jean Gautier Dalché*. Nice: Annales de la Faculté des Lettres et Sciences Humaines, 1983.

Evans-Pritchard, E. E. *The Nuer: A Description of the Modes of Livelihood and Political Institutions of a Nilotic People*. Oxford: Clarendon, 1940.

Fallers, Lloyd A. *Inequality: Social Stratification Reconsidered*. Chicago: U of Chicago P, 1973.

Fallers, Lloyd A., ed. *The King's Men*. London: Oxford UP, 1964.

Farnsworth, William O. *Uncle and Nephew in the Old French Chansons de Geste*. New York: Columbia UP, 1913.

Finley, M. I. *The World of Odysseus*. London: Chatto, 1956.

Fischer, Claude S. "The Dispersion of Kinship Ties in Modern Society: Contemporary Data and Historical Speculation." *JFH* 7 (1982): 353–75.

Flanagan, James G. "Hierarchy in Simple Egalitarian Societies." *ARA* 18 (1989): 245–66.

Fletcher, Richard. *The Quest for El Cid*. New York: Knopf, 1990.

Foley, John Miles, ed. *Oral Tradition in Literature*. Columbia: U of Missouri P, 1986.

Foley, John Miles, and Robert P. Creed, eds. *Oral Traditional Literature: A Festschrift for Albert Bates Lord*. Columbus, OH: Slavica, 1981.

Forde, Daryll. "Double Descent Among the Yakö." Bohannan and Middleton, *Kinship* 179–91. Abr., rpt. of chs. 3, 4 of his *Yakö Studies*. London: Oxford UP, 1964.

Forster, Robert, and Orest Ranum, eds. *Family and Society: Selections from the Annales*. Baltimore: Johns Hopkins UP, 1976.

Fortes, Meyer. *Kinship and the Social Order: The Legacy of Lewis Henry Morgan*. Chicago: Aldine, 1969.

Fortes, Meyer, and E. E. Evans-Pritchard. Introduction. Fortes and Evans-Pritchard 1–23.

——, eds. *African Political Systems*. London: Oxford UP, 1940.

Foster, George M. "Cofradía and Compadrazgo in Spain and South America." *SJA* 9 (1953): 1–28.

Fox, Dian. "Pero Vermúez and the Politics of the Cid's Exile." *MLR* 78 (1983): 319–27.

Fox, Robin. *Kinship and Marriage: An Anthropological Perspective*. Baltimore and Harmondsworth: Penguin, 1967.

Fraker, Charles F. "Sancho II: Epic and Chronicle." *Romania* 95 (1974): 467–507.

Freeman, J. D. "On the Concept of the Kindred." Bohannan and Middleton, *Kinship* 255–56.

Fried, Morton H. *The Evolution of Political Society*. New York: Random, 1967.

——. "State. The Institution." *IESS* 15: 143–50.

Friedman, Jonathan, and M. J. Rowlands, eds. *The Evolution of Social Systems*. London: Duckworth, 1977.

Friedrich, Paul. "Proto-Indo-European Kinship." *Ethnology* 5 (1966): 1–36.

*Fuero Juzgo en latín y castellano*. Ed. of Real Academia Española. Madrid: Ibarra, 1815.

Gagarin, Michael. *Early Greek Law*. Berkeley: U of California P, 1986.

Gallais, Pierre, and Yves-Jean Riou, eds. *Mélanges offerts à René Crozet à l'occasion de son soixante-dixième anniversaire*. 2 vols. Poitiers: Société d'Etudes Médiévales, 1966.

Ganshof, F. L. *El feudalismo*. Trad. Félix Formosa. Barcelona: Ariel, 1963.

Garci-Gómez, Miguel. "The Economy of *Mio Cid*." Keller 227–36.

——. *"Mio Cid": estudios de endocrítica*. Barcelona: Planeta, 1975.

García de Cortázar, José Angel. *La época medieval*. 3rd ed. Vol. 2 of *Historia de España Alfaguara*. Madrid: Alfaguara, 1976.

García de Valdeavellano, Luis. "Las instituciones feudales en España." Appendix to Ganshof 229–300.

——. *Orígenes de la burguesía en la edad media española*. Madrid: Espasa-Calpe, 1969.

García Gallo, Alfonso. "El carácter germánico de la épica y del derecho en la edad media española." *AHDE* 25 (1955): 583–679.

García González, Juan. "El matrimonio de las hijas del Cid." *AHDE* 31 (1961): 531–68.

Gardner, Jane F. *Women in Roman Law and Society*. Bloomington: Indiana UP, 1986.

Geary, John S. "Old and New Problems in Cid Studies." *RPh* 37 (1983): 175–87.

Geary, John S., Charles Faulhaber, et al., eds. *Florilegium Hispanicum: Medieval and Golden Age Studies Presented to Dorothy Clotelle Clarke*. Madison: Hispanic Seminary of Medieval Studies, 1983.

Gerbert, Marie-Claude. "Majorat, stratégie familiale et pouvoir royal en Castille." *Espagnes Médiévales (Mélanges Dalché)* 257–76.

Gerli, E. Michael, and Harvey L. Sharrer, eds. *Hispanic Medieval Studies in Honor of Samuel G. Armistead*. Madison: Hispanic Seminary of Medieval Studies, 1992.

Gibert Sánchez, Rafael. "El consentimiento familiar en el matrimonio según el derecho medieval español." *AHDE* 18 (1947): 706–61.

# Bibliography

Giddens, Anthony. *Central Problems in Social Theory*. Berkeley: U of California P, 1979.

——. "Class Structuration and Class Consciousness." Giddens and Held 157–74. Rpt. from Giddens, *Class Structure of the Advanced Societies*. 2nd ed. London: Hutchinson, 1980. 105–17, 296–311.

——. *The Constitution of Society*. Berkeley: U of California P, 1984.

Giddens, Anthony, and David Held, eds. *Classes, Power and Conflict*. Berkeley: U of California P, 1982.

Gies, Frances, and Joseph Gies. *Marriage and the Family in the Middle Ages*. New York: Harper, 1987.

Gifford, Douglas J. "European Folk-Tradition and the 'Afrenta de Corpes.'" Deyermond, *"Mio Cid"* 49–62.

Glass, David V., and D. E. C. Eversley, eds. *Population in History: Essays in Historical Demography*. London: Arnold, 1965.

Glick, Thomas. *Islamic and Christian Spain in the Early Middle Ages*. Princeton: Princeton UP, 1979.

Gluckman, Max. "Judicial Process: Comparative Aspects." *IESS* 8: 291–97.

——. "The Kingdom of the Zulu of South Africa." Fortes and Evans-Pritchard 25–55.

Gluckman, Max, and Fred Eggan, eds. *Political Systems and the Distribution of Power*. Association of Social Anthropologists of the Commonwealth, Monographs 2. London: Tavistock, 1965.

Goldhamer, Herbert. "Social Mobility." *IESS* 14: 429–38.

Goldthorpe, J. E. *An Introduction to Sociology*. Cambridge: Cambridge UP, 1974.

González Jiménez, Manuel. "Frontier and Settlement in the Kingdom of Castile (1085–1350)." Bartlett and MacKay 49–74.

Goody, Jack. "Bridewealth and Dowry in Africa and Eurasia." Goody and Tambiah 1–58.

——, ed. *The Character of Kinship*. Cambridge: Cambridge UP, 1973.

——. "Class and Marriage in Africa and Eurasia." *American Journal of Sociology* 76 (1971): 585–603.

——. "The Classification of Double Descent Systems." *Current Anthropology* 2 (1961): 3–12.

——. "Descent Groups." *IESS* 8: 401–08.

——. *The Development of the Family and Marriage in Europe*. Cambridge: Cambridge UP, 1983.

——. "The Evolution of the Family." Laslett and Wall 103–24.

——. "Inheritance, Property, and Women: Some Comparative Considerations." Goody, Thirsk and Thompson 10–36.

——. "Strategies of Heirship." *CSSH* 15 (1973): 3–20.

Goody, Jack, and S. J. Tambiah, eds. *Bridewealth and Dowry*. Cambridge Papers in Social Anthroplogy 7. Cambridge: Cambridge UP, 1973.

Goody, Jack, Joan Thirsk, and E. P. Thompson, eds. *Family and Inheritance*. Cambridge: Cambridge UP, 1976.

Gordon, Alan M., and Evelyn Rugg, eds. *Actas del Sexto Congreso Internacional de Hispanistas celebrado en Toronto del 22 al 26 de agosto de 1977*. Toronto: Dept. of Spanish and Portuguese, U of Toronto, 1980.

Gough, Kathleen. "Mappilla: North Kerala." Schneider and Gough 415–42.

——. "Nayar: Central Kerala." Schneider and Gough 298–384.

——. "Nayar: North Kerala." Schneider and Gough 385–414.

——. "Variation in Interpersonal Kinship Relationships." Schneider and Gough 577–613.

Grassotti, Hilda. *Las instituciones feudo-vasalláticas en León y Castilla*. 4 vols. Spoleto: Centro Italiano di Studi sull'Alto Medioevo, 1969.

——. "La ira regia en León y Castilla." *CHE* 41–42 (1965): 5–135.

——. "Para la historia del botín y las parias en León y Castilla." *CHE* 39–40 (1964): 43–132.

——. "Otra vez sobre señores y vasallos." *Homenaje Millares Carlo* 117–28.

Gudeman, Stephen. "Anthropological Economics: The Question of Distribution." *ARA* 7 (1978): 347–77.

——. "The *Compadrazgo* as a Reflection of the Natural and Spiritual Person: The Curl Prize Essay, 1971." *Proceedings of the Royal Anthropological Institute* (1972): 45–71.

Guglielmi, Nilda. "Cambio y movilidad social en el *Cantar de Mio Cid*." *Anales de Historia Antigua y Medieval* 12 (1963–64): 43–65.

Guichard, Pierre. *Structures sociales "orientales" et "occidentales" dans l'Espagne musulmane*. Paris: Mouton, 1977.

Gulliver, P. H. "On Mediators." Hamnett 15–52.

Hajnal, John. "European Marriage Patterns in Perspective." Glass and Eversley 101–43.

Hall, John W. "Feudalism in Japan—A Reassessment." *CSSH* 5 (1962): 15–51.

Hallet, Judith. *Fathers and Daughters in Roman Society.* Princeton: Princeton UP, 1984.

Hammel, Eugene A. "The Comparative Method in Anthropological Perspective." *CSSH* 22 (1980): 145–55.

Hammel, Eugene A., and Peter Laslett. "Comparing Household Structure over Time and Between Cultures." *CSSH* 16 (1974): 73–109.

Hamnett, Ian, ed. *Social Anthropology and Law.* Association of Social Anthropologists of the Commonwealth, Monographs 14. London: Academic, 1977.

Harney, Michael. "Class Conflict and Primitive Rebellion in the *Poema de Mio Cid*." *O* 12 (1987): 171–219.

——. "Estates Theory and Status Anxiety in the *Libro de los estados* and Other Medieval Spanish Texts." *REH* 23 (1989): 1–29.

——. "Movilidad social, bandolerismo y la emergencia del estado en el *Poema de Mio Cid*." Resina, *Mythopoesis* 65–101.

Harrel, Steven, and Sara A. Dickey. "Dowry Systems in Complex Societies." *Ethnology* 24 (1985): 105–20.

Harris, David R. "Settling Down: An Evolutionary Model for the Transformation of Mobile Bands into Sedentary Communities." Friedman and Rowlands 401–17.

Hart, Thomas. "Hierarchical Patterns in the *Cantar de Mio Cid*." *Romanic Review* 53 (1962): 162–73.

Hatch, Elvin. "Theories of Social Honor." *AA* 91 (1989): 341–53.

Heers, Jacques. *Family Clans in the Middle Ages.* Trans. Barry Herbert. Amsterdam: North-Holland, 1977.

Heper, Metin. "The State and Public Bureaucracies: A Comparative and Historical Perspective." *CSSH* 27 (1985): 86–110.

Herlihy, David. "The Family and Religious Ideologies in Medieval Europe." *JFH* 12 (1987): 3–17.

——. "The Making of the Medieval Family: Symmetry, Structure and Sentiment." *JFH* 8 (1983): 116–30.

——. *Medieval Households.* Cambridge: Harvard UP, 1985.

Hilton, Rodney H. *Class Conflict and the Crisis of Feudalism: Essays in Medieval Social History.* Ronceverte: Hambledon, 1985.

Hindess, Barry, and Paul Q. Hirst. *Pre-capitalist Modes of Production.* London and Boston: Routledge, 1975.

Hinojosa y Naveros, Eduardo de. "El derecho en el *Poema del Cid*." *Homenaje Menéndez y Pelayo* 2: 541–81.

———. "La fraternidad artificial en España." *Obras*. 2 vols. Madrid: Ministerio de Justicia/CSIC, 1948. 2: 259–78.

Hobsbawm, Eric J. *Bandits*. Rev. ed. New York: Pantheon, 1981.

———. *Primitive Rebels*. New York: Praeger, 1963.

*Homenaje a don Agustín Millares Carlo*. 2 vols. Gran Canaria: Caja de Ahorros de Gran Canaria, 1975.

*Homenaje a Menéndez y Pelayo*. 2 vols. Madrid: Librería General de Victoriano Suárez, 1899.

Homer. *The Odyssey of Homer*. Trans. Richmond Lattimore. New York: Harper, 1967.

Honigmann, J. J., ed. *Handbook of Social and Cultural Anthropology*. New York: Rand, 1974.

Hook, David. "The Conquest of Valencia in the *Cantar de Mio Cid*." *BHS* 50 (1974): 120–26.

———. "On Certain Correspondences between the *Poema de Mio Cid* and Contemporary Legal Instruments." *Iberoromania* ns 11 (1980): 31–53.

Horrent, Jules. *Historia y poesía en torno al «Cantar del Cid»*. Barcelona: Ariel, 1973.

Hughes, Diane Owen. "From Bridewealth to Dowry in Mediterranean Europe." *JFH* 3 (1978): 262–96.

Hunt, Robert, ed. *Personalities and Cultures: Readings in Psychological Anthropology*. Garden City: Natural History, 1967.

*International Encyclopedia of the Social Sciences*. David L. Sills, ed. 17 vols. New York: MacMillan, 1968.

Irigaray, Luce. *This Sex Which Is Not One*. Ithaca: Cornell UP, 1985.

Isidore of Seville. *Etymologiae*. Ed. W. M. Lindsay. 2 vols. Oxford: Clarendon, 1911.

Jackson, William T. H., ed. *European Writers: The Middle Ages and the Renaissance, I: Prudentius to Medieval Drama; II: Petrarch to Renaissance Short Fiction*. New York: Scribner's, 1983.

Jones, Joseph R., ed. *Medieval, Renaissance and Folklore Studies in Honor of John Esten Keller*. Newark, DE: Juan de la Cuesta, 1980.

Jones, Michael, ed. *Gentry and Lesser Nobility in Late Medieval Europe*. Gloucester: Sutton; New York: St. Martin's, 1986.

Kapferer, Bruce, ed. *Transaction and Meaning: Directions in the Anthropology of Exchange*. Philadelphia: Institute of Human Study, 1976.

Karsten, Rafael. "Blood Revenge and War Among the Jibaro Indians of Eastern Ecuador." Bohannan, *Law and Warfare* 303–25.

Keen, Maurice. "Robin Hood—Peasant or Gentleman?" *P&P* 19 (1961): 7–15.

——. *The Outlaws of Medieval Legend*. Rev. ed. London and New York: Routledge, 1987.

Keller, Hans-Erich, ed. *Romance Epic: Essays on a Medieval Literary Genre*. Studies in Medieval Culture 24. Kalamazoo: Medieval Institute Publications, 1987.

Kertzer, David I. "Anthropology and Family History." *JFH* 9 (1984): 201–16.

——. "Household History and Sociological Theory." *AnnRevS* 17 (1991): 155–79.

Kertzer, David I., and Caroline Brettell. "Advances in Italian and Iberian Family History." *JFH* 12 (1987): 87–120.

Klass, Morton. *Caste: The Emergence of the South Asian Social System*. Philadelphia: Institute for the Study of Human Issues, 1980.

Krader, Lawrence. *Formation of the State*. Englewood Cliffs: Prentice, 1968.

Lacarra, José María. "En torno a la propagación de la voz «hidalgo»." *Homenaje Millares Carlo*, 2: 43–53.

Lacarra, María Eugenia. *El «Poema de Mio Cid»: realidad histórica e ideología*. Madrid: Porrúa Turanzas, 1980.

Ladero Quesada, Miguel Angel, ed. *En la España medieval: estudios en memoria del profesor D. Salvador de Moxó*. 2 vols. Madrid: Universidad Complutense, 1982.

Lapesa, Rafael. "Sobre el *Cantar de Mio Cid*, crítica de críticas: cuestiones históricas." Tate 55–66.

Laslett, Peter. "The History of the Family." Laslett and Wall 1–73.

——. "Characteristics of the Western Family Considered over Time." *JFH* 2 (1977): 89–115.

Laslett, Peter, and Richard Wall, eds. *Household and Family in Past Time*. Cambridge: Cambridge UP, 1972.

Laumann, Edward O., Paul M. Siegel, and Robert W. Hodge, eds. *The Logic of Social Hierarchies*. Chicago: Markham, 1970.

Le Goff, Jacques. "The Symbolic Ritual of Vassalage." In *Time, Work and Culture in the Middle Ages*. Trans. Arthur Goldhammer. Chicago: U of Chicago P, 1980. 237–87.

Lea, Henry Charles. "The Wager of Battle." Bohannan, *Law and Warfare* 233–53.

Leach, Edmund. "Anthropology. Comparative Method." *IESS* 1: 339–45.

———. "Caste, Class and Slavery: The Taxonomic Problem." Laumann et al. 83–94.

———. *Political Systems of Highland Burma*. Boston: Beacon, 1965. Orig. publ. 1954.

———. *Rethinking Anthropology*. London: Athlone, 1961.

Lenski, Gerhard. *Power and Privilege*. New York: McGraw, 1966.

Lerner, Daniel. "Modernization. Social Aspects." *IESS* 10: 386–95.

Levine, Robert A. "The Internalization of Political Values in Stateless Societies." Hunt 185–203.

Lévi-Strauss, Claude. *The Elementary Structures of Kinship*. Rev. ed. Trans. James Harle Bell and John Richard von Sturmer. Ed. Rodney Needham. Boston: Beacon, 1969.

———. "Structural Analysis." *Structural Anthropology*. Trans. Claire Jacobson and Brooke Grundfest Schoeff. New York: Basic, 1963.

Levy, Harry L. "Inheritance and Dowry in Classical Athens." Pitt-Rivers, *Mediterranean Countrymen* 137–43.

Lewis, Archibald. *Knights and Samurai: Feudalism in Northern France and Japan*. London: Smith, 1974.

———. "The Midi, Buwayhid Iraq, and Japan: Some Aspects of Comparative Feudalisms. A.D. 946–1055." *CSSH* 2 (1966): 47–53.

Lewis, I. M., ed. *History and Social Anthropology*. Association of Social Anthropologists of the Commonwealth, Monographs 7. London: Tavistock, 1968.

Leyser, Karl. "The German Aristocracy from the Ninth to the Early Twelfth Century: A Historical and Cultural Sketch." *P&P* 41 (1968): 25–53.

———. "Maternal Kin in Early Medieval Germany: A Reply." *P&P* 49 (1970): 126–34.

Lidz, Victor, and Talcott Parsons, eds. *Readings on Premodern Societies*. Englewood Cliffs: Prentice, 1972.

Lisón-Tolosana, Carmelo. *Belmonte de los Caballeros: A Sociological Study of a Spanish Town*. Oxford: Clarendon, 1966.

255

Lomax, Derek W. "The Date of the *Poema de Mio Cid*." Deyermond, *"Mio Cid"* 73–81.

López Estrada, Francisco. *Panorama crítico sobre el "Poema del Cid."* Madrid: Castalia, 1982.

Lopreato, Joseph, and Lionel S. Lewis, eds. *Social Stratification: A Reader*. New York: Harper, 1974.

Lord, Albert. "The Merging of Two Worlds: Oral and Written Poetry as Carriers of Ancient Values." Foley, *Oral Tradition* 19–64.

——. *The Singer of Tales*. New York: Atheneum, 1974. Rpt. of Harvard Studies in Comparative Literature 24. Cambridge: Harvard UP, 1960.

Lourie, Elena. "A Society Organized for War: Medieval Spain." *P&P* 35 (1966): 54–76.

Lynch, Joseph H. *Godparents and Kinship in Early Modern Europe*. Princeton: Princeton UP, 1986.

MacKay, Angus. "The Ballad and the Frontier in Later Medieval Spain." *BHS* 53 (1976): 15–33.

——. "The Lesser Nobility in the Kingdom of Castile." Michael Jones 159–80.

——. *Spain in the Middle Ages: From Frontier to Empire*. London: MacMillan, 1977.

Maddicott, J. R. "The Birth and Settings of the Ballads of Robin Hood." *English Historical Review* 93 (1978): 276–99.

Madero Eguía, Marta. "El riepto y su relación con la injuria, la venganza y la ordalía (Castilla y León, siglos XIII y XIV)." *His* 47 (1987): 805–61.

Magnotta, Miguel. *Historia y bibliografía de la crítica sobre el «Poema de Mio Cid» (1750–1871)*. North Carolina Studies in Romance Languages and Literatures 145. Chapel Hill: U of North Carolina, Dept. of Romance Languages, 1976.

——. "Per Abbat y la tradición oral o escrita en el *Poema de Mio Cid*: un ensayo histórico-crítico." *HR* 43 (1975): 293–309.

Mallory, James. "A Short History of the Indo-European Problem." *JIES* 1 (1973): 21–65.

Marín, Nicolás. "Señor y vasallo, una cuestión disputada en el *Cantar de Mio Cid*." *Romanische Forschungen* 86 (1974): 451–61.

Marriot, McKim, and Ronald B. Inden. "Caste Systems." *Encyclopedia Britannica*. 15th ed. 1974. 3: 982–91.

Marshall, Gloria A. "Marriage. Comparative Analysis." *IESS* 10: 8–19.

Martínez, J. Victorio. "Nota sobre la épica medieval española: el motivo de la rebeldía." *Revue Belge de Philologie et d'Histoire* 50 (1972): 777–92.

Martínez Marcos, Esteban. *Las causas matrimoniales en las "Partidas" de Alfonso el Sabio.* Salamanca: CSIC, 1966.

Matras, Judah. "Comparative Social Mobility." *AnnRevS* 6 (1980): 401–31.

*Il Matrimonio nella Società altomedievale.* Settimane di studio del Centro Italiano di Studi sull'Alto Medioevo. Spoleto: Presso la Sede del Centro, 1977.

Mauss, Marcel. *The Gift.* Trans. Ian Cunnison. New York: Norton, 1967.

Mayer, Adrian C. *Caste and Kinship in Central India.* London: Routledge, 1960.

———. "The Significance of Quasi-Groups in the Study of Complex Societies." Banton 97–122.

McGovern, John F. "The Rise of New Economic Attitudes—Economic Humanism, Economic Nationalism—During the Later Middle Ages and the Renaissance. A.D. 1200–1500." *Traditio* 26 (1970): 217–53.

Mead, Margaret. *Cooperation and Competition among Primitive Peoples.* New York: McGraw, 1937.

Meillassoux, Claude. *Anthropologie économique des Gouro de Côte d'Ivoire.* Paris and The Hague: Mouton, 1964.

———. *Maidens, Meal and Money.* Cambridge: Cambridge UP, 1981.

Meinhard, H. H. "The Patrilineal Principle in Early Teutonic Kinship." Beattie and Lienhardt 1–29.

Melena, José L., ed. *Symbolae Ludovico Mitxelena septuagenario oblatae.* 2 vols. Vitoria: Instituto de Ciencias de la Antigüedad, 1985.

Menéndez Pidal, Ramón, ed. *Cantar de Mio Cid: texto, gramática y vocabulario.* Rev. ed. 3 vols. Madrid: Espasa-Calpe, 1944–46.

———. *En torno al Poema del Cid.* Barcelona: EDHASA, 1963.

———. *La España del Cid.* 5th ed. 2 vols. Madrid: Espasa-Calpe, 1956. 1st ed. Madrid: Plutarco, 1929.

———, ed. *Primera Crónica General.* 2nd ed. 2 vols. Madrid: Gredos, 1955.

Menéndez Pidal, Ramón, ed. *Reliquias de la poesía épica española.* 2nd ed. Ed. Diego Catalán. Reliquias de la Epica Hispánica 1. Madrid: Cátedra-Seminario Menéndez Pidal, Gredos, 1980. Orig. publ. 1951.

Merêa, Manuel Paulo. "O dote nos documentos dos seculos XI–XII." *EDHM* 1 (1952): 59–130.

——. "Notas sobre o poder paternal no direito hispánico ocidental." *EDHM* 2 (1953): 83–112.

——. "Sobre a palavra «arras»." *EDHM* 1 (1952): 131–41.

Meyer, Paul, ed. *Histoire de Guillaume le Maréchal.* 3 vols. Paris: Société de l'Histoire de France, 1891, 1894, 1901.

Michael, Ian, ed. *El Poema de Mio Cid.* 2nd ed. Madrid: Castalia, 1984.

Miletich, John S. "Folk Literature, Related Forms, and the Making of the *Poema de Mio Cid.*" *La Corónica* 15 (1987): 186–96.

——, ed. *Hispanic Studies in Honor of Alan D. Deyermond: A North American Tribute.* Madison: Hispanic Seminary of Medieval Studies, 1986.

——. "Medieval Spanish Epic and European Narrative Traditions." *La Corónica* 6 (1978): 90–96.

Mintz, Sidney W., and Eric R. Wolf. "An Analysis of Ritual Co-Parenthood (Compadrazgo)." *SJA* 6 (1950): 341–68.

Mitterauer, Michael, and Rinhard Sieder. *The European Family: Patriarchy to Partnership from the Middle Ages to the Present.* Trans. Karla Oosterveen and Manfred Horzinger. Oxford: Blackwell, 1982.

Montgomery, Thomas. "Assonance, Word, and Thought in the *Poema del Cid.*" *JHP* 11 (1986): 5–22.

——. "Mythopoeia and Myopia: Colin Smith's *The Making of the Poema de Mio Cid.*" *JHP* 8 (1983): 7–16.

——. "The 'Poema del Cid' and the Potentialities of Metonymy." *HR* 59 (1991): 421–36.

——. "The *Poema de Mio Cid*: Oral Art in Transition." Deyermond, *"Mio Cid"* 91–112.

——. "The Rhetoric of Solidarity in the *Poema del Cid.*" *MLN* 102 (1987): 191–205.

——. "The Uses of Writing in the Spanish Epic." *La Corónica* 15 (1987): 179–85.

Montoro, Adrian G. "La épica medieval española y la 'estructura trifuncional' de los indoeuropeos." *Cuadernos Hispanoamericanos* 95 (1974): 554–71.

Moreta, Salustiano. *Malhechores-Feudales: Violencia, antagonismos y alianzas de clases en Castilla, siglos XIII–XIV.* Madrid: Cátedra, 1978.

Moseley, K. P., and Immanuel Wallerstein. "Precapitalist Social Structures." *AnnRevS* 4 (1978): 259–90.

Mosley, Alejandro. "De Vivar a Valencia: el ascenso épico del que en buena hora nació." Unpublished ms.

Moxó, Salvador de. *Repoblación y sociedad en la España cristiana medieval.* Madrid: Rialp, 1979.

Murdock, George Peter. "Cognatic Forms of Organization." Bohannan and Middleton, *Kinship* 235–53.

Murray, Alexander. *Germanic Kinship Structure.* Toronto: Pontifical Institute of Medieval Studies, 1983.

Myers, Oliver T. "Multiple Authorship of the *Poema de Mio Cid*: A Final Word?" Deyermond, *"Mio Cid"* 113–28.

Nader, Laura. "Conflict. Anthropological Aspects." *IESS* 3: 236–42.

Nash, Manning. "Economic Anthropology." *IESS* 4: 359–65.

Needham, Rodney, ed. *Rethinking Kinship and Marriage.* Association of Social Anthropologists of the Commonwealth, Monographs 11. London: Tavistock, 1971.

Newman, Katherine S. *Law and Economic Organization: A Comparative Study of Preindustrial Societies.* Cambridge: Cambridge UP, 1983.

Noble, Peter, Lucie Polak, and Claire Isoz, eds. *The Medieval Alexander Legend and Romance Epic: Essays in Honour of David J. A. Ross.* Millwood, NY: Krauss, 1982.

North, Robert C. "Conflict. Political Aspects." *IESS* 3: 226–32.

O'Callaghan, Joseph F. *A History of Medieval Spain.* Ithaca: Cornell UP, 1975.

Ong, Walter J. *Orality and Literacy.* London: Methuen, 1982.

Orderic Vitalis. *The Ecclesiastical History.* Ed. and trans. Marjorie Chibnall. 6 vols. Oxford: Clarendon, 1972.

Ossowski, Stanislav. *Class Structure in the Social Consciousness.* Trans. Sheila Patterson. London: Routledge, 1963.

*Oxford English Dictionary.* 2nd ed. Ed., comp. J. A. Simpson and E. S. C. Weiner. Oxford: Clarendon, 1989.

Pardo, Aristóbulo. "La imagen del rey en el *Cantar de Mio Cid*." Keller 213–25.

Parkin, Frank. "Social Closure and Class Formation." Giddens and Held 175–84. Rpt. from *The Marxist Theory of Class: A Bourgeois Critique* (London: Tavistock, 1979) 44–54.

Parsons, Talcott. *Societies.* Englewood Cliffs: Prentice, 1966.

Pastor de Togneri, Reyna. *Conflictos sociales y estancamiento económico en la España medieval.* Barcelona: Ariel, 1973.

——. "Historia de las familias en Castilla y León (siglos X–XIV) y su relación con la formación de los grandes dominios eclesiásticos." *CHE* 43–44 (1967): 88–118.

Patai, Rafael. *Society, Culture and Change in the Middle East.* 3rd ed. Philadelphia: U of Pennsylvania P, 1969.

Pattison, D. G. "The Cid and Alcocer." *BHS* 60 (1983): 49–51.

Pavlović, Milija N. "Oralist Vision and Neo-Traditionalist Revision: A Review Article." *MLR* 86 (1991): 867–84.

Pavlović, Milija N., and Roger M. Walker. "Money, Marriage and the Law in the *Poema de Mio Cid.*" *MÆ* 51 (1982): 197–212.

——. "A Reappraisal of the Closing Scenes of the *Poema de Mio Cid*, I: The *Rieptos.*" *MÆ* 58 (1989): 1–16.

——. "A Reappraisal of the Closing Scenes of the *Poema de Mio Cid*, II: The Duels." *MÆ* 58 (1989): 189–205.

——. "Roman Forensic Procedure in the *Cort* Scene in the *Poema de Mio Cid.*" *BHS* 60 (1983): 95–107.

Pearson, Roger. "Some Aspects of Social Mobility in Early Historic Indo-European Societies." *JIES* 1 (1973): 155–62.

Pellegrini, Giovan Battista. "Terminologia matrimoniale." *Matrimonio Società altomedievale* 1: 43–91.

Peristiany, J. G., ed. *Honour and Shame: The Values of Mediterranean Society.* Chicago: U of Chicago P, 1966.

——. Introduction. Peristiany, *Honour and Shame* 9–18.

Perroy, Edouard. "Social Mobility among the French *noblesse* in the Late Middle Ages." *P&P* 21 (1962): 25–38.

Pershits, Abraham I. "Tribute Relations." Seaton and Cleassen 149–56.

Pescador, Carmela. "La caballería popular en León y Castilla." *CHE* 33–34 (1961): 101–238; *CHE* 35–36 (1962): 156–201; 37–38 (1963): 88–198; 39–40 (1964): 169–260.

Phillpotts, Bertha Surtees. *Kindred and Clan in the Middle Ages and After.* Cambridge: Cambridge UP, 1913.

Piers, Gerhart, and Milton B. Singer. *Shame and Guilt.* New York: Norton, 1971.

Pitt-Rivers, Julian, ed. "Honour and Social Status." Peristiany, *Honour and Shame* 21–77.

——. "The Kith and the Kin." Goody, *Character* 89–105.

——. *Mediterranean Countrymen: Essays in the Social Anthropology of the Mediterranean.* Paris–The Hague: Mouton, 1963.

——. "Pseudo-Kinship." *IESS* 8: 408–13.

Polanyi, Karl. "The Economy as Instituted Process." Polanyi et al. 243–70.

——. *Primitive, Archaic, and Modern Economies.* Ed. George Dalton. Boston: Beacon, 1968.

Polanyi, Karl, Conrad M. Arensberg, and Harry W. Pearson, eds. *Trade and Market in the Early Empires.* Glencoe, IL: Free, 1957.

Posner, Richard A. *Law and Literature: A Misunderstood Relation.* Cambridge: Harvard UP, 1988.

Pospisil, Leopold. *The Anthropology of Law: A Comparative Theory.* New Haven: HRAF, 1974. Rpt. of orig. ed. New York: Harper, 1971.

Poulantzas, Nicos. "On Social Classes." Giddens and Held 101–11. Abbr. rpt. of article in *New Left Review* 78 (1973): 27–35, 37–39, 47–50.

Powers, James F. *A Society Organized for War.* Berkeley: U of California P, 1988.

Quintanilla Raso, María Concepción. "Estructuras sociales y familiares y papel político de la nobleza cordobesa (siglos XIV y XV)." Ladero Quesada 331–52.

Radcliffe-Brown, A. R. "On Joking Relationships." *Structure and Function in Primitive Society.* New York: Free, 1965. Orig. publ. 1952.

Radcliffe-Brown, A. R., and Daryll Forde, eds. *African Systems of Kinship and Marriage.* London: Oxford UP, 1950.

Raheja, Gloria Goodwin. *The Poison in the Gift.* Chicago: U of Chicago P, 1988.

Ramsoy, Odd. "Friendship." *IESS* 6: 12–17.

Redfield, Robert. "Primitive Law." Bohannan, *Law and Warfare* 3–24.

Reig, Carola, ed. *El cantar de Sancho II y cerco de Zamora. Revista de Filología Española,* anejo 37. Madrid: CSIC, 1947.

Resina, Joan Ramon. "El honor y las relaciones feudales en el *Poema de Mio Cid.*" *REH* 18 (1984): 417–28.

——, ed. *Mythopoesis: literatura, totalidad, ideología.* Barcelona: Anthropos, 1992.

Reuter, Timothy, ed. *The Medieval Nobility.* Oxford: North-Holland, 1978.

Rheinstein, Max. "Comparative Law and Legal Systems." *IESS* 9: 204–10.

Rheubottom, David B. " 'Sisters First': Betrothal Order and Age at Marriage in Fifteenth-Century Ragusa." *JFH* 13(1988): 359–76.

Richter, A. L., ed. *Corpus Juris Canonici.* 2 vols. Leipzig: Tauchniz, 1839.

Rodríguez-Puértolas, Julio. "El *Poema de Mio Cid*: nueva épica y nueva propaganda." Deyermond, *"Mio Cid"* 141–59.

Rosell, Cayetano, ed. *Crónicas de los reyes de Castilla.* Biblioteca de Autores Españoles 66, 68, 70. 3 vols. Madrid: Rivadeneyra, 1875, 1877, 1878.

Rosenfield, Eva. "Social Stratification in a 'Classless' Society." Lopreato and Lewis 134–42. Rpt. from *American Sociological Review* 16 (1951): 766–74.

Rosenhaft, Eve. "History, Anthropology and the Study of Everyday Life." *CSSH* 29 (1987): 99–105.

Rosenthal, Joel T. "Marriage and the Blood Feud in 'Heroic' Europe." *British Journal of Sociology* 17 (1966): 133–44.

Royer de Cardinal, Susana. "Tensiones sociales en la baja edad media castellana." *CHE* 65–66 (1981): 277–358.

Rubin, Zick. "Do American Women Marry Up?" Laumann et al. 633–43.

Ruiz Domenec, José E. "Estrategias matrimoniales y sistemas de alianza entre Castilla y Cataluña en el siglo XII." *His* 40 (1980): 271–84.

Runciman, W. G. "Accelerating Social Mobility: The Case of Anglo-Saxon England." *P&P* 104 (1984): 3–30.

Sahlins, Marshall. "On the Ideology and Composition of Descent Groups." *Man* 65 (1965): 104–07.

———. "The Segmentary Lineage: An Organization of Predatory Expansion." Cohen and Middleton 89–119. Rpt. from *AA* 63 (1961): 332–45.

———. *Social Stratification in Polynesia.* Seattle: U of Washington P, 1958.

Saltman, Michael. "Feudal Relationships and the Law: A Comparative Enquiry." *CSSH* 29 (1987): 514–32.

Sánchez Albornoz, Claudio. *España: un enigma histórico.* 2 vols. Buenos Aires: Sudamericana, 1956.

San Martín, Antonio de, ed. *Los códigos españoles, concordados y anotados.* 12 vols. Madrid, 1872–73.

Scheffler, Harold W. *"The Elementary Structures of Kinship,* by Claude Lévi-Strauss: A Review Article." *AA* 72 (1970): 251–68.

——. "Kinship, Descent, and Alliance." Honigmann 747–93.

Schlegel, Alice, and Rohn Eloul. "Marriage Transactions: Labor, Property, Status." *AA* 90 (1988): 291–309.

Schmid, Karl. "Heirat, Familienfolge, Geschlechterbewusstsein." *Matrimonio Società altomedievale* 1: 103–37.

——. "The Structure of the Nobility in the Earlier Middle Ages." Reuter 37–59.

Schneider, David M., and E. Kathleen Gough. *Matrilineal Kinship.* Berkeley: U of California P, 1961.

Schneider, Jane. "Of Vigilance and Virgins: Honor, Shame and Access to Resources in Mediterranean Societies." *Ethnology* 10 (1971): 1–24.

Schusky, Ernest L. *Manual for Kinship Analysis.* 2nd ed. New York: Holt, 1972.

Searle, Eleanor. *Predatory Kinship and the Creation of Norman Power, 840–1066.* Berkeley: U of California P, 1988.

Seaton, S. Lee, and Henri J. M. Claessen, eds. *Political Anthropology: The State of the Art.* The Hague: Mouton, 1979.

Service, Elman R. *Origins of the State and Civilization: The Process of Cultural Evolution.* New York: Norton, 1975.

Shils, Edward. "Charisma." *IESS* 2: 386–90.

——. "Deference." Laumann et al. 420–48.

Singer, A. "Marriage Payments and the Exchange of People." *Man* 8 (1973): 80–92.

Slatta, Richard W., ed. *Bandidos: The Varieties of Latin American Banditry.* Contributions in Criminology and Penology 14. New York: Greenwood, 1987.

Smith, Colin. "The Choice of the Infantes de Carrión as Villains in the *Poema de Mio Cid." JHP* 4 (1980): 105–18.

——. "Epics and Chronicles: A Reply to Armistead." *HR* 51 (1983): 409–28.

——. *The Making of the "Poema de Mio Cid."* Cambridge: Cambridge UP, 1983.

——, ed. *Poema de Mio Cid.* Oxford: Clarendon, 1972.

Smith, Michael G. "Political Anthropology: Political Organization." *IESS* 12: 193–202.

Smith, Raymond T. "Anthropology and the Concept of Social Class." *ARA* 13 (1984): 467–94.

——. "The Matrifocal Family." Goody, *Character* 121–44.

Soliday, Gerald L., Tamara K. Hareven, et al., eds. *History of the Family and Kinship: A Select International Bibliography*. Millwood, NY: Kraus International, 1980.

Sorokin, Pitirim. *Social and Cultural Mobility*. Glencoe, IL: Free, 1959.

Southall, Aidan. "The Segmentary State in Africa and Asia." *CSSH* 30 (1988): 52–82.

——. "Stateless Society." *IESS* 15: 157–68.

Southwold, Martin. "Meanings of Kinship." Needham 35–56.

Spitzer, Leo. "¡Dios, qué buen vasallo si oviesse buen señor!" *RFH* 8 (1946): 132–36.

——. "Sobre el carácter histórico del *Cantar de Mio Cid*." *NRFH* 2 (1948): 105–17.

Stock, Brian. *Implications of Literacy*. Princeton: Princeton UP, 1983.

Stokes, Sally. "The Language of Kinship in the *Poema de Mio Cid*." M.A. Thesis. U of Texas, 1989.

Strayer, Joseph P. *On the Medieval Origins of the Modern State*. Princeton: Princeton UP, 1970.

*Studia Philologica. Homenaje a Dámaso Alonso*. 3 vols. Madrid: Gredos, 1960–63.

Tambiah, Stanley J. "Dowry and Bridewealth, and the Property Rights of Women in Southeast Asia." Goody and Tambiah 59–169.

Tannenbaum, Arnold S. "Leadership. Sociological Aspects." *IESS* 9: 101–07.

Tate, R. Brian, ed. *Essays on Narrative Fiction in the Iberian Peninsula in Honour of Frank Pierce*. London: Dolphin, 1982.

Terray, Emmanuel. *Marxism and "Primitive" Societies*. Trans. M. Klopper. New York and London: Monthly Review, 1972.

Tilly, Charles. *Big Structures, Large Processes, Huge Comparisons*. New York: Russel Sage Foundation, 1984.

——. "Family History, Social History, and Social Change." *JFH* 12 (1987): 319–30.

——, ed. *The Formation of National States in Western Europe*. Princeton: Princeton UP, 1975.

——. "Reflections on the History of European State-Making." Tilly, *Formation* 3–83.

——. "Western State-Making and Theories of Political Transformation." Tilly, *Formation* 601–38.

Turnbull, Colin. *The Mountain People*. New York: Knopf, 1973.

Ubieto Arteta, Antonio. *El «Cantar de Mio Cid» y algunos problemas históricos*. Valencia: Anúbar, 1973.

van Hoecke, Willy, and Andries Welkenhuysen, eds. *Love and Marriage in the Twelfth Century*. Mediaevalia Lovaniensia, ser. 1, Studia, 8. Louvain: Leuven UP, 1981.

Vaquero, Mercedes. "El cantar de la Jura de Santa Gadea y la tradición del Cid como vasallo rebelde." *O* 15 (1990): 47–84.

——. "The Tradition of the 'Cantar de Sancho II' in Fifteenth-Century Historiography." *HR* 57 (1989): 137–54.

Verdery, Katherine. "A Comment on Goody's *Development of the Family and Marriage in Europe*." *JFH* 13 (1988): 265–70.

Verkauteren, Fernand. "A Kindred in Northern France in the Eleventh and Twelfth Centuries." Reuter 87–101. Trans., rpt. of "Une Parentèle dans la France du Nord aux XI$^e$ et XII$^e$ siècles." *Moyen Age* 69 (1963): 223–45.

Walker, Roger M. "The Role of the King and the Poet's Intentions in the *Poema de Mio Cid*." Deyermond, *Hamilton Studies* 257–66.

Waltman, Franklin M., ed., comp. *Concordance to "Poema de Mio Cid."* University Park, PA: Pennsylvania State UP, 1972.

Watkins, Frederick M. "State. The Concept." *IESS* 15: 150–57.

Webber, Ruth House. "The *Cantar de Mio Cid*: Problems of Interpretation." Foley, *Oral Tradition* 65–88.

——. "Hispanic Oral Literature: Accomplishments and Perspectives." *Oral Tradition* 1 (1986): 344–80.

Weber, Max. "Bureaucracy." Weber, *From Max Weber* 196–244.

——. "Class, Status, and Party." Weber, *From Max Weber* 180–95.

——. *From Max Weber: Essays in Sociology*. Ed., trans. H. H. Gerth and C. Wright Mills. New York: Oxford UP, 1946.

——. "The Nature of Charismatic Authority and Its Routinization." Eisenstadt, *On Charisma* 48–65.

——. "Structures of Power." Weber, *From Max Weber* 159–79.

Weinstein, Eugene A. "Adoption." *IESS* 1: 96–100.

Werner, Karl Ferdinand. "Liens de parenté et noms de personne." Duby and Le Goff 25–34.

West, Geoffrey. "King and Vassal in History and Poetry: A Contrast Between the *Historia Roderici* and the *Poema de Mio Cid*." Deyermond, *"Mio Cid"* 195–208.

Whitehead, Frederic, ed. *La Chanson de Roland*. Oxford: Blackwell, 1970.

Whyte, Martin King. *The Status of Women in Preindustrial Societies*. Princeton: Princeton UP, 1978.

Williams, Raymond. *The Country and the City*. New York: Oxford UP, 1973.

——. *Keywords*. Rev. ed. New York: Oxford UP, 1983.

Winch, Robert F. "Marriage. Family Formation." *IESS* 10: 1–8.

Wolf, Eric. *Europe and the People Without History*. Berkeley: U of California P, 1982.

——. "Kinship, Friendship, and Patron-Client Relations in Complex Societies." Banton 1–22.

Wright, Henry T. "Recent Research on the Origin of the State." *ARA* 6 (1977): 379–97.

Wright, Quincy. *The Study of War*. Chicago: U of Chicago P, 1959.

Wuthnow, Robert. "Processes of Early State Development: A Review Article." *CSSH* 28 (1986): 107–13.

# Index